Along Ohio's Historic Route 20

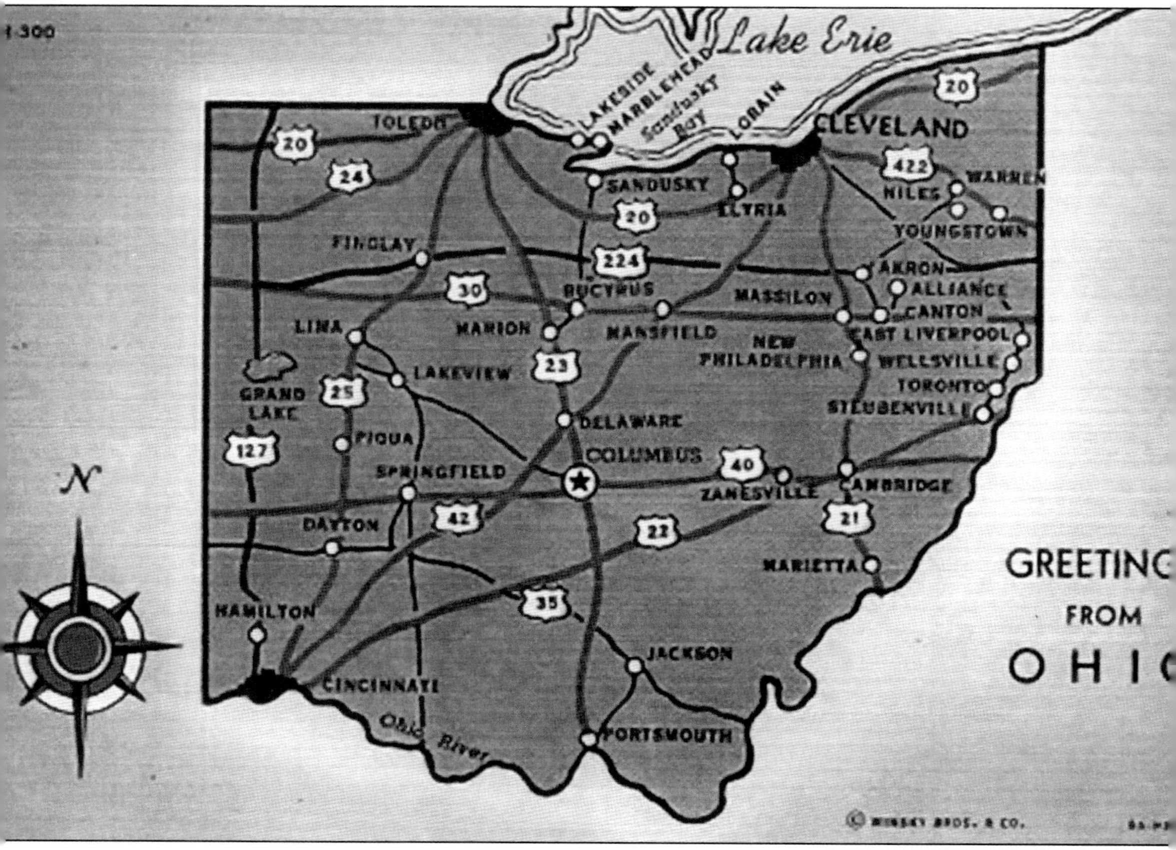

Historic Route 20 across Northern Ohio. From 1926, when it was designated a federal highway, until the arrival of the Interstate Highway System, historic Route 20 was northern Ohio's principal artery for both commercial and leisure travel. (Author's collection.)

On the Front Cover: The catchy slogan "Hungry Hubby?—So Am I" attracted customers to the Speed-Way Inn and Cabin Court. Blowing a horn for service summoned an attendant, typically wearing a neatly pressed uniform, cap, and leather clip-on bow tie. In addition to filling the tank, he would clean the windshield and check the car's oil, radiator, and tire pressure. (Author's collection.)

On the Back Cover: Roadside diners designed to resemble railroad cars were fixtures along early highways. Typical fare included chili, pancakes, burgers, and the ever-popular blue plate special, which consisted of generous portions of meat, vegetables, gravy, bread, and a drink, usually costing less than $1. (Author's collection.)

POSTCARD HISTORY SERIES

Along Ohio's Historic Route 20

Michael J. Till

ARCADIA
PUBLISHING

ISBN 978-1-4671-1042-6

Published by Arcadia Publishing
Charleston, South Carolina

Printed in the United States of America

Library of Congress Control Number: 2013936670

For all general information contact Arcadia Publishing at:
Telephone 843-853-2070
Fax 843-853-0044
E-mail sales@arcadiapublishing.com
For customer service and orders:
Toll-Free 1-888-313-2665

Visit us on the Internet at www.arcadiapublishing.com

To all who remember the crowding and heat in the backseat of the family sedan before the days of air-conditioning, iPods, and smartphones

Contents

Acknowledgments

This book would not have been possible were it not for civic leaders and business owners in the early 1900s who recognized the value of picture postcards in promoting their communities to the ever-expanding motoring public. These visual and historical records provide invaluable insights into "the way it was," when two-lane highways and mom-and-pop tourist courts were state of the art.

Thanks also to the vendors of vintage postcards for their help. Many people searched for Route 20 cards for me, which is greatly appreciated. The same is true for persons responsible for modern websites describing towns and historical sites on Route 20. I have relied heavily on their descriptions and wish to acknowledge their contributions.

Local librarians and the staffs of county historical societies and museums along Route 20 were especially helpful in directing me to interesting information about the road. Many shared personal memories of the postcard sites, and if someone did not know the answer to a question, their telephone call to a longtime resident of the community usually produced the information. Thus, many grandparents, uncles, aunts, and community elders indirectly contributed to this book.

Last, but certainly not least, I wish to thank my wife, Christine, for her help. A librarian herself, she knew sources of information and how to access them. She was also an excellent collaborator as we drove along Route 20 researching specific sites. Many of her observations have been incorporated into the captions of this book.

All images are from the author's personal collection.

Introduction

Route 20 in Ohio was part of the first interstate highway legislation enacted by Congress. It was the result of the landmark Federal-Aid Highway Act of 1923, which recognized the rapid growth in popularity of motor vehicles for both personal and commercial transportation, and addressed the need for better organization of the country's highway system. Funding for the development and maintenance of seven percent of each state's highway system was awarded provided that the designated roads were "interstate in character," meaning simply that the roads must connect with similarly designated roads in their adjacent states. Thus, the original interstate highways were not new, but rather existing roads that met the stated criteria.

Officials charged with the responsibility of determining which roads should be included completed their task in 1923, and in 1926 these roads were designated as federal highways; the numbering system adopted at the time is still in use today. Major east-west routes were assigned a number ending in 0, and the numbering sequence went from north to south. To avoid the unique number 0, the northernmost road was given the designation 2, and the remaining roads were designated 10, 20, 30, all the way to 90.

Highways 2 and 10 extended only from the Midwest to the West Coast. From 1926 to 1940, Route 20 extended from Boston to the east entrance of Yellowstone National Park. In 1940, the western section was completed to Newport, Oregon, making Route 20 the northernmost of the true cross-country highways, and with a total length of 3,365 miles it was the longest. Although not as famous as its cousins Route 30, much of which followed the course of the original Lincoln Highway, or Route 66, which is not a true cross-country highway, Route 20 has served with equal importance in the evolution of motor traffic in United States.

Highway officials in Ohio chose wisely for Route 20, recognizing that the road was destined to become the primary commercial and recreational highway in northern Ohio. It would connect the entire northeastern United States to Cleveland and, from there, Chicago and farther west. Route 20 was planned to be a major contributor to the economic health of the entire state, with special emphasis on the north. It would be the overland link to the Great Lakes ports from Conneaut to Toledo, expand commercial development in Cleveland and its surrounding suburbs, connect the population to major educational, health, and cultural venues, and be a farm-to-market road in Ohio's rural districts. The road was also planned to bring tourists to the state's many attractions. For almost half a century, until it was superseded by the present Interstate Highway System, Route 20 fulfilled its role with distinction.

Although much of its former traffic has now been taken over by the interstate highways, Route 20 is unique in that most of its original configuration has remained intact. Many early highways were destroyed when the interstates were built. The original roadbed and the adjacent structures were simply bulldozed away to make room for four-lane superhighways. Higher speeds were attained at the expense of idyllic views of farms, fields, and small towns, together with the memories they evoked. In Ohio, and throughout the entire country, Route 20 is the exception. The interstates have been placed roughly parallel to historic Route 20 rather than directly on top of it. Thus, one can still travel historic Route 20 much as our ancestors did in decades gone by.

The purpose of this book is to give a glimpse of the early days of automobile travel, a time when two-lane highways were state of the art and Main Street was the focal point of most communities. Urban sprawl, big-box stores, and franchised restaurants and motels had not yet entered our imagination. The book follows a drive on historic Route 20 across Ohio from east to west as closely as possible to its original route, when motorists got a close-up view of the towns and cities along the path of their journey and took advantage of the stores, restaurants, service stations, and tourist accommodations in the communities. The route was determined by following travel guides and road maps from the 1920s to the 1940s as accurately as possible and extrapolating information from them to current streets and roads. Whenever possible, local knowledge of the route is included. The overall objective is to provide a guide for anyone wishing to replicate the experience of driving across Ohio on Route 20 in the pre-interstate era.

City officials and individual merchants were quick to recognize the value of advertising their wares to the traveling public. Inexpensive or even free picture postcards were a popular way to advertise cities. Professionally produced picture postcards provided a convenient record of the trip, and they were typically less expensive and of higher quality than travelers could produce with their own cameras. Thus, many picture postcards found their way into personal scrapbooks, and others were sent to friends and relatives back home. The postcards show main streets, service stations, diners, tourist homes, cabin courts, and early motels. Notable scenic and historic locations along the route also are included.

All scenes in this book were located either directly on Route 20 or within a few miles of the highway and thus easily accessible to early travelers. In many instances, the sites still exist, although many no longer serve their original purpose. While certain sections of the original highway have been realigned and widened to four lanes, and some towns now have bypass options, in most places where this has occurred the roads that carried the original Route 20 still exist. Local numerical or street name designations may have been assigned, but with a bit of effort one can still follow historic Route 20 across the state. It is a drive well worth taking.

One

Along Lake Erie

Historic Route 20 entered Ohio in the extreme northeastern corner of the state, and for most of the 50 miles from the Pennsylvania-Ohio border to Cleveland's suburbs it was rarely more than three to four miles from the south shore of Lake Erie. This section, originally known as the Connecticut Western Reserve, was the result of the charter granted by England to Connecticut during the Colonial period. All land extending directly west from Connecticut was included. After the American Revolution, much of the original Connecticut charter was ceded to the federal government or sold to other states, but Connecticut retained the title to this area. Even after this section became part of Ohio, the name Western Reserve continued to be used.

Early immigrants recognized the potential for agriculture and commerce in the area, and homesteaders established farms, which were soon followed by villages. The proximity to the lake provided opportunities for expanded commerce. Conneaut and Ashtabula developed into two of the most important ports on the entire Great Lakes, receiving and shipping iron ore, lumber, coal, and manufactured goods from all the Great Lakes to the Eastern states, the Midwest, and Canada. This made the highway connecting the lakeside cities the natural path to follow when Route 20 was designated in 1926.

Lake Erie's beautiful sandy beaches and plentiful sunshine contributed to making the area a major tourist destination. Hardly a mile goes by without evidence of an early tourist accommodation. The quaint main streets and residential neighborhoods testify to the high quality of life of the citizens, to which Route 20 contributed significantly. Most Lake Erie communities can boast of significant historical structures, including homes, churches, and civic buildings, and many are listed in the National Register of Historic Places. Due to their strategic position near Lake Erie, many communities contributed to the Underground Railroad, providing assistance to escaped slaves making their way across the lake to Canada.

As the dominant northern highway from 1926 through the early 1950s, Route 20 served northeastern Ohio both as a commercial highway and as the road pleasure-seekers took to visit the many historical and lakeshore attractions near it.

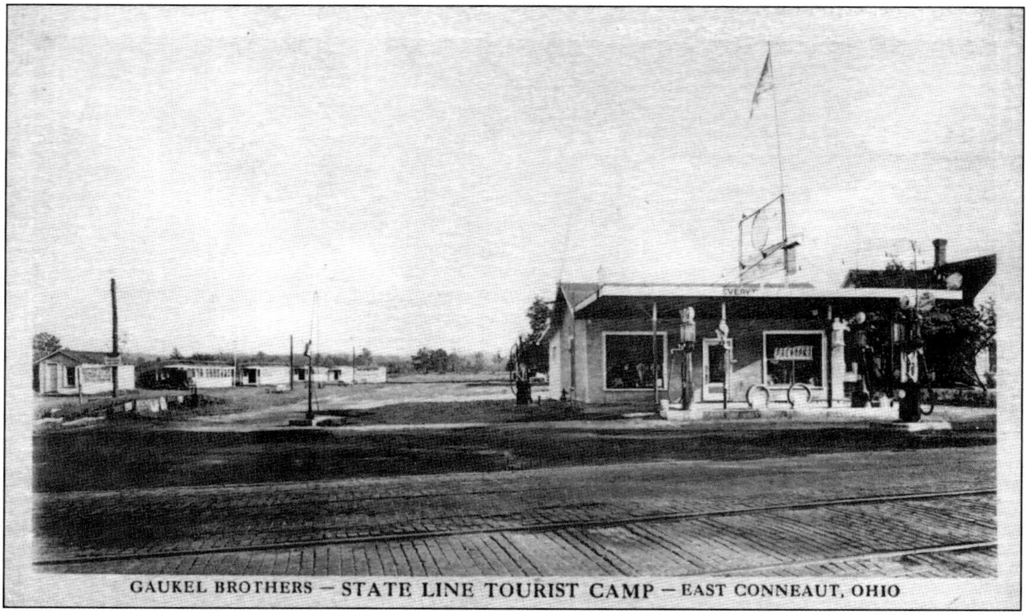

GAUKEL BROTHERS STATE LINE TOURIST CAMP, EAST CONNEAUT. This roadside establishment was on Route 20 only a short distance west of the Pennsylvania-Ohio state line. The sign on the canopy informed travelers that Gaukel's offered "everything for self and car," and the back of the card advertised "service that brings you back with a smile." Overnight amenities included private cottages, a community cookhouse, and a service station.

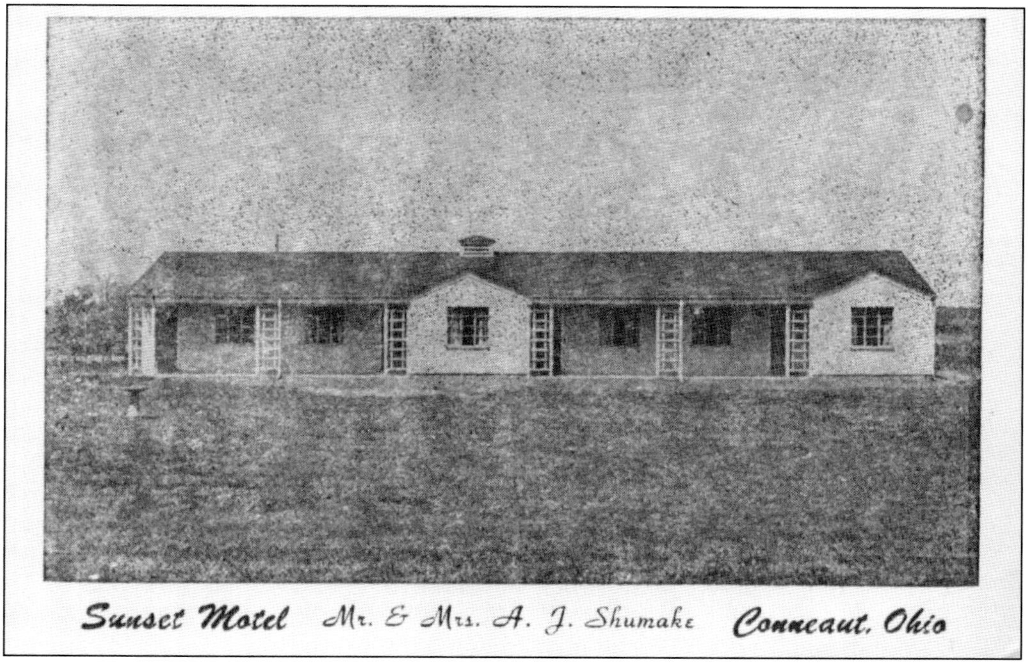

SUNSET MOTEL, ROUTE 20, CONNEAUT. Most early motel owners described the advantages of their properties, often in flowery terms, to entice travelers to stop for the night. Mr. and Mrs. A.J. Shumake apparently hoped this photograph alone would be sufficient. No description of the motel's other amenities is provided on the back of the card.

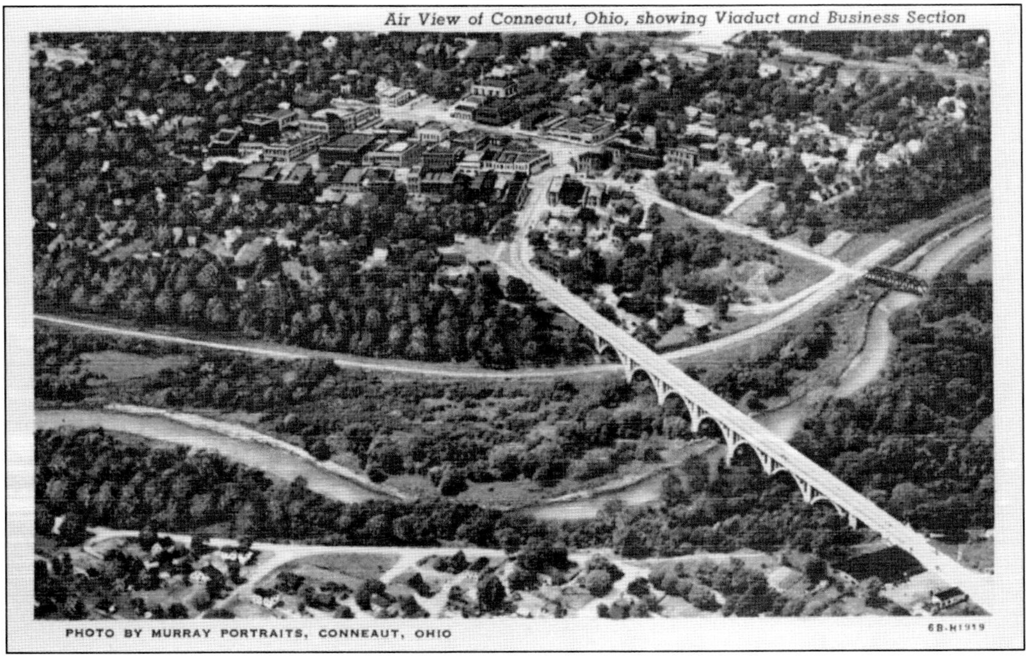

AERIAL VIEW OF BUSINESS DISTRICT AND VIADUCT, CONNEAUT. The 1,300-foot Conneaut Viaduct opened in 1924. It spanned Conneaut Creek and the Nickel Plate Railroad. The name of the street at that time was Chicago-Buffalo Road. The photograph above, taken in the 1930s, shows Route 20 coming from the east, crossing the viaduct, and then making a left turn on Main Street, where it passed through Conneaut's business district. The double view on the postcard below shows the viaduct from both the valley and surface levels. Both scenes illustrate the size and intricate concrete-arch design of the viaduct, which carried Route 20 traffic throughout its 80-year lifetime.

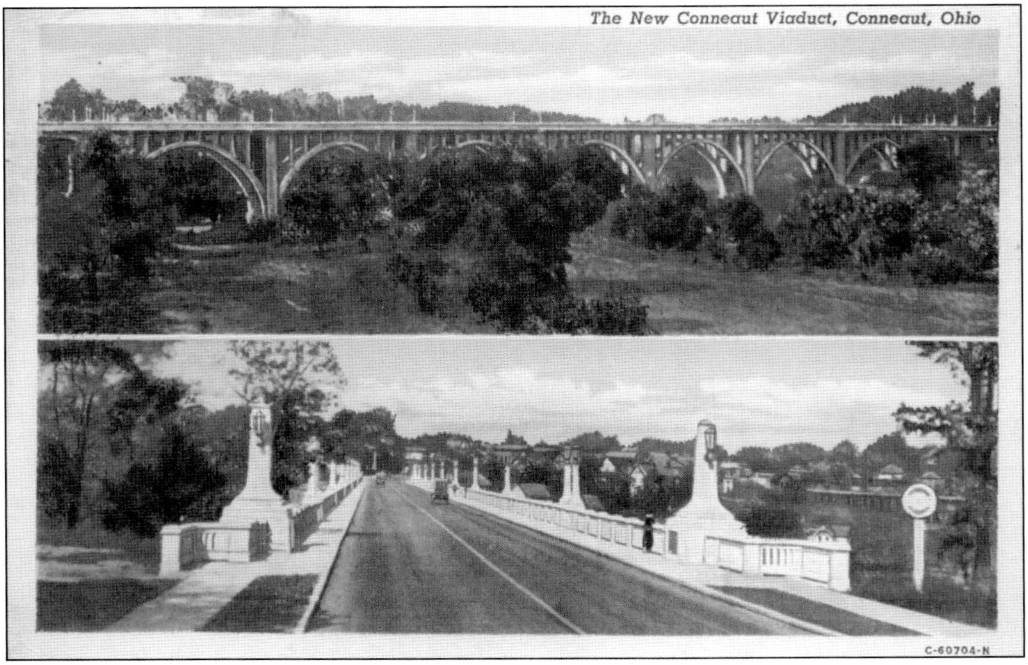

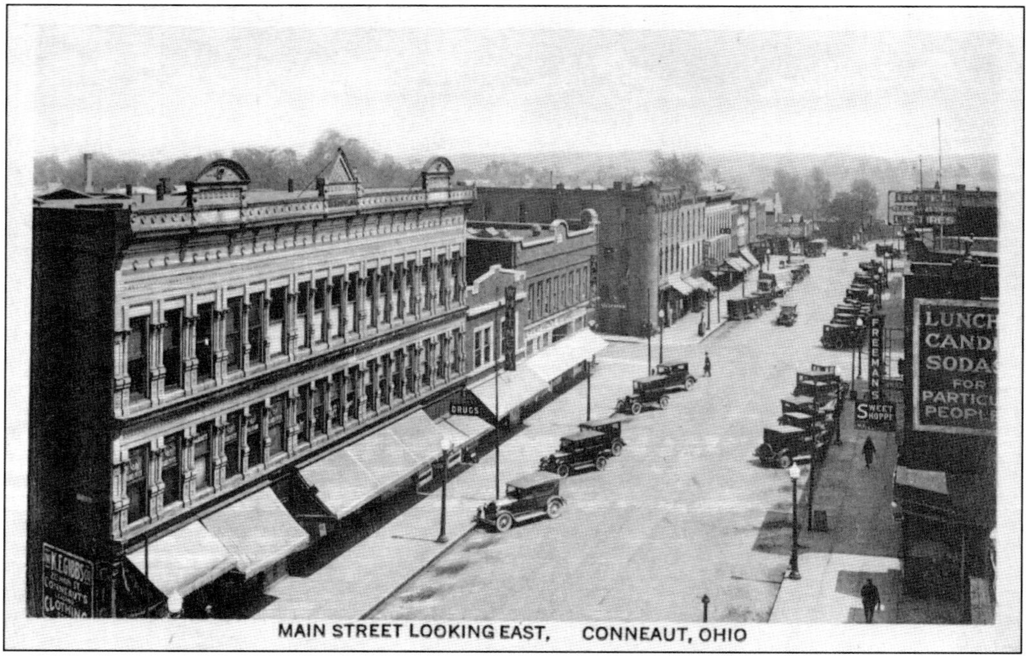

MAIN STREET LOOKING EAST, CONNEAUT. All the necessities of the day were available along Main Street in Conneaut in the 1930s. The left side of the street included clothing stores, drugstores, department stores, and cigar stores. On the right, shoppers could purchase tires, and "particular people" could enjoy lunch, candy, and sodas at Freeman's Sweet Shoppe. Before the days of traffic congestion, diagonal parking was used on the main streets of most cities.

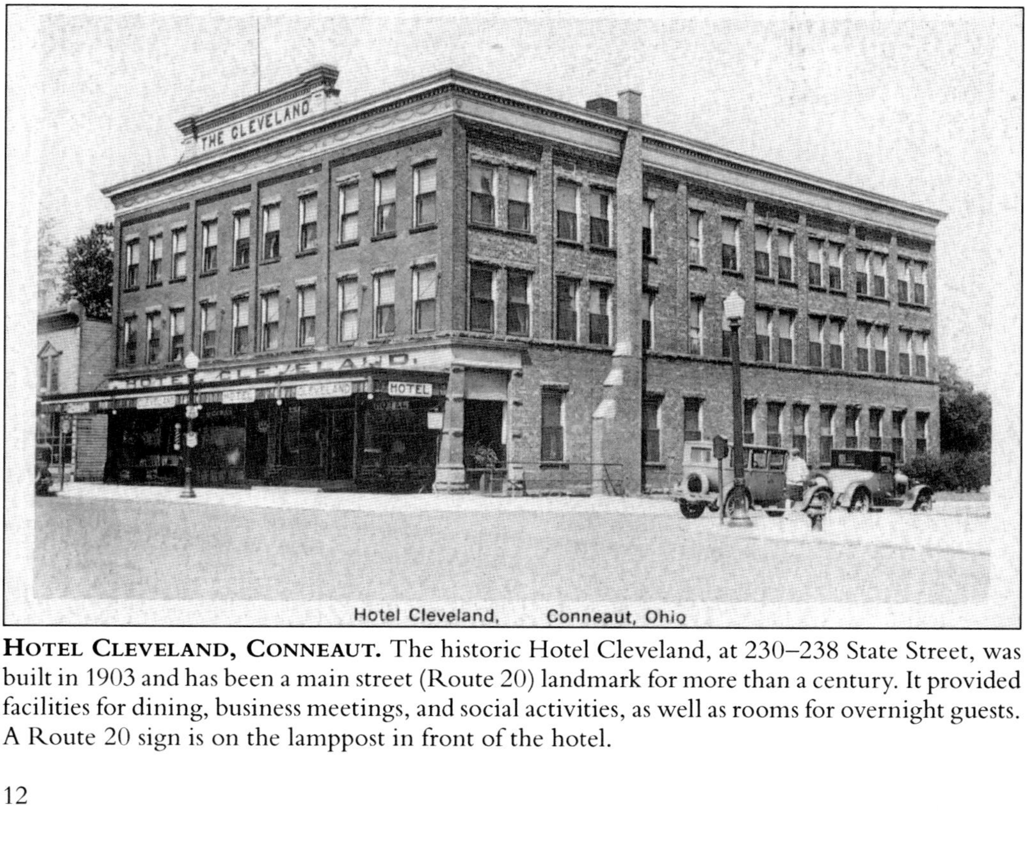

HOTEL CLEVELAND, CONNEAUT. The historic Hotel Cleveland, at 230–238 State Street, was built in 1903 and has been a main street (Route 20) landmark for more than a century. It provided facilities for dining, business meetings, and social activities, as well as rooms for overnight guests. A Route 20 sign is on the lamppost in front of the hotel.

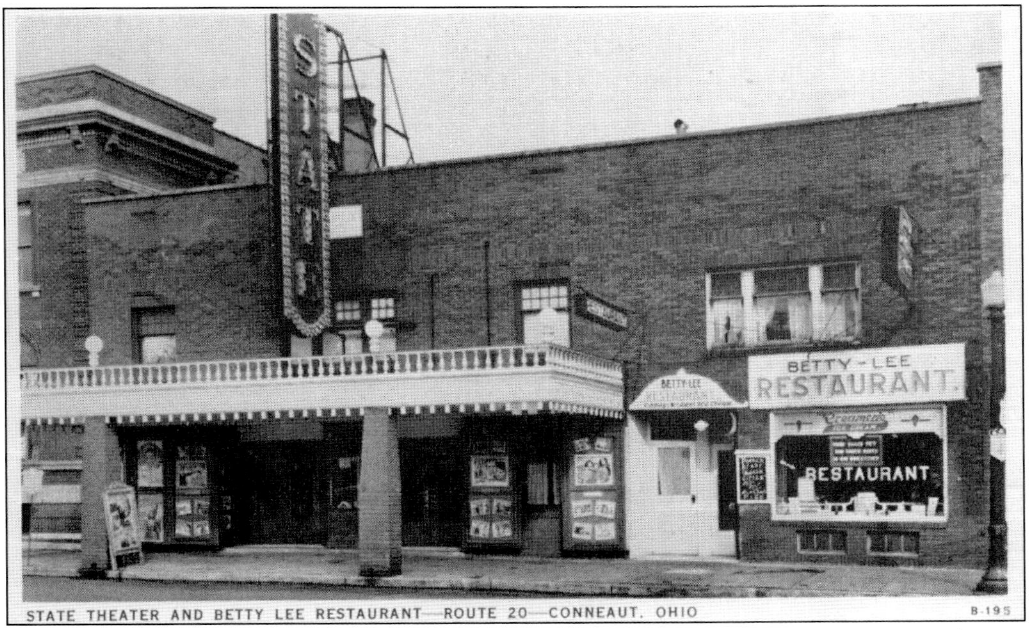

State Theater and Betty-Lee Restaurant, Main Street, Conneaut. Travelers on Route 20 who chose to spend the night in Conneaut could enjoy a good meal at Betty-Lee's Restaurant and then take in a movie next door at the State Theater. The theater's facade was typical of the day, with its elaborate, well-lighted canopy and movie placards on both sides of the entrance.

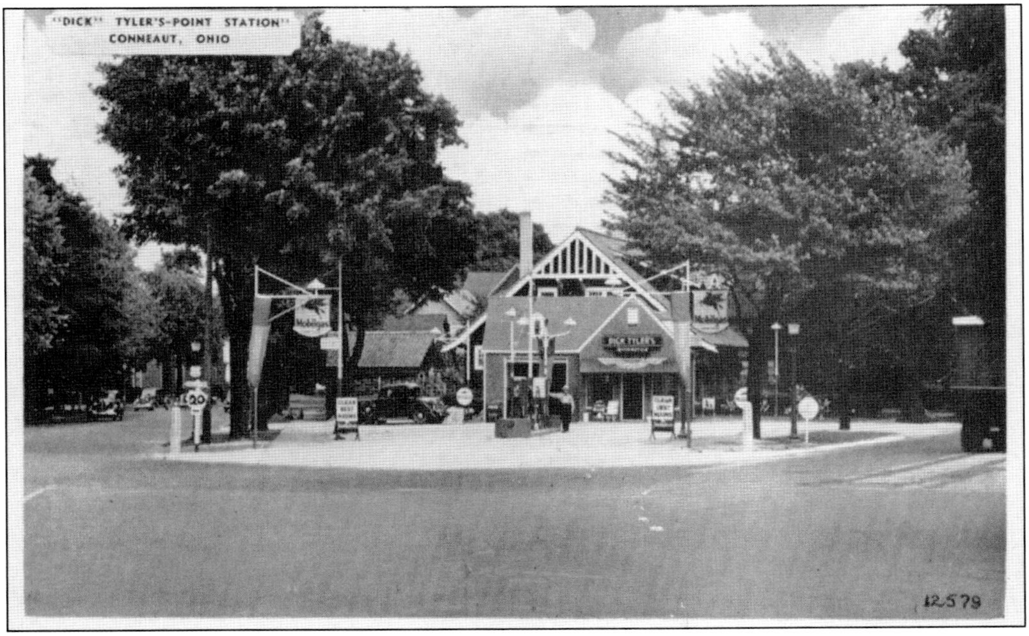

Dick Tyler's Point Station, Conneaut. The term "point" typically indicates a prominent intersection where streets meet at an angle. At the point in Conneaut, Dick Tyler's service station featured Mobilgas products and proudly proclaimed "Clean Rest Rooms" on two signs. A makeshift Route 20 sign is on the left, and the official Route 20 shield is visible a few feet farther down the street.

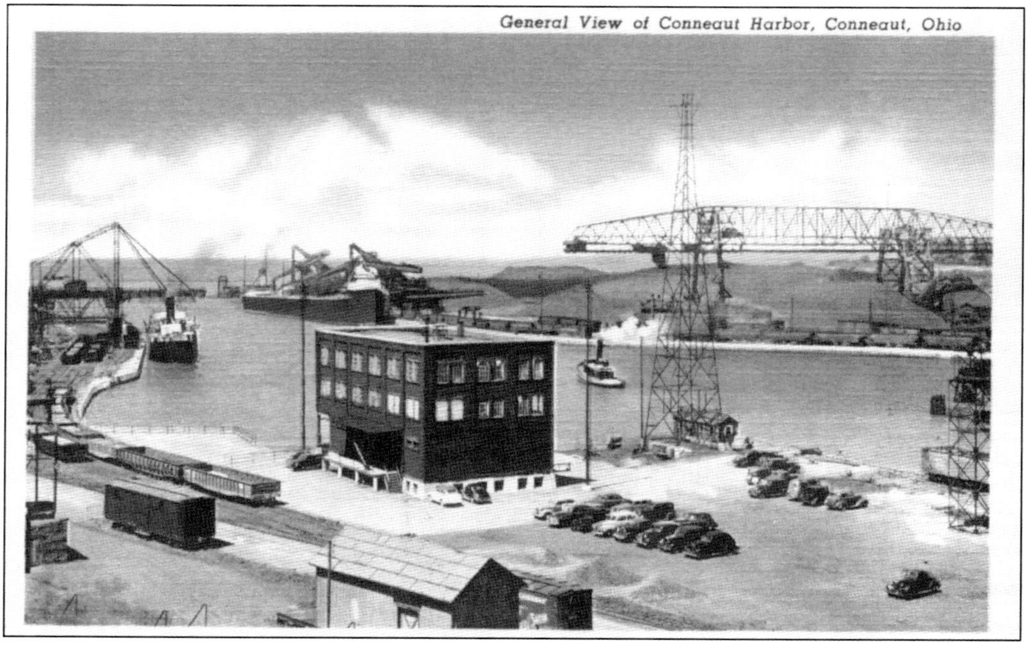

CONNEAUT HARBOR, LAKE ERIE, CONNEAUT. Prior to the opening of the St. Lawrence Seaway, which gave large ships direct access to middle America, many natural resources— including lumber, coal, grain, and iron ore—and manufactured goods were shipped through Lake Erie ports, where they were then transferred to railroads for distribution throughout the Eastern states. Conneaut and its neighbor Ashtabula were prime beneficiaries of the Great Lakes shipping industry.

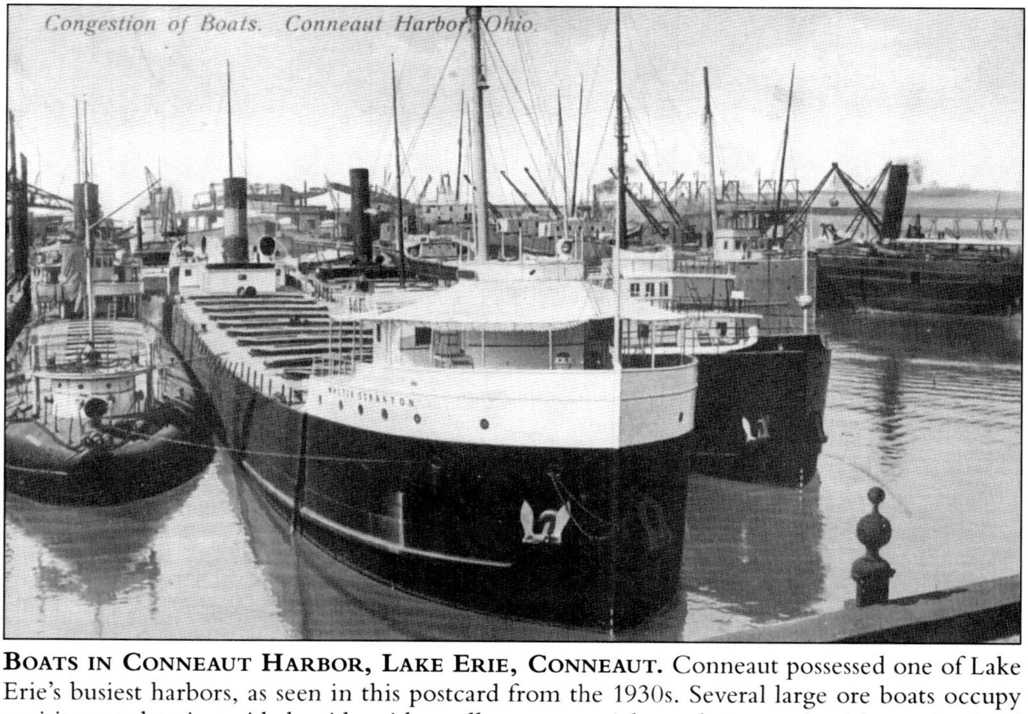

BOATS IN CONNEAUT HARBOR, LAKE ERIE, CONNEAUT. Conneaut possessed one of Lake Erie's busiest harbors, as seen in this postcard from the 1930s. Several large ore boats occupy positions at the piers, side by side with smaller commercial vessels. Large derricks used to load and unload cargo are in the background.

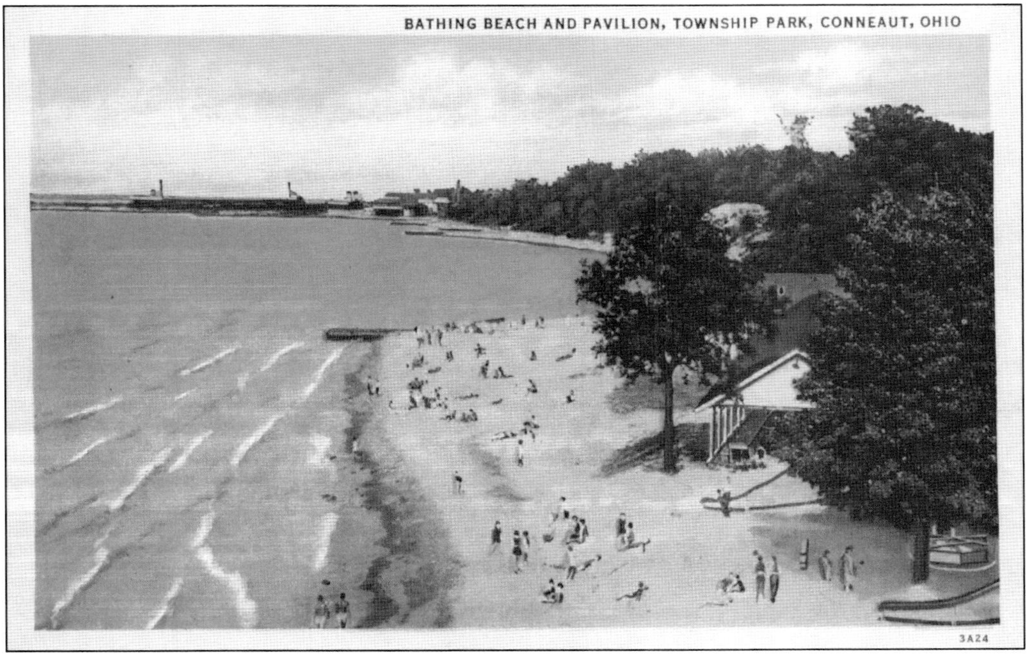

BATHING BEACH AND PAVILION, TOWNSHIP PARK, CONNEAUT. Conneaut's seven-mile-long sandy beach offered excellent swimming, boating, fishing, and other water sports popular with local citizens and visitors. A portion of the industrial port connecting Conneaut with other Great Lakes ports is in the distance. At least one ore boat is moored at the pier.

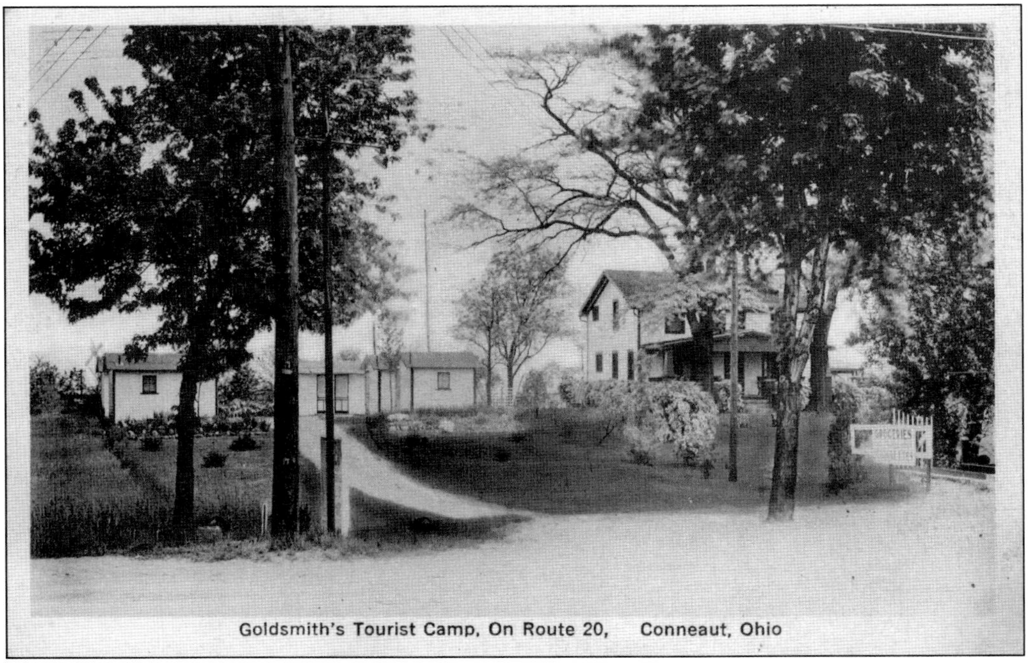

GOLDSMITH'S VALLEY VIEW TOURIST CAMP, CONNEAUT. This complete tourist camp offered showers, groceries, cigarettes, a camp kitchen, running water, and natural-gas heat. The sender of this card wrote that after dinner they were going uptown to a show, possibly at Conneaut's State Theater.

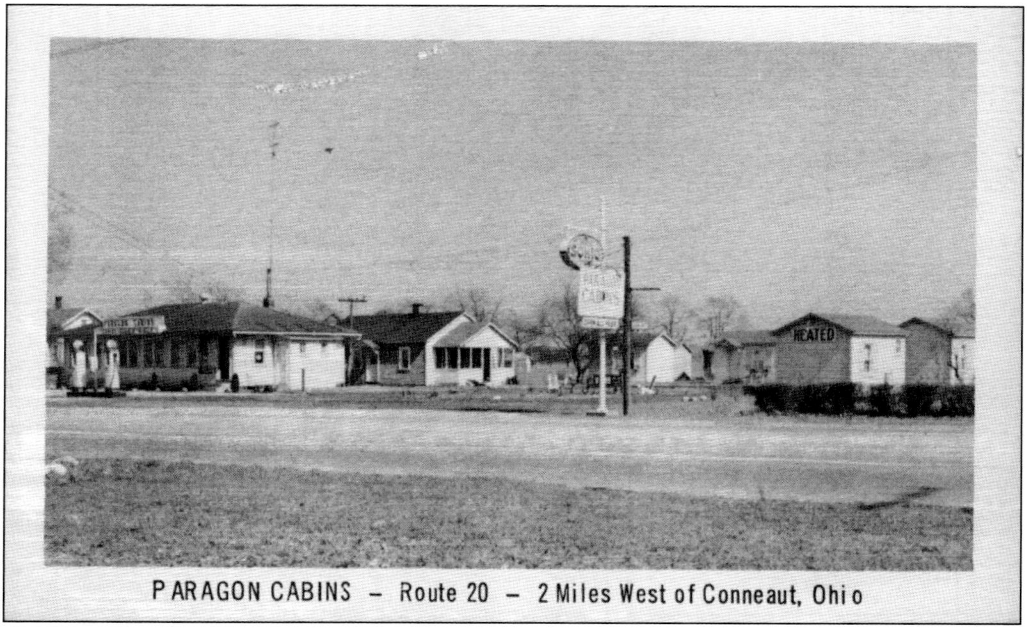

PARAGON CABINS, CONNEAUT. The large sign in the center informed travelers that the Paragon was open all year and that Sohio Oil products were featured at the two-pump service station. Guests were accommodated in individually heated cabins on the grounds.

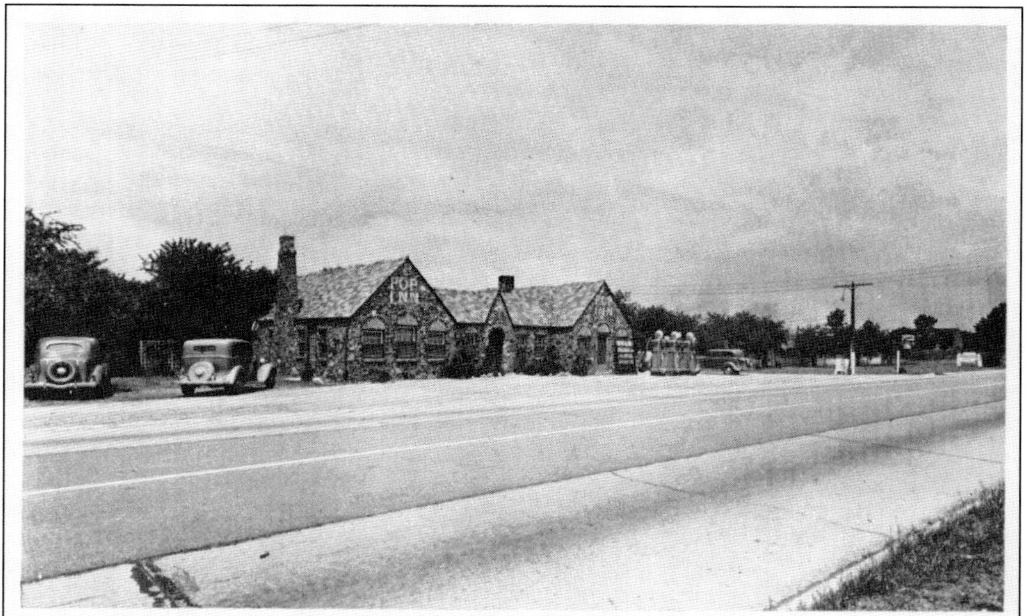

POP-INN, NORTH KINGSVILLE. "Pop-Inn" is engraved in stone above the doors on both wings of this building. The attractive roadside establishment provided one-stop service for motorists on Route 20. A service station, restaurant, and tourist court were all available. The several cars in front of the building in this 1930s photograph indicate business was good that day. The Pop-Inn is now the North Kingsville municipal building.

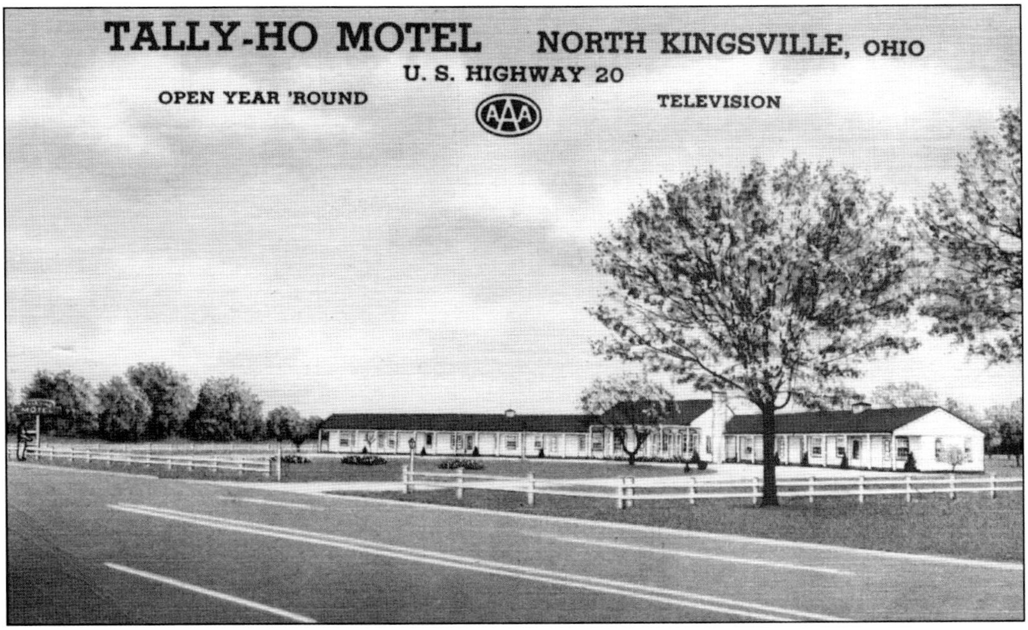

Tally-Ho Motel, North Kingsville. The Tally-Ho is another motel that took advantage of its Route 20 location close to Lake Erie recreation. The back of the card states that it was "seven miles east of Ashtabula, five miles west of Conneaut, and one mile from Lake Erie." The covered porch and landscaped grounds provided a pleasant setting for travelers.

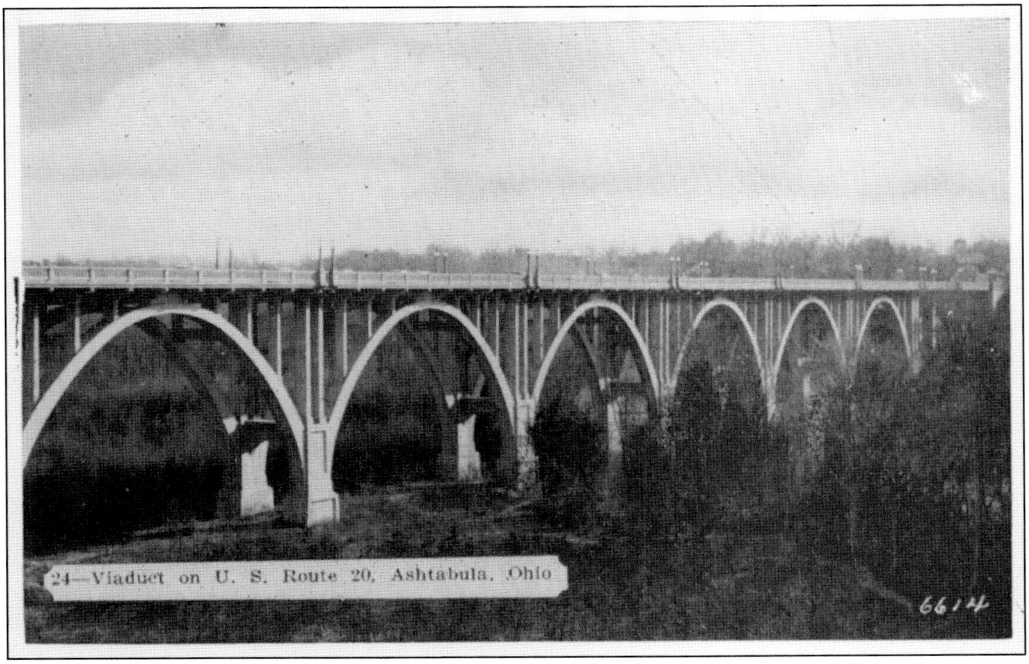

Route 20 Viaduct, Ashtabula. This historical viaduct east of the Ashtabula business district was built between 1926 and 1928 and carried Route 20 for almost 75 years after the federal highway was designated in 1926. A new viaduct, named in honor of Rev. Sam Wells Jr., a Baptist minister and longtime civic activist, was opened in November 2000, at which time this viaduct was razed.

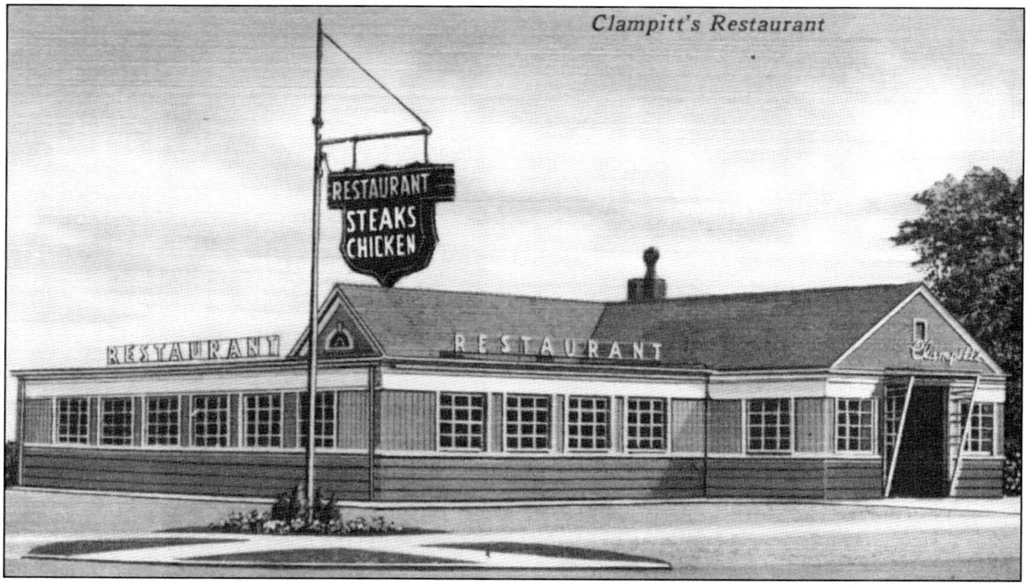

Clampitt's Restaurant, 4110 Park Avenue, Ashtabula. Clampitt's proudly proclaimed that it was "the home of delicious food at popular prices." Its favorable location at the junction of Route 20, Routes 83 and 46, and Main Avenue, near the Ashtabula viaduct, ensured a steady flow of patrons. The postcard also includes its distance from four cities on Route 20: "Buffalo—135; Erie—45; Cleveland—56; and Toledo—172."

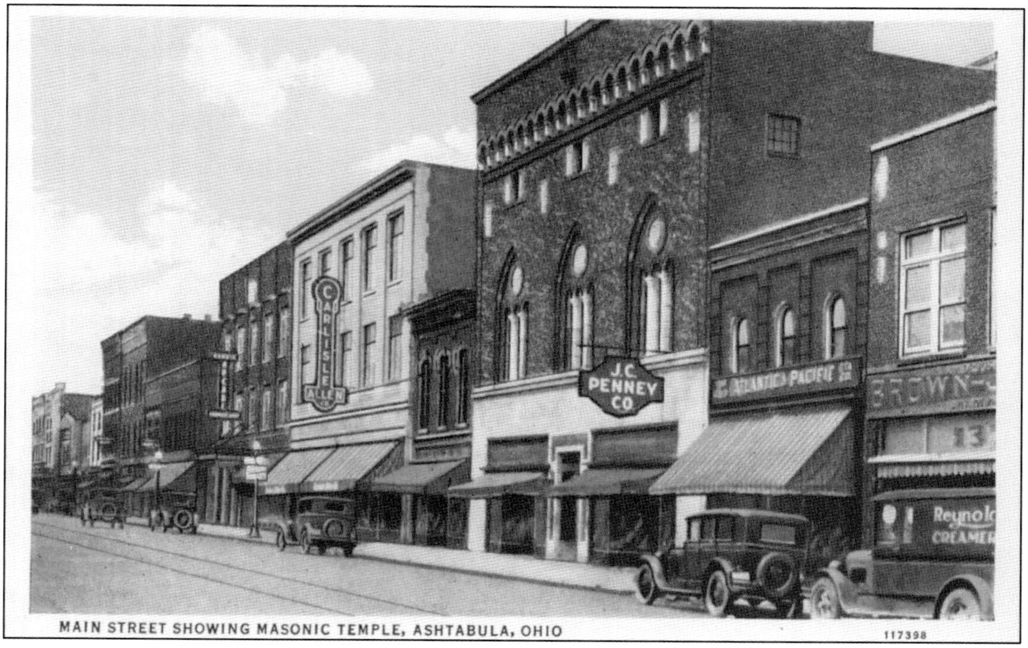

Main Street, Ashtabula. Other postcards and maps identify this thoroughfare as Main Avenue rather than Main Street. In either case, it was the main artery of Ashtabula's business district. Trolleys were still in use when this photograph was taken, although the increasing popularity of automobiles is evident. Local outlets of two companies that grew into major American chain stores are also seen: J.C. Penney Co. and the Great Atlantic & Pacific Tea Company (A&P), which were next to each other.

ASHTABULA HOTEL, 4726 MAIN AVENUE, ASHTABULA. The Ashtabula Hotel was a fixture in Ashtabula's business district and a significant contributor to the city's economy throughout the early decades of the 1900s. It was the site of business and social events and was a resting place for highway travelers and persons engaged in the maritime commerce in Ashtabula's large harbor. The hotel's fancy lobby is seen below. The large stone pillars, ornate balconies, and oversized furniture are reminiscent of medieval castles. The Hotel Ashtabula is in the National Register of Historic Places.

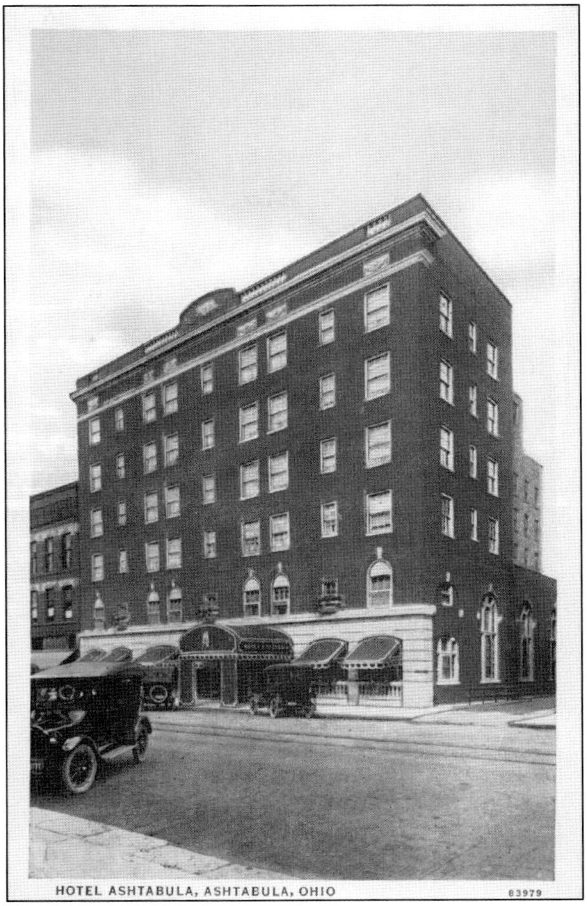

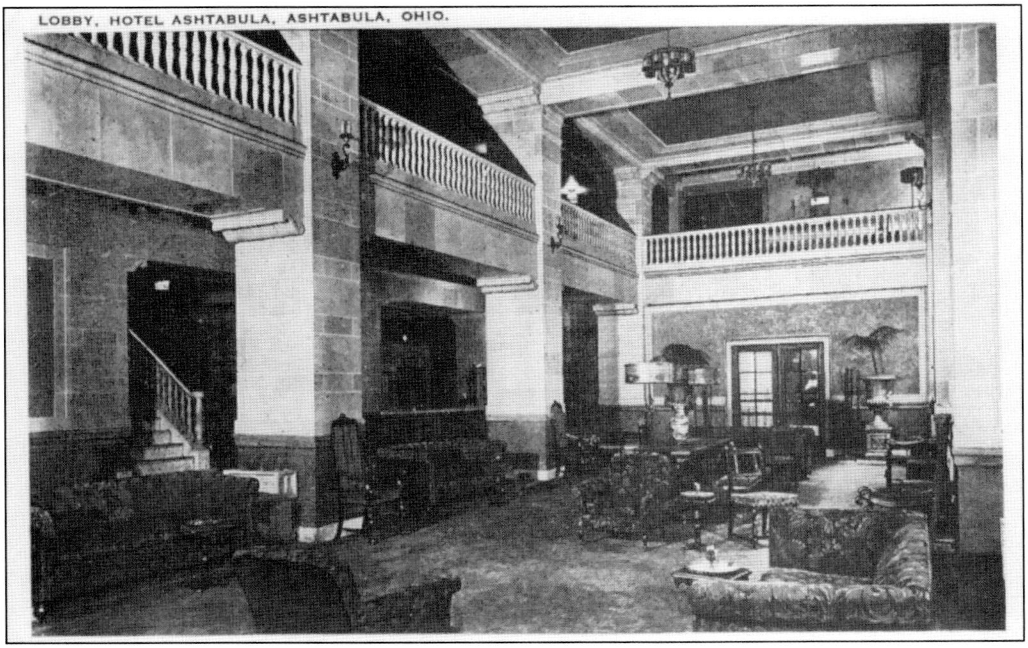

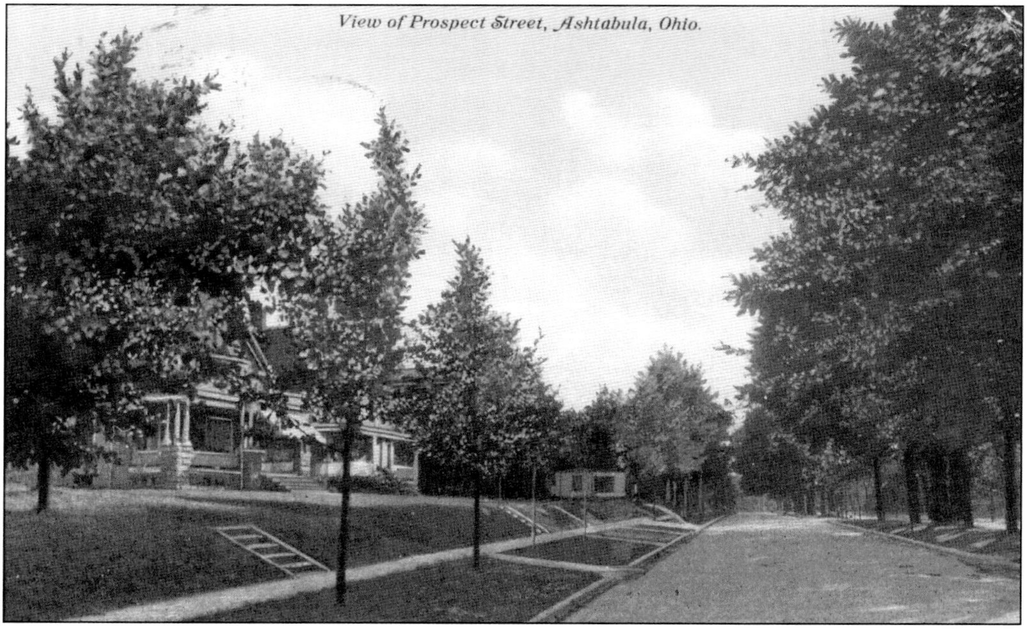

PROSPECT STREET, ASHTABULA. Route 20 followed Prospect Street as it proceeded west through Ashtabula. Most of the homes on this pleasant residential street had front porches that were characteristic of homes in the 1920s and 1930s. The large trees and well-cared-for lawns were indicative of the prosperity of this neighborhood.

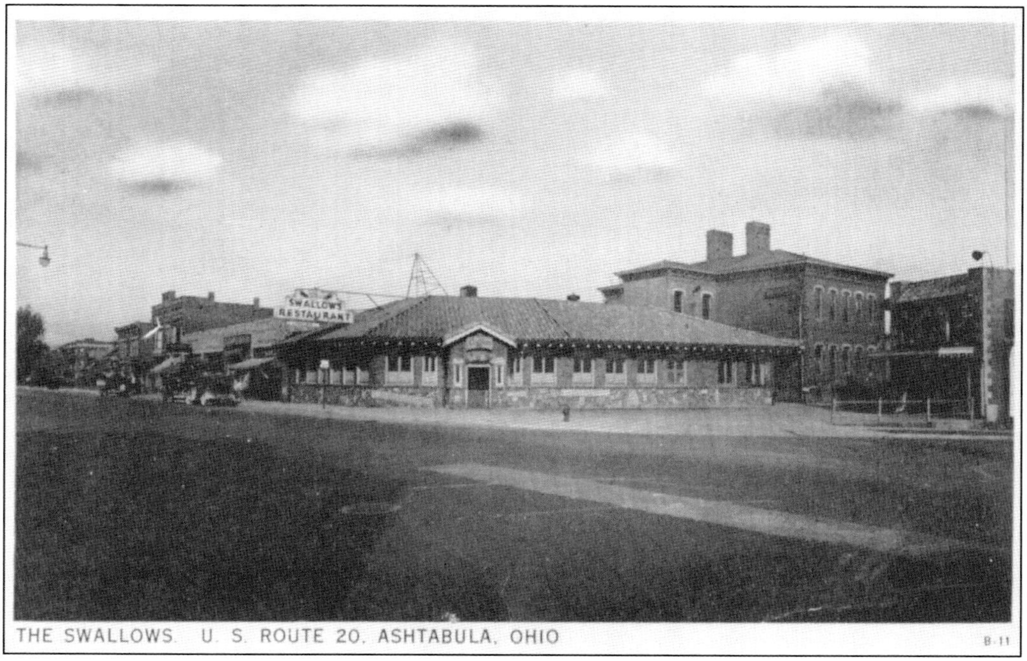

THE SWALLOWS RESTAURANT, ASHTABULA. Located toward the western edge of Ashtabula, the Swallows proclaimed that it was "known from coast to coast." The back of the card added that it was "truly a haven for gourmets, specializing in prime roast beef, steaks, chops and seafood, served in a manner you will approve." It continued, "Come sometime, won't you? Take Route 20 right into Ashtabula—you can't miss our sign."

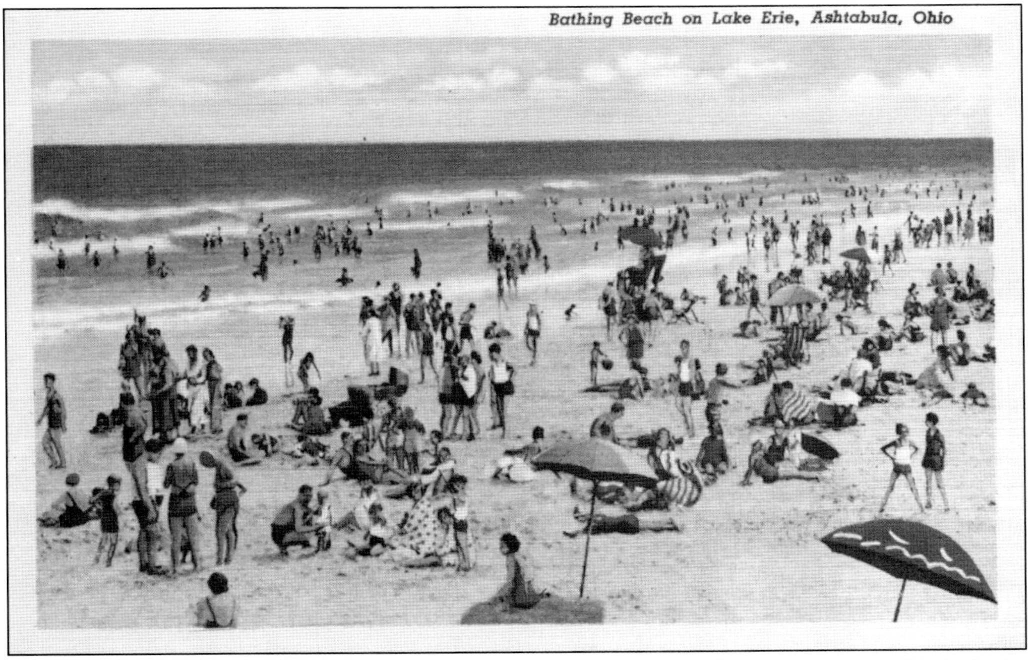

BATHING BEACH AND PAVILION, LAKE ERIE, ASHTABULA. Both east and west of Ashtabula, Route 20 paralleled the south shore of Lake Erie, usually no more than one or two miles from the lake. Beaches extended for miles along the shoreline, as seen above. In addition to sun and sand, the lakeshore in Ashtabula offered excellent opportunities for boating, fishing, and other water sports. Among the most popular attractions was the dance pavilion at Lake Shore Park, seen below, where famous orchestras and dance bands provided music. Picnic grounds and cabins for large and small groups made the beach at Ashtabula the ideal location for local residents to spend the day or for vacationers to come for lengthier stays.

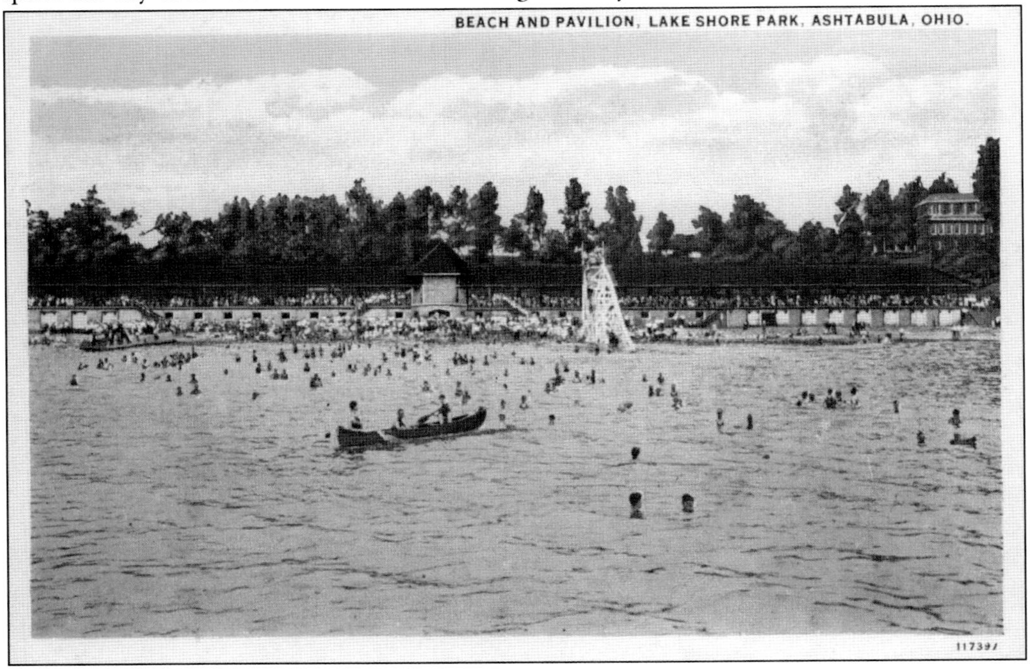

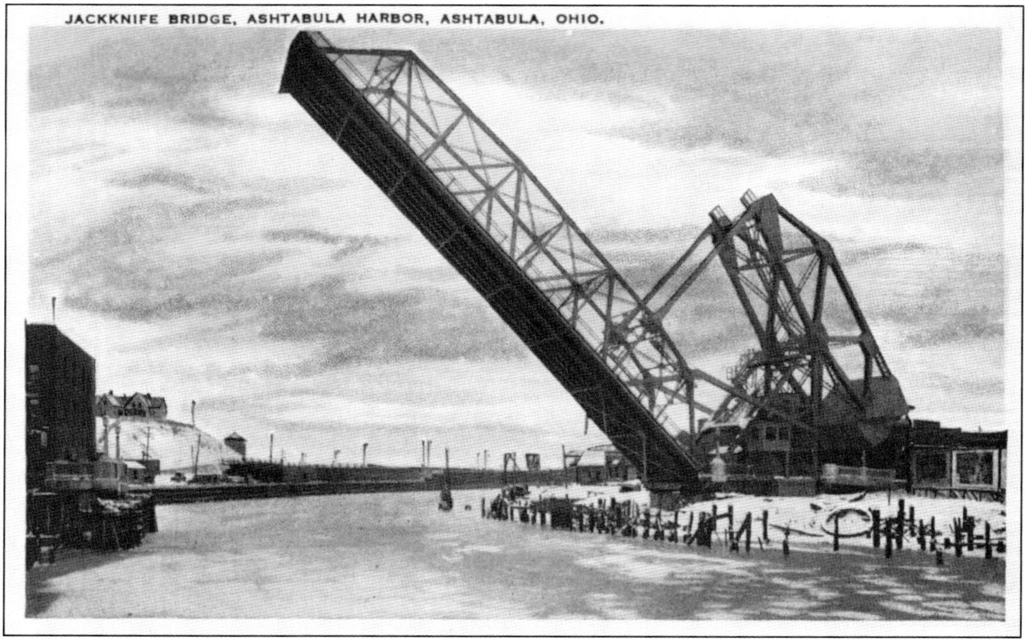

JACKKNIFE BRIDGE, ASHTABULA HARBOR. Another popular attraction in Ashtabula harbor is seen on this postcard. Children were especially excited to watch the famous Jackknife Bridge, completed in 1925, open to allow larger boats access to the Ashtabula River. The unique bridge design employed a counterbalancing mechanism at one end, which enabled the entire roadbed to be elevated.

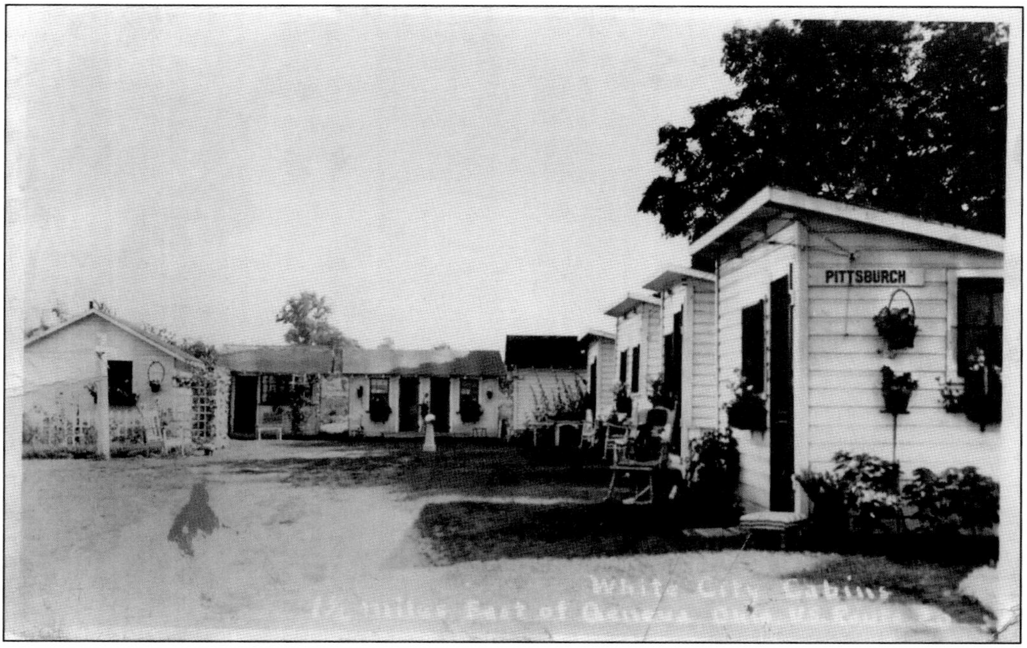

WHITE CITY CABINS, ROUTE 20, GENEVA. This postcard shows the Pittsburgh unit and others at this early tourist camp. The proprietors did their best to beautify the court, adorning each cabin with potted plants and providing comfortable chairs so guests could sit outside.

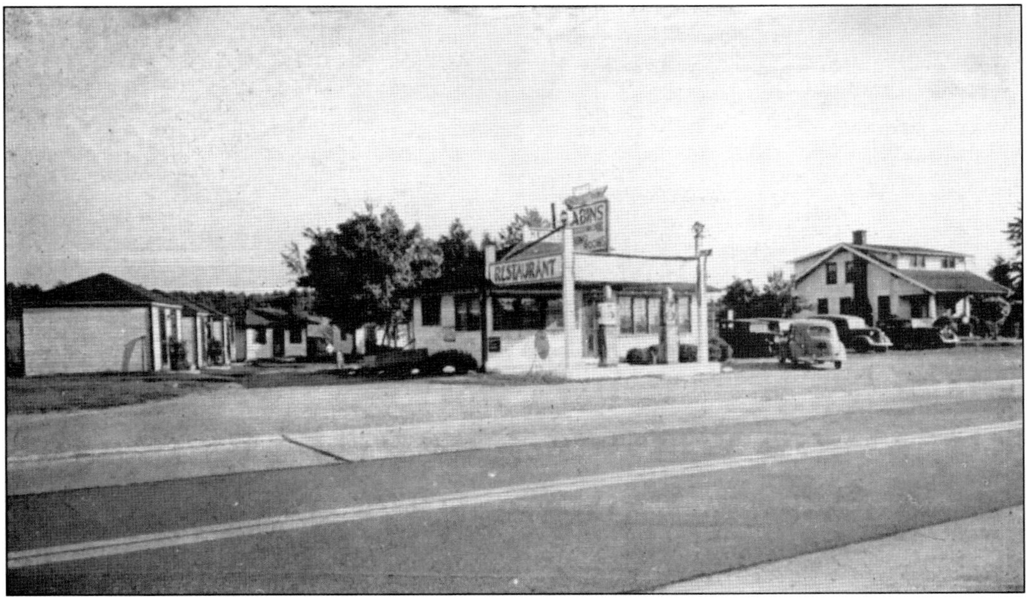

Unc'l Sams Modern Cabins, Geneva. This is another example of the small gas station/restaurant/cabins combination typical of the early days of Route 20. The owner probably lived in the house on the right.

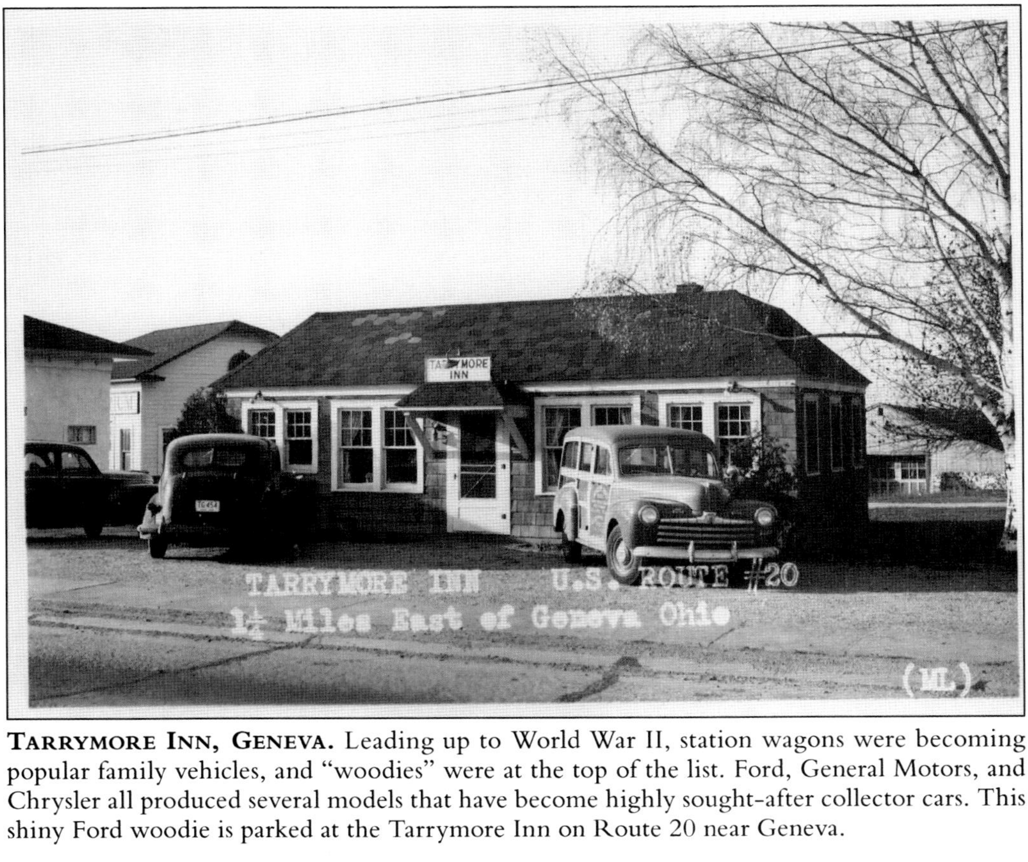

Tarrymore Inn, Geneva. Leading up to World War II, station wagons were becoming popular family vehicles, and "woodies" were at the top of the list. Ford, General Motors, and Chrysler all produced several models that have become highly sought-after collector cars. This shiny Ford woodie is parked at the Tarrymore Inn on Route 20 near Geneva.

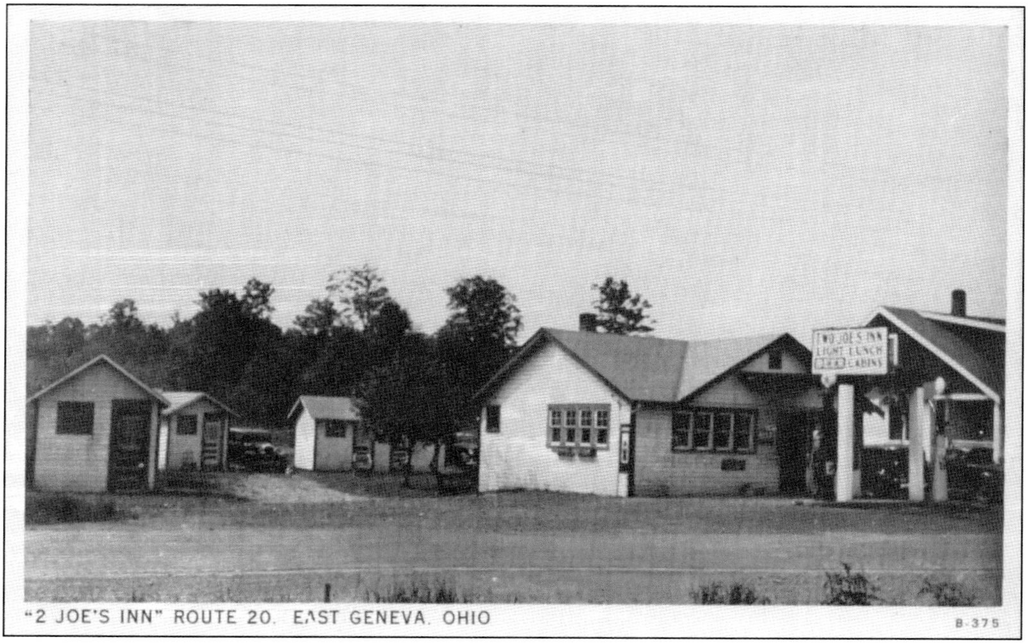

2 JOE'S INN, GENEVA. The sign above the service island informed Route 20 motorists that light lunches and cabins were available. Beer was also highlighted, indicating that Prohibition had ended when this photograph was taken. Bathroom facilities were located in the main service station building and in traditional outhouses on the property.

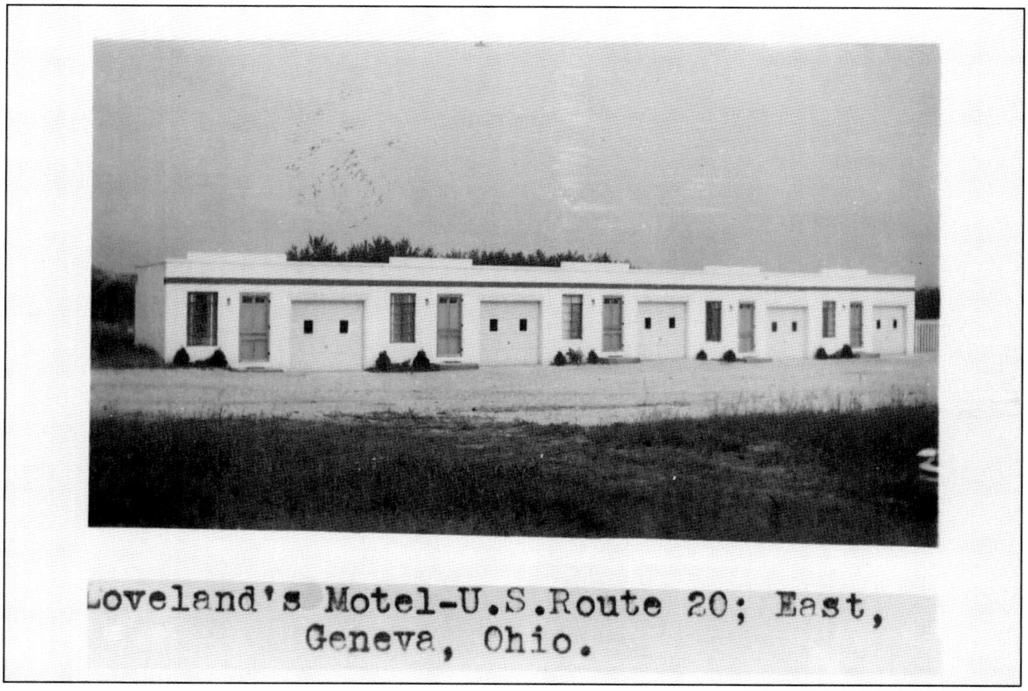

LOVELAND'S MOTEL, ROUTE 20 EAST, GENEVA. No information is printed on the back of this card, and it is difficult to identify features that would attract travelers to this stark and treeless early motel, especially because there were several tourist accommodations nearby.

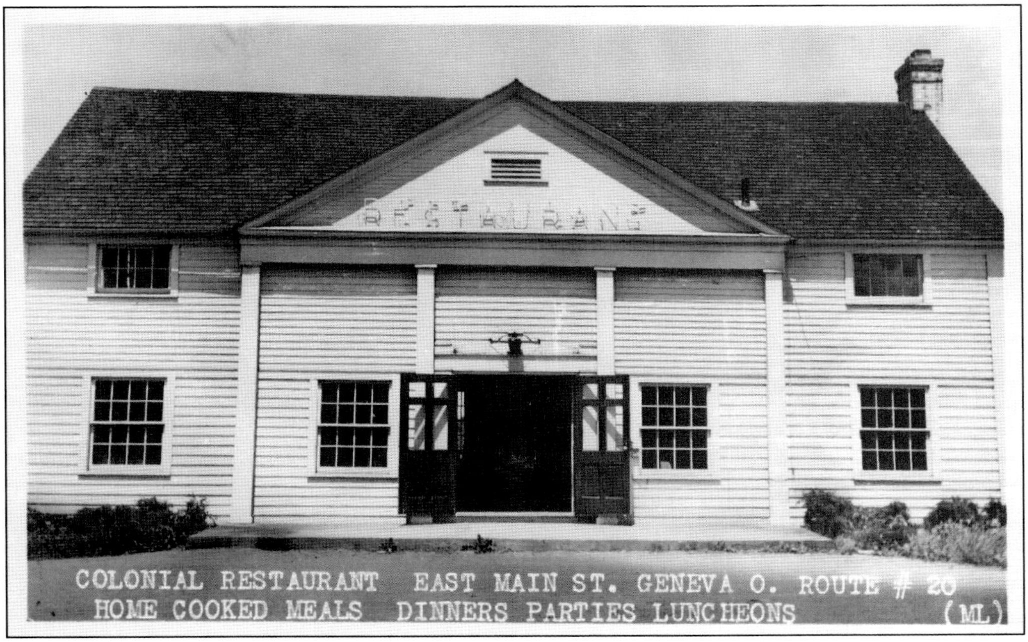

COLONIAL RESTAURANT, EAST MAIN STREET, GENEVA. The architectural style of this restaurant no doubt accounted for its name. The phrase "home cooking" was used often in restaurant advertisements of the day. It usually meant generous helpings of basic staples like chicken, beef, pork, and vegetables.

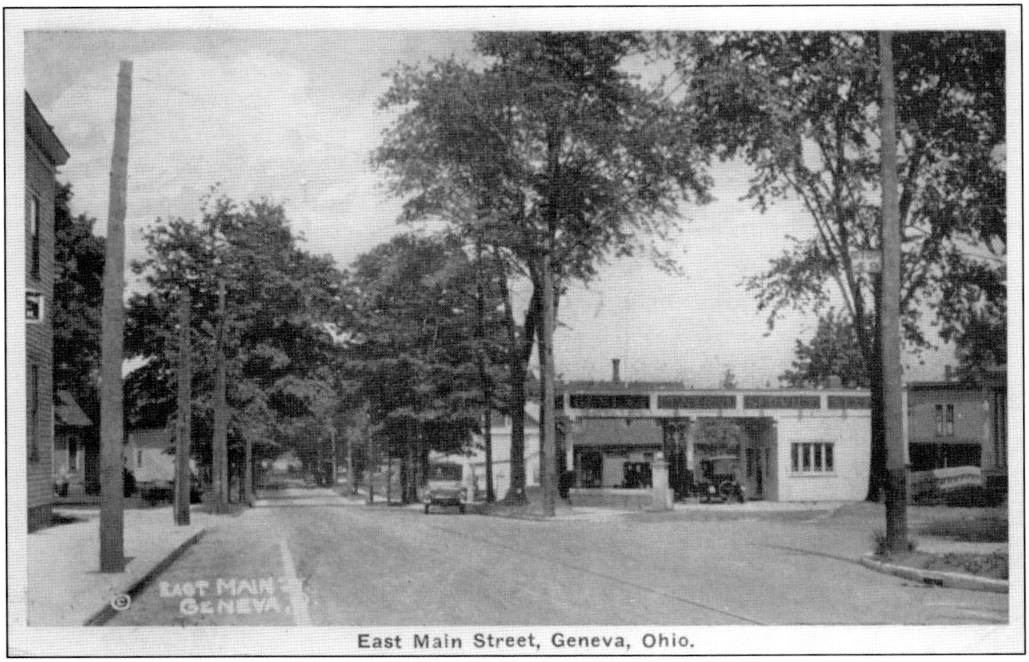

East Main Street, Geneva, Ohio.

EAST MAIN STREET, GENEVA. This neighborhood service station occupied a prominent position on East Main Street in Geneva in the late 1920s. The business blended in well with the residences on the tree-lined street. The writer of this card told her friend that she was on vacation and had a bad sunburn. She was most likely enjoying one of the nearby Lake Erie beaches.

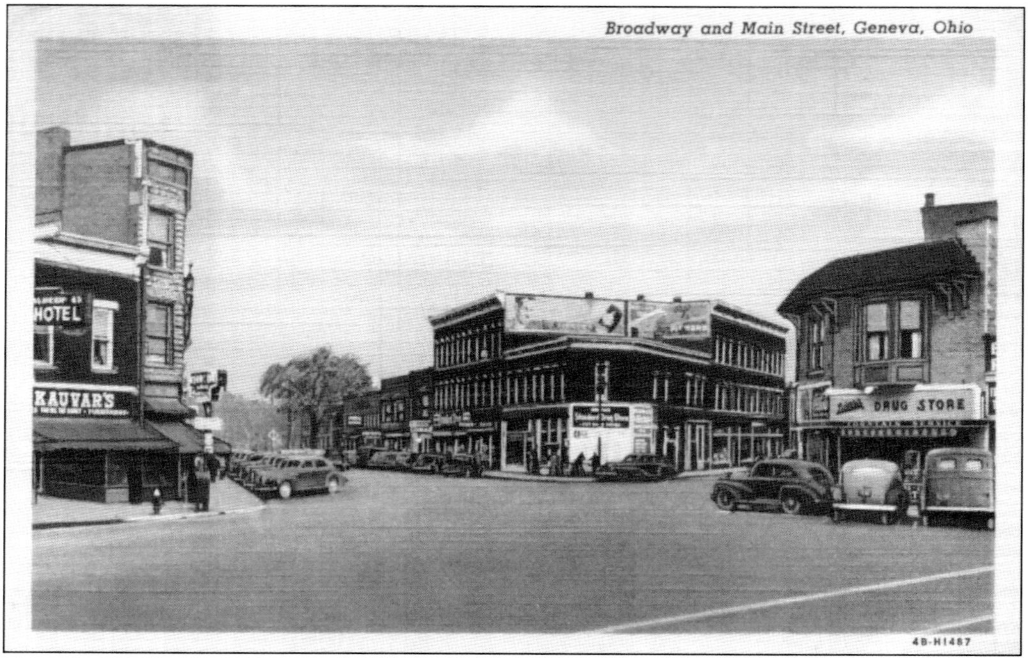

Broadway and Main Street, Geneva. Route 20 followed Main Street in an east-west direction through Geneva, and Broadway was a main north-south street. The intersection of these two streets shows a very traditional picture of small-town America in the 1930s. There were competing drugstores on either side of the intersection, as well as a hotel and a furniture store.

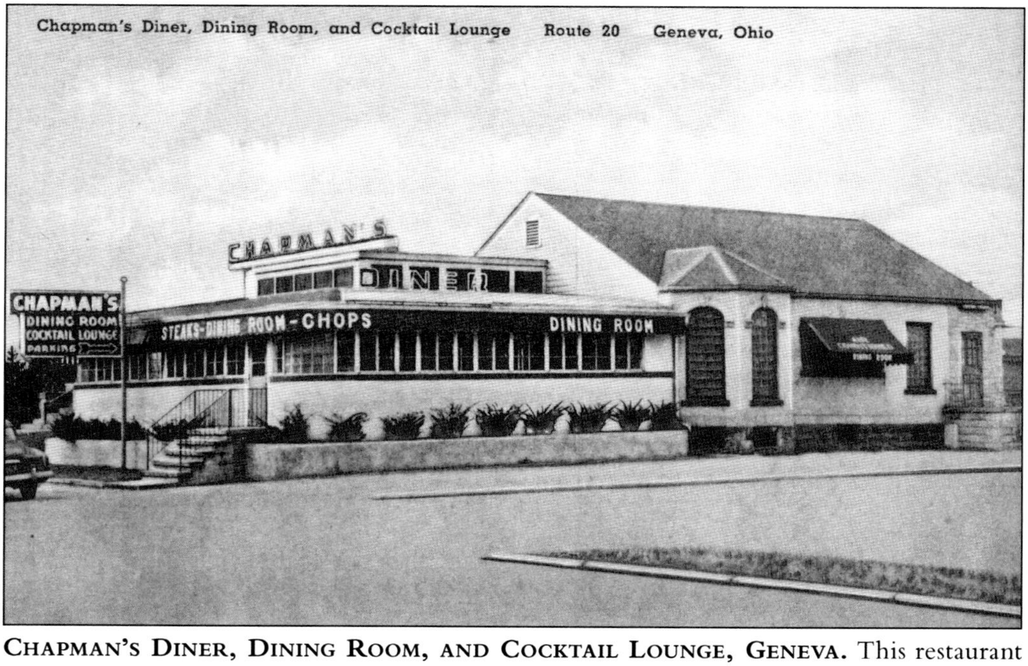

Chapman's Diner, Dining Room, and Cocktail Lounge, Geneva. This restaurant was located in Geneva's downtown business district, at 103 West Main Street, and was a popular place for travelers and locals to dine or enjoy a cocktail. Central air-conditioning, which was quite new when this postcard was produced, was prominently featured in its advertising and added to the restaurant's attractiveness.

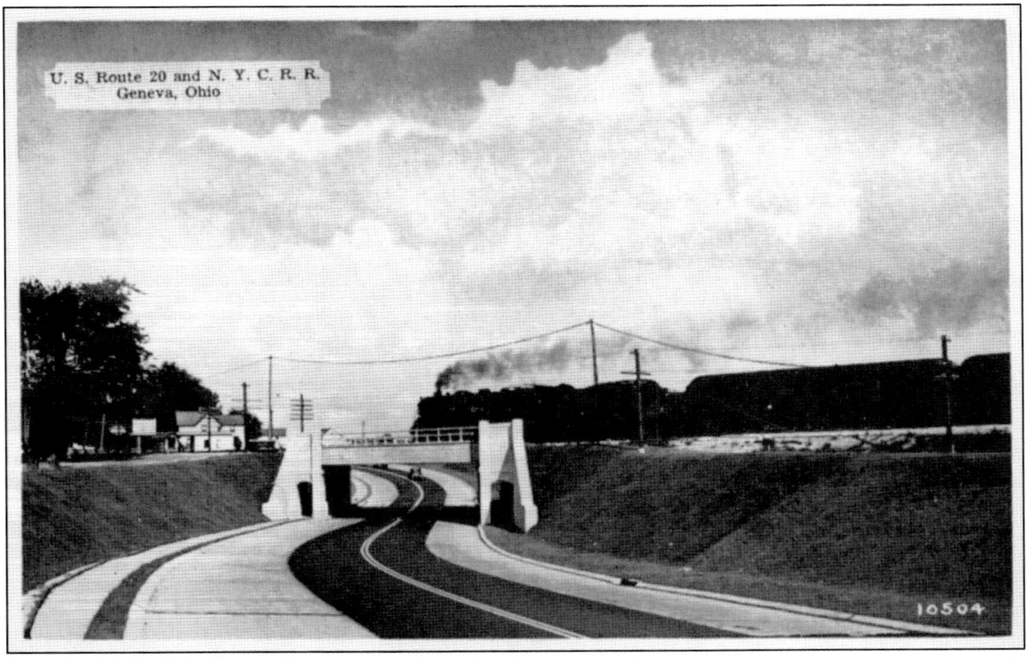

ROUTE 20 AND THE NYCRR, GENEVA. This scene near Geneva in the 1930s unwittingly portends the future of passenger train service in the United States. Modern concrete highways, capable of carrying automobile traffic long distances at rapid speeds, gradually displaced trains as the preferred method of personal transportation.

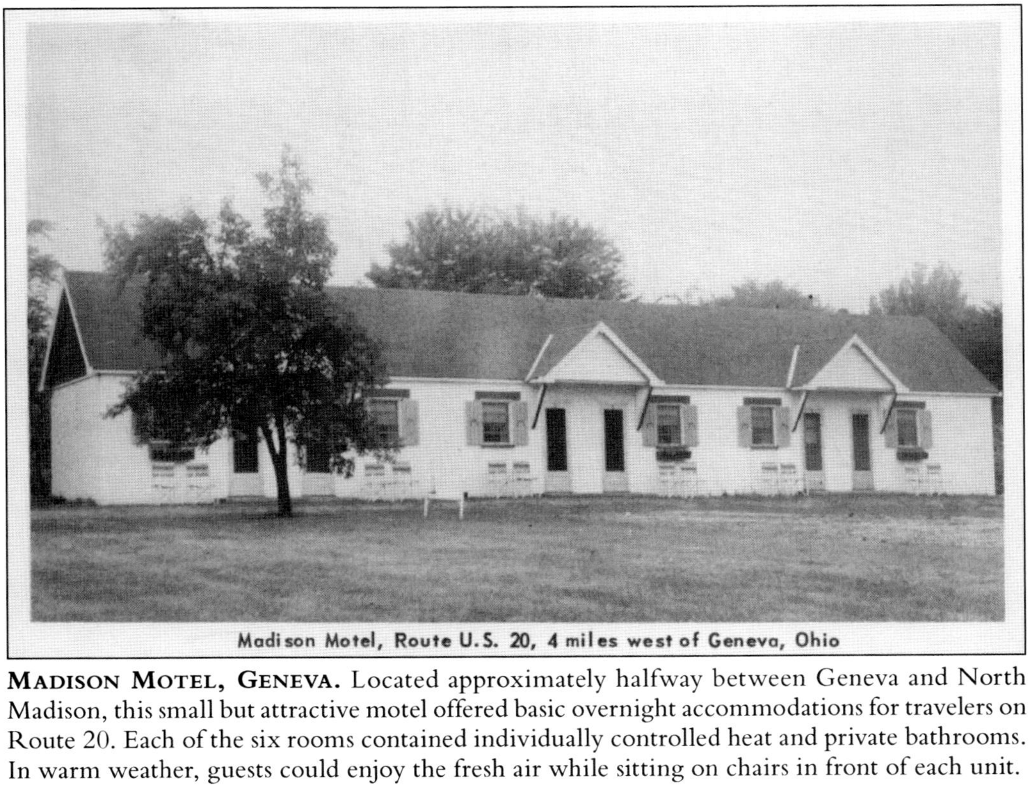

MADISON MOTEL, GENEVA. Located approximately halfway between Geneva and North Madison, this small but attractive motel offered basic overnight accommodations for travelers on Route 20. Each of the six rooms contained individually controlled heat and private bathrooms. In warm weather, guests could enjoy the fresh air while sitting on chairs in front of each unit.

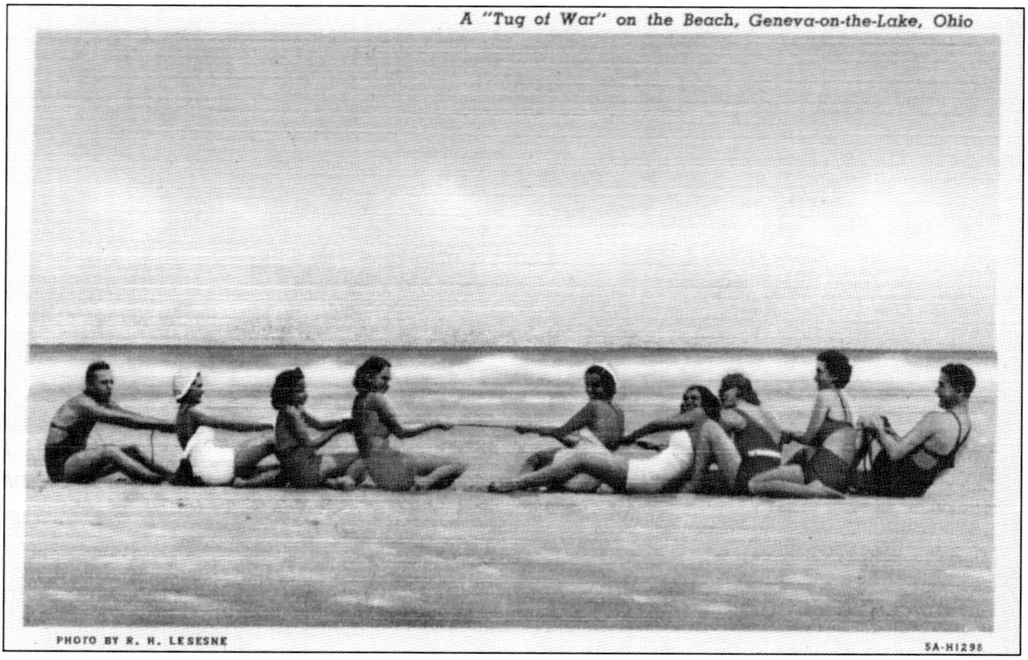

GENEVA-ON-THE-LAKE. The community of Geneva-on-the-Lake, adjacent to Geneva and only a short distance north of Route 20, has long been a popular destination on the south shore of Lake Erie. It is one of the oldest resort communities in Ohio, and at one time it was the site of summer cottages owned by such luminaries as John D. Rockefeller, Henry Ford, and Harvey Firestone. The community offered miles of sandy beaches, swimming, boating, fishing, and golfing. Above, two groups of bathers enjoy a game of tug-of-war on the beach. Note the 1920s-style bathing suits worn by the men anchoring the teams at either end. Eddie's Grill, below, was the place to go for burgers, hot dogs, and ice cream or simply to enjoy lakeside fun.

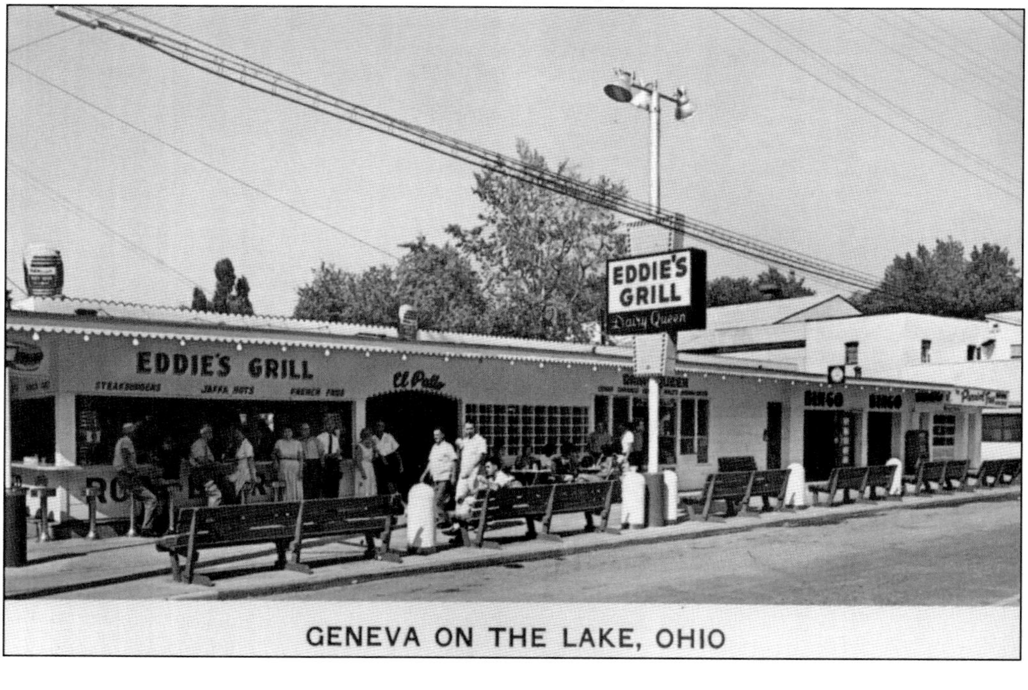

Two

East of Cleveland

As Route 20 continued westward toward Cleveland in the 1920s and 1930s, the region became progressively more urban, but as the postcards in this chapter illustrate, the urban sprawl so well known today was still in its infancy. Big-box stores and chain hotels were still many years in the future. Tourist camps, motels, small service stations, and mom-and-pop restaurants and diners were the roadside businesses. The most notable accessions to urbanization were trolley tracks, which extended from the center of the city into the suburbs. Communities were blending together, and definite geographic city limits were becoming more difficult to determine. For typical travelers, especially those going directly through the cities, this did not present a problem, as Route 20 signs were prominently displayed, and the road proceeded directly from town to town along the way.

Mentor Avenue was the dominant thoroughfare through this region of Ohio, originating in Painesville and, with only a few local interruptions, continuing on to Cleveland's eastern city limits. Each of the communities through which Mentor Avenue passed presented the traveler with lovely neighborhoods, interesting architecture, and vibrant main streets. Among Mentor Avenue's many attractions was the beautiful campus and historical buildings that comprised Lake Erie College in Painesville. Also in Painesville, the Randell Tavern (now Rider's Inn) opened its doors to travelers in 1810. In its colorful history, it served hundreds of guests who arrived by stagecoach, trains, and later by automobile.

Farther on, in the town of Mentor, the James Garfield National Historic Site recognizes the home of the 20th president. He conducted the majority of his presidential campaign via speeches delivered from his front porch. President Garfield's remarks were transmitted to newspapers by reporters stationed on his front lawn, giving rise to the name of Garfield's estate, Lawnfield. Also located at Lawnfield is the Garfield Presidential Library, established in 1881 by Garfield's family four years after his assassination.

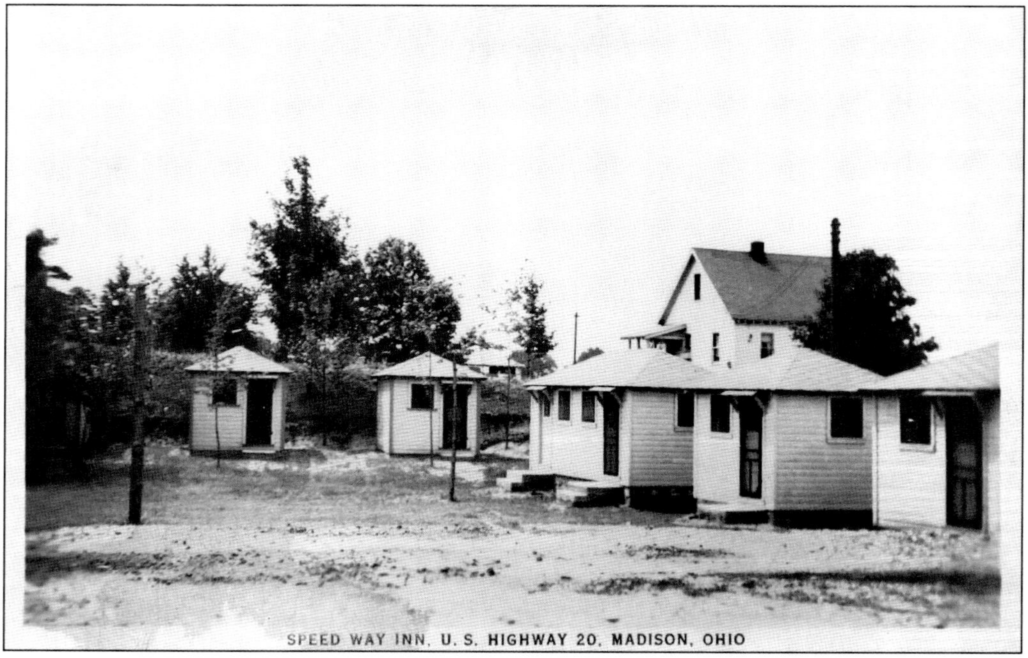

SPEED-WAY INN, ROUTE 20, NORTH MADISON. This postcard shows the cabin accommodations of the Speed-Way Inn, also seen on the front cover of this book. The cabins at Speed-Way were among the smallest along the entire length of Route 20.

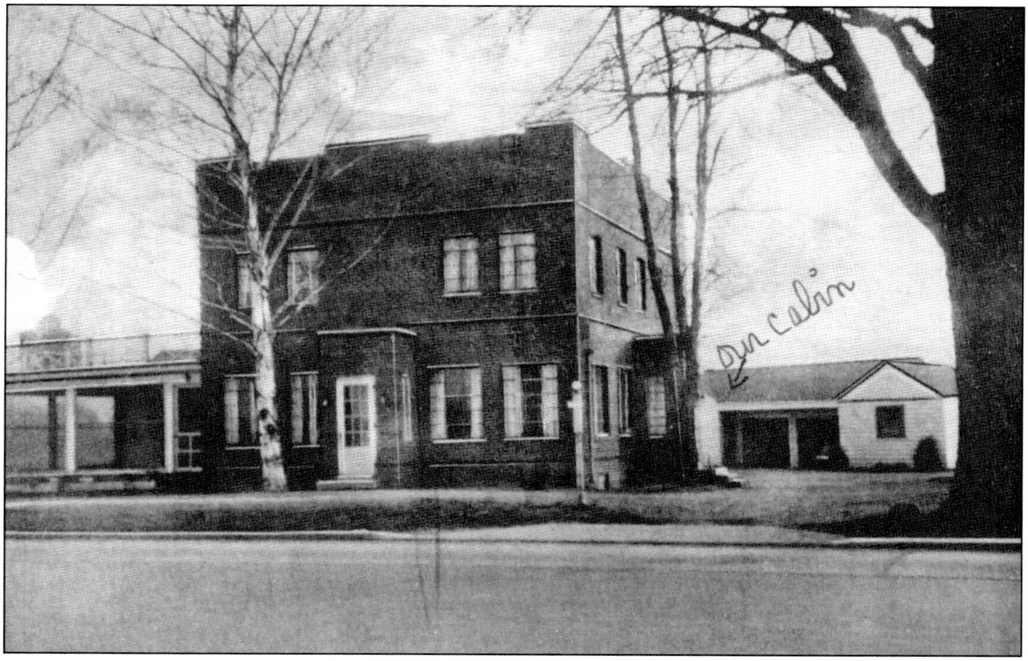

BRANCH'S CIRCLE INN, ROUTE 20, NORTH MADISON. Indoor and outdoor seating were available at this 1940s restaurant that proudly advertised serving 80 to 100 breakfasts and dinners daily. While the sender made no comment on the food, she did mark the cabin where they had spent the night. She also reported some common woes of early automobile travel: "A flat tire, a short in one headlight, and the radio don't [*sic*] work."

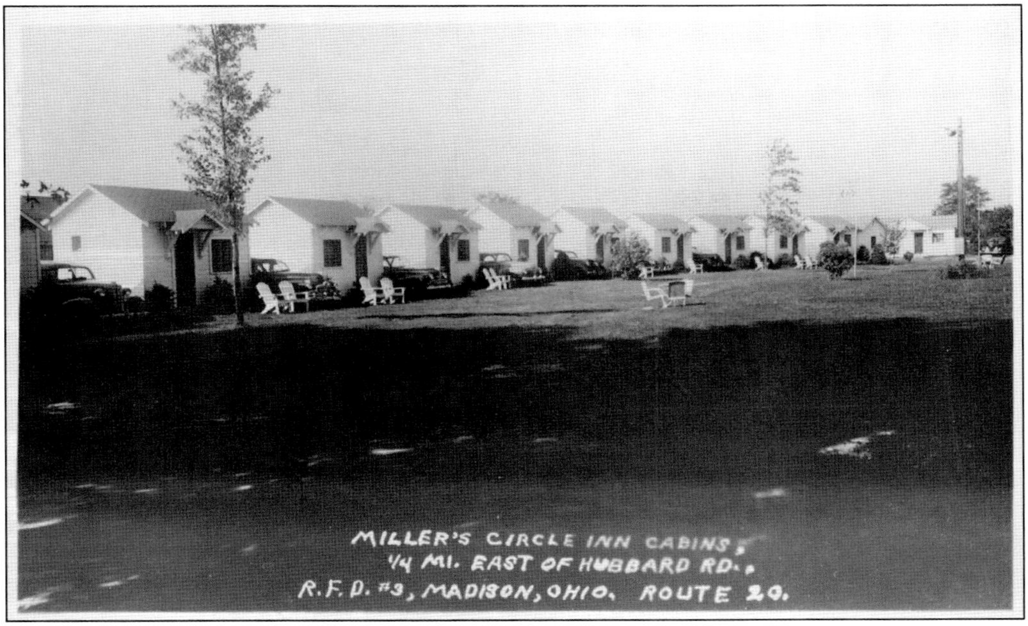

MILLER'S CIRCLE INN, MADISON. The popularity of Miller's Circle Inn, a quarter mile east of Hubbard Road, is evidenced by the number of cars parked by the cabins. Almost all of the cabins are occupied. As was typical of tourist courts from that era, guests could enjoy the fresh air in Adirondack chairs in front of each cabin.

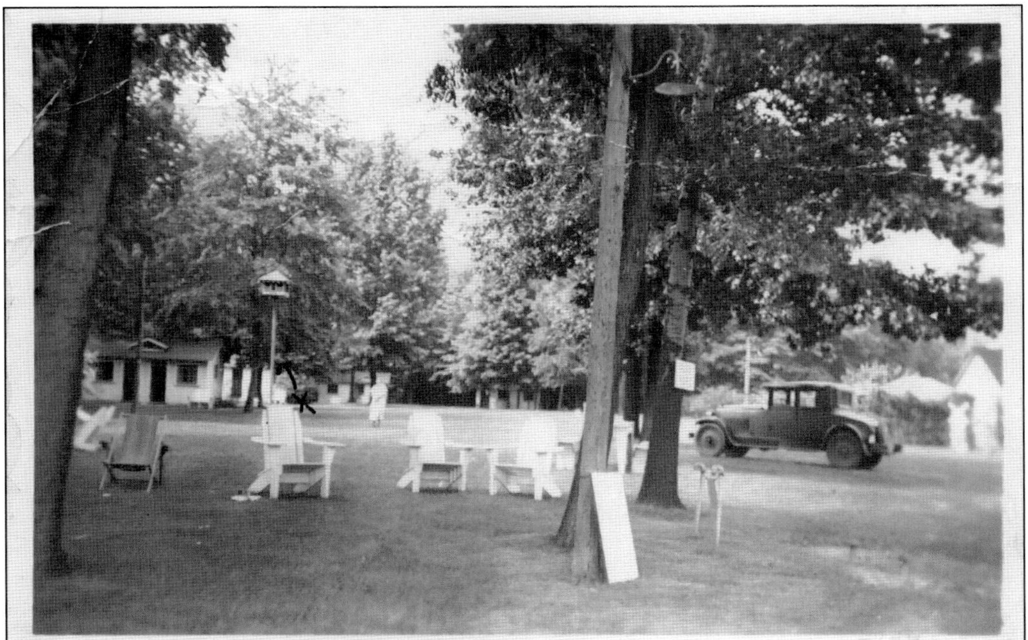

WHITE SWAN INN AND CABINS, MADISON. The caption on the back of this card described its location as between Geneva and Painesville, as well as it being spacious, shaded, and restful. The photograph supports that description, and guests certainly enjoyed relaxing on the lawn. The automobile dates the photograph to the late 1920s.

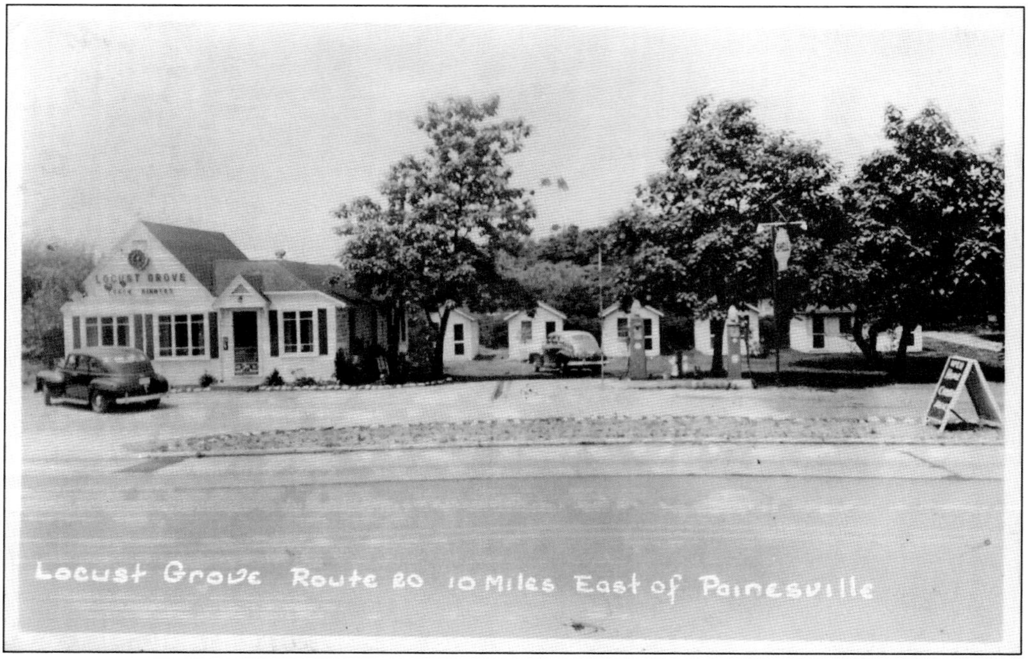

Locust Grove, Painesville. Guests at this tourist court and service station could fill up with Shell gasoline before continuing on their journey. This card was mailed in May 1947. The writer was spending the night in the cabin on the end. Using a common term of the day, she reported that everything was "swell" but that it sure had been cold, and they all were nearly frozen.

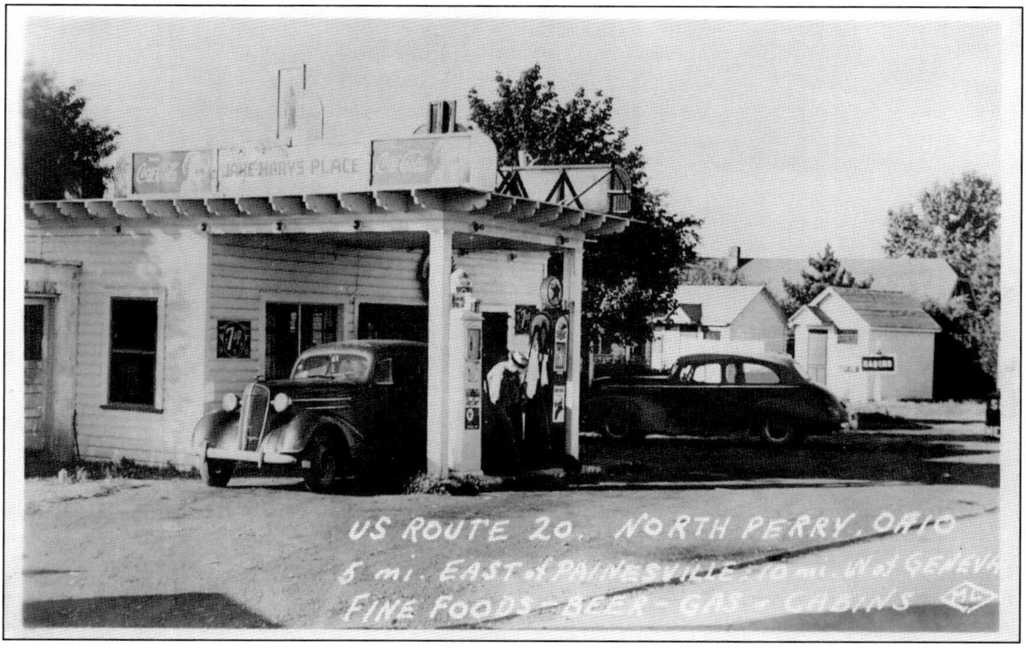

Jake-Mary's Place, between North Perry and Painesville. Jake and Mary appear to have operated a no-frills establishment, and they were straightforward in describing the services they offered. Tourists who stopped here could expect the basics: fine food, beer, gas, and cabins. As with the previous card, it was identified as being between Geneva and Painesville.

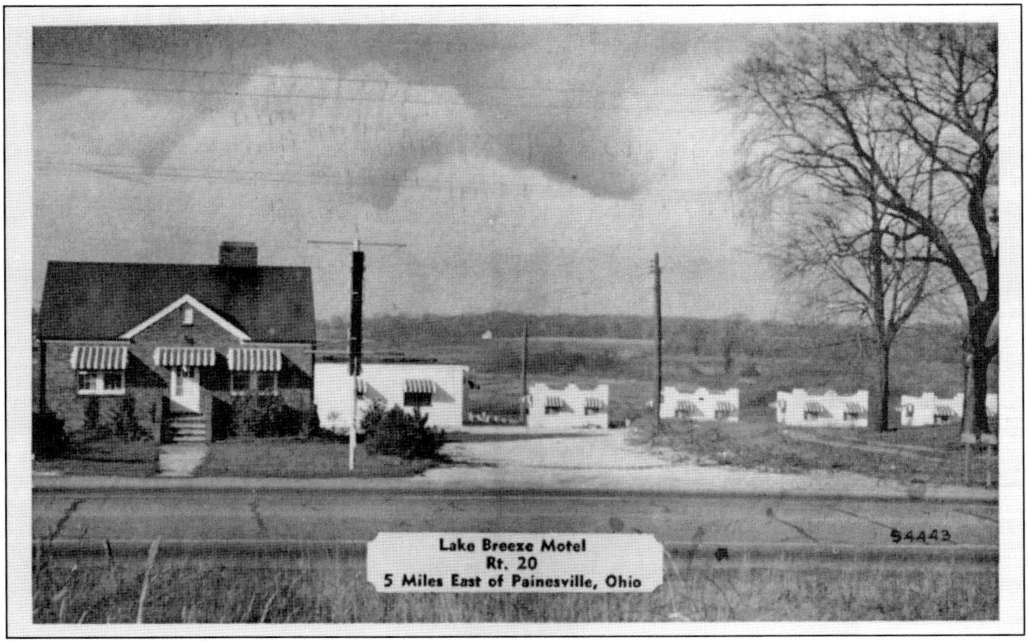

Lake Breeze Cabins, Painesville. The proximity of Route 20 to Lake Erie is reflected in the name of this 1940s motel. The lake was less than two miles north of the highway. The site is described as being 45 miles east of Cleveland and "300 feet" from the highway.

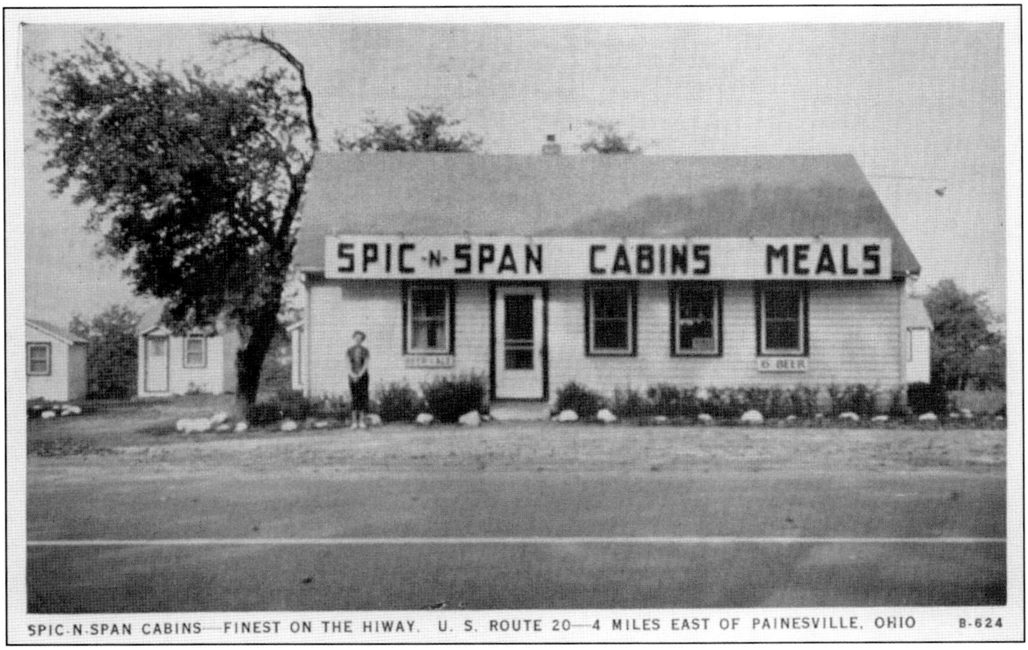

Spic-N-Span Cabins, Route 20, Painesville. Many early mom-and-pop tourist accommodations attempted to attract travelers with a catchy name. The owners of this cabin camp chose Spic-N-Span, indicating cleanliness and neatness, which were certainly desirable qualities in a roadside cabin camp.

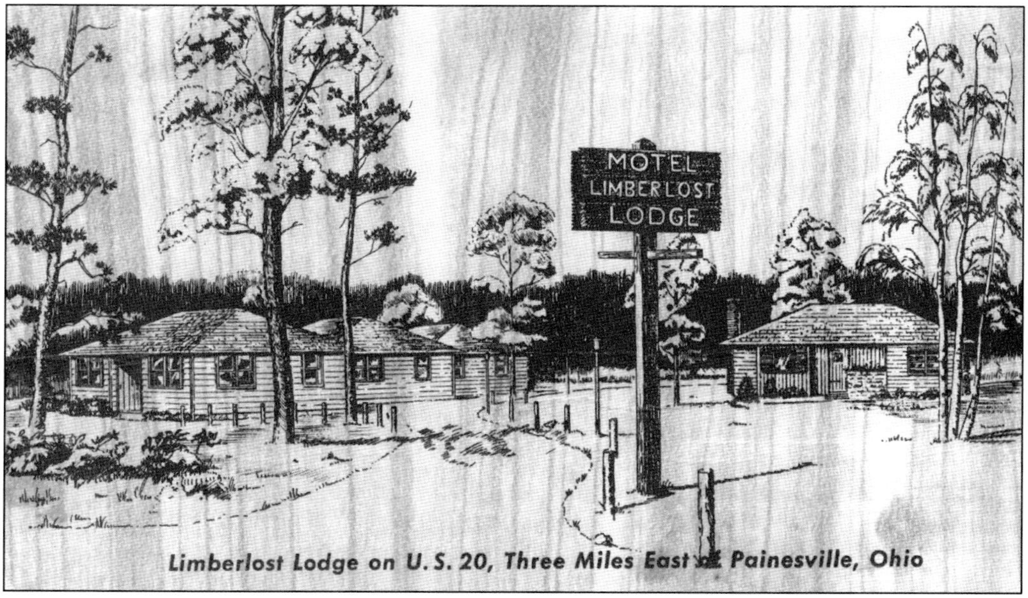

LIMBERLOST LODGE, ROUTE 20, PAINESVILLE. This 1940s lodge advertised, "We're Different. Open and airy for summer comfort. Cozy and warm in winter. Always restful." The lodge offered cedar-paneled rooms with maple furnishings and combination baths. Single and double rooms were available, as were two-room suites with connecting doors that could accommodate parties of up to six people.

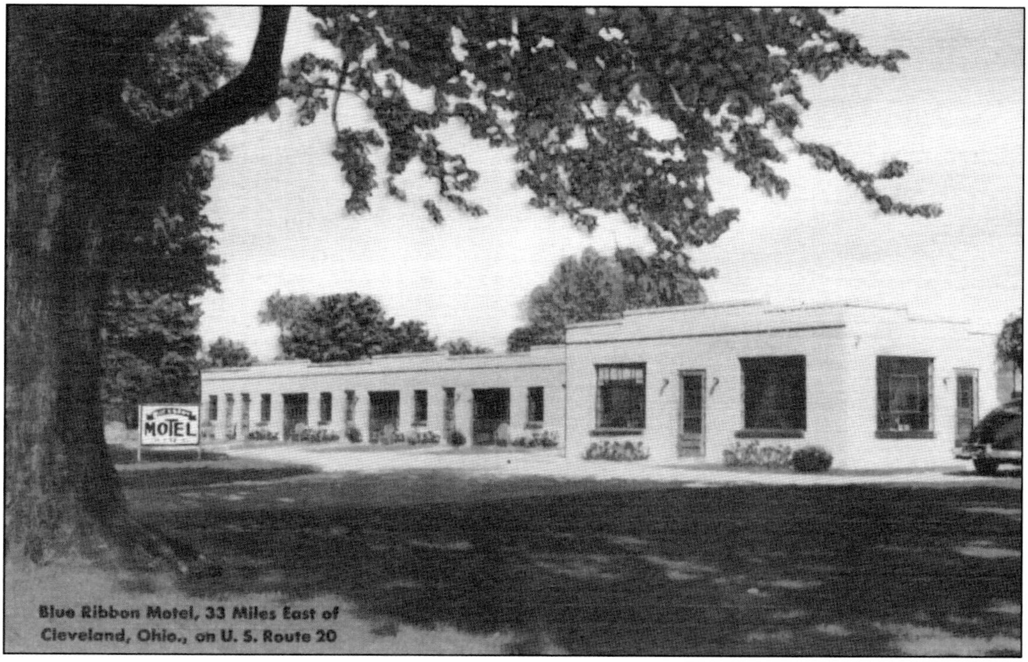

BLUE RIBBON MOTEL, ROUTE 20, PAINESVILLE. This small motel was designed in the Art Deco style popular in the 1940s, and unlike most tourist courts and early motels, each unit included a garage. The owners likely felt the mention of Cleveland on the front of the card would be a greater attraction to motorists than its actual location in Painesville.

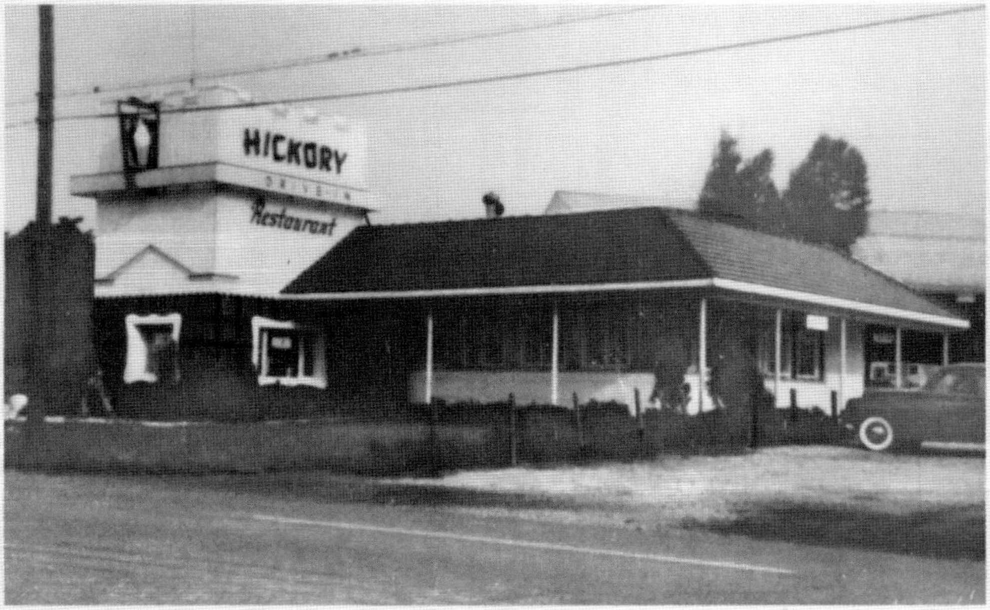

HICKORY DRIVE-IN RESTAURANT, 1 MILE EAST OF PAINESVILLE, OHIO ON U.S. ROUTE 20

HICKORY DRIVE-IN RESTAURANT, PAINESVILLE. The postcard above shows a popular restaurant in Painesville, which was among the first to offer drive-in service. The cartoon postcard below promoted hickory chicken dinners, recommended by "Col. Reuster." There is no date on either card, but the sign reads, "All you can eat for $1.75, children 75¢." The restaurant featured nationally known Dairy Queen products, indicating that the postcards were from the 1940s. Dairy Queen was founded in 1938 and underwent rapid expansion in the 1940s.

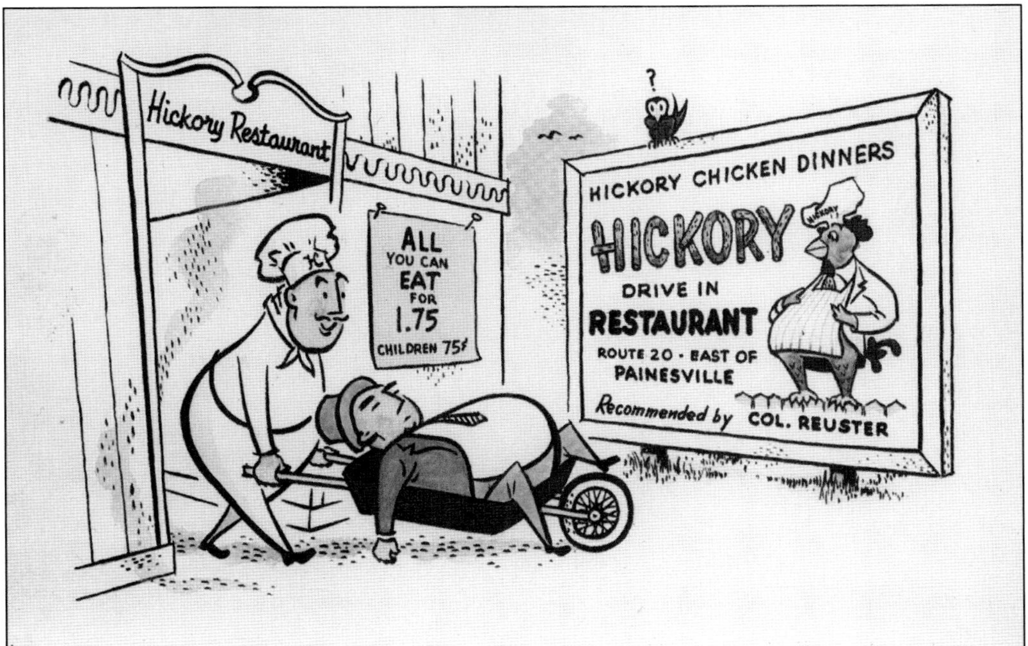

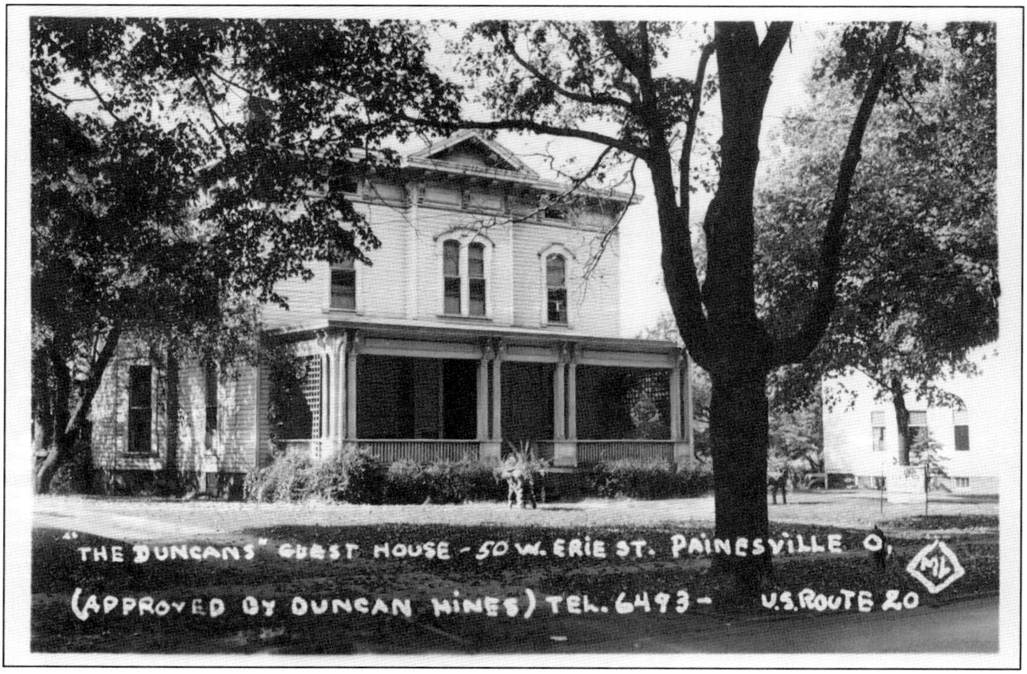

THE DUNCANS GUEST HOUSE, PAINESVILLE. The Duncans Guest House at 50 West Erie Street was typical of homes built in the early 1900s that were converted into tourist facilities. Residents enjoyed cool breezes on the front porch before the introduction of air-conditioning. The owners took meticulous care of the lawn, which added to the attractiveness of the facility. The home was "approved by Duncan Hines."

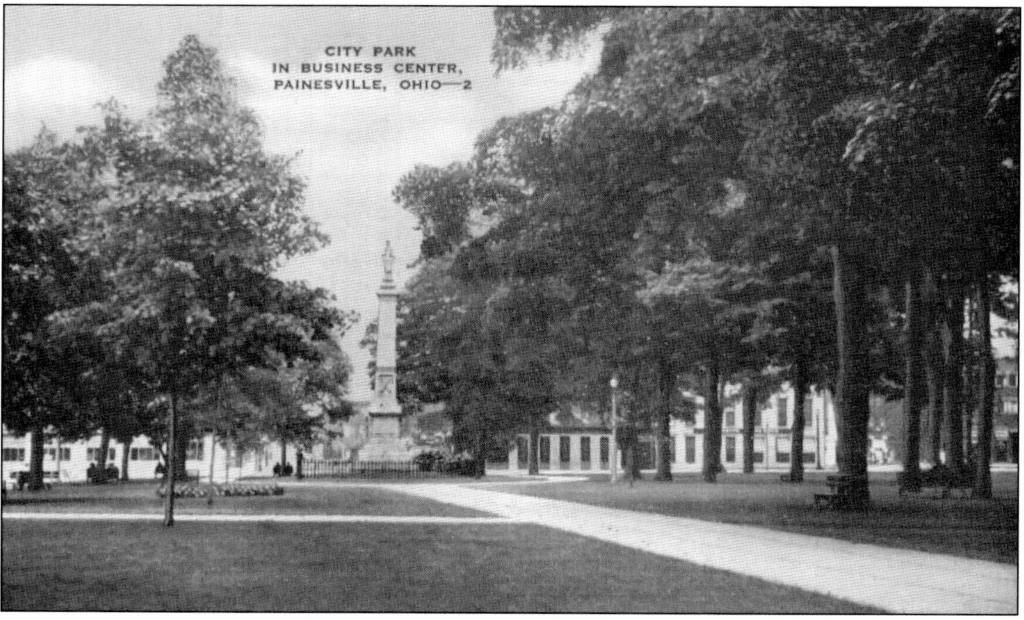

CITY PARK, PAINESVILLE. Many communities that Route 20 passed through were planned around a central public square, with business and residential districts spreading away from the central core. Painesville had a particularly attractive square. Expert landscaping, beautiful flowers, and mature trees made this park the ideal place to relax, meet friends, or listen to a band concert.

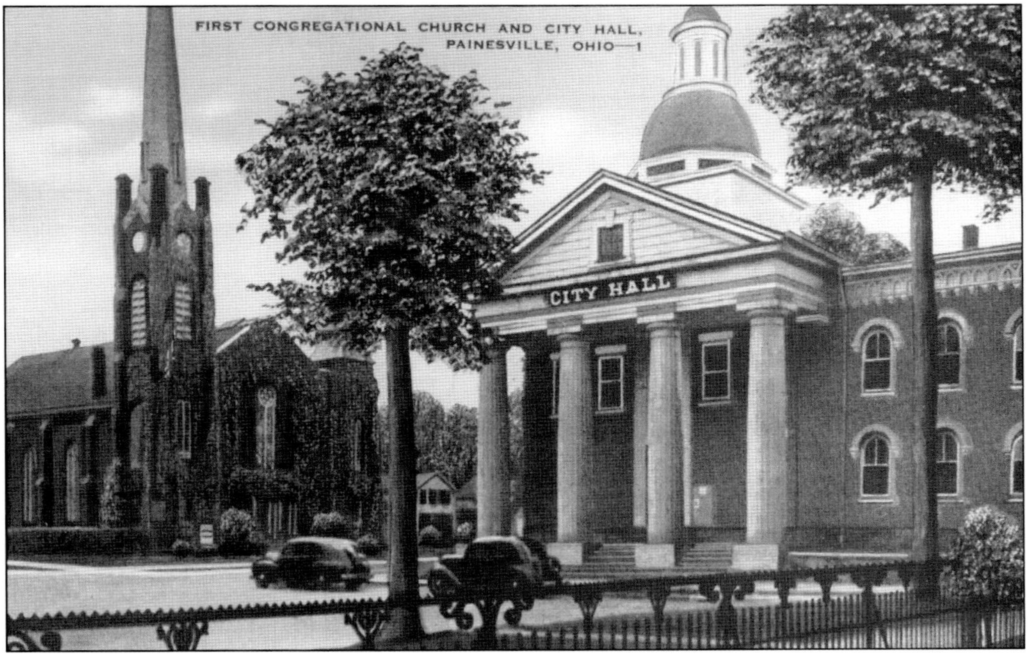

FIRST CONGREGATIONAL CHURCH, CITY HALL, AND LAKE COUNTY COURTHOUSE, PAINESVILLE. Three of Painesville's landmark buildings are seen in these two postcards. All are within the Mentor Avenue Historical District, which is listed in the National Register of Historic Places. The First Congregational Church (above) was organized in 1810. As the membership increased, the original church was replaced in 1862 by the present building. The second building is Painesville's city hall, which was constructed in 1840 and originally served as the county courthouse. The stately new courthouse (right) has been the seat of government in Lake County since it was dedicated in 1909. The eagle at the top of the cupola is 145 feet high and has a 14-foot wingspan.

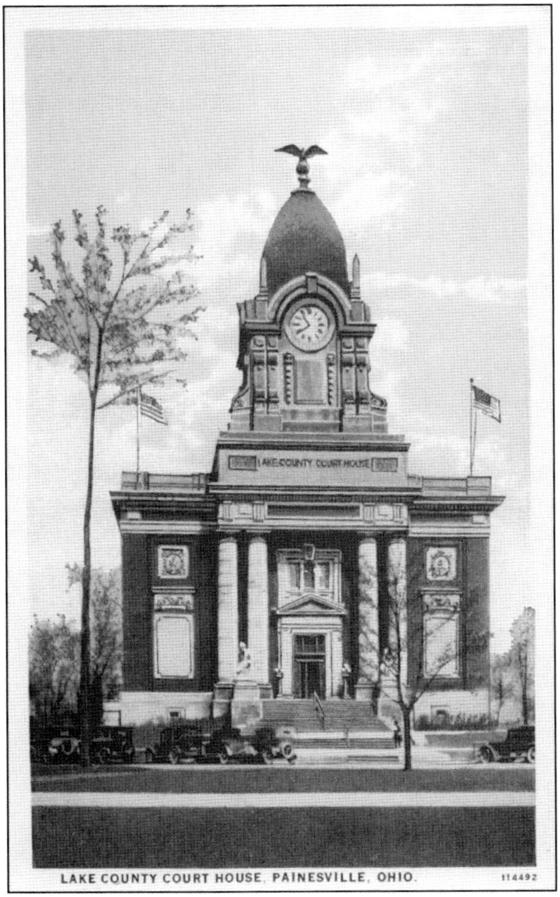

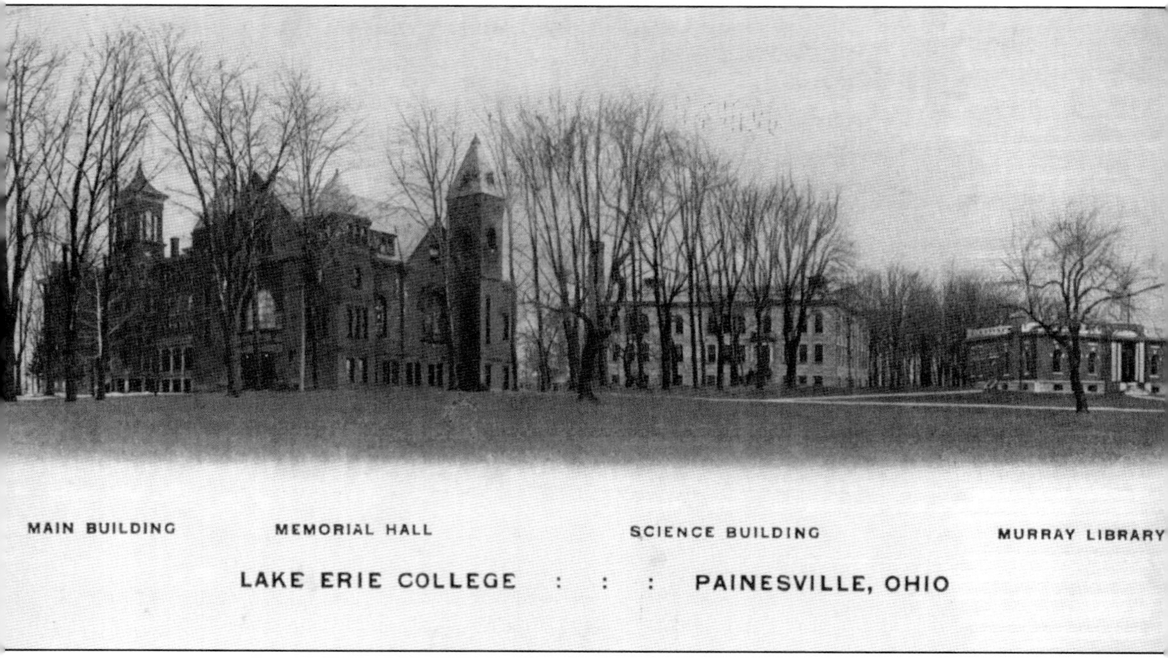

LAKE ERIE COLLEGE, PAINESVILLE. Lake Erie College occupies a 50-acre campus fronting Route 20. It is one of the oldest institutions for higher learning in the Western Reserve. Founded in 1856 as the Lake Erie Female Seminary, the college was commonly referred to as Lake Erie College, and that name was formally adopted in 1898. For the first 80 years of its existence, it only admitted females; the first men were permitted to enroll in 1935. Lake Erie College has long been distinguished for its excellent equine studies program, which attracts students from around the world. Four of the college's notable buildings are seen on this card.

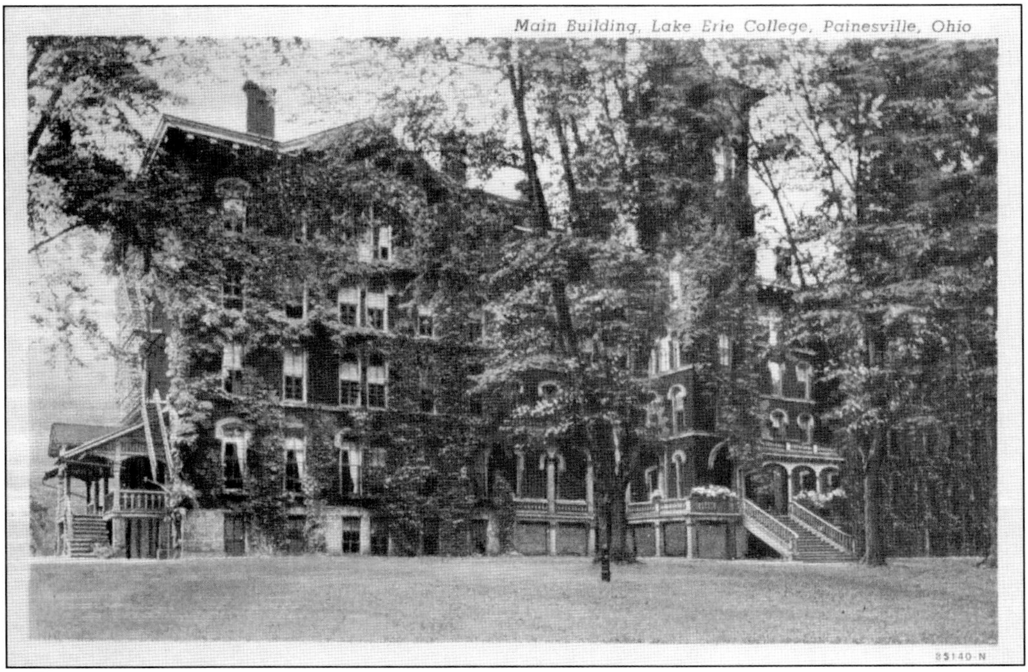

MAIN BUILDING, LAKE ERIE COLLEGE, PAINESVILLE. The building on this postcard, also known as College Hall, was the first constructed on the campus. It was completed in 1859 and remains the focal point of the campus and a landmark on Mentor Avenue in Painesville. Today, it serves as the administration building for the college. It is listed in the National Register of Historic Places.

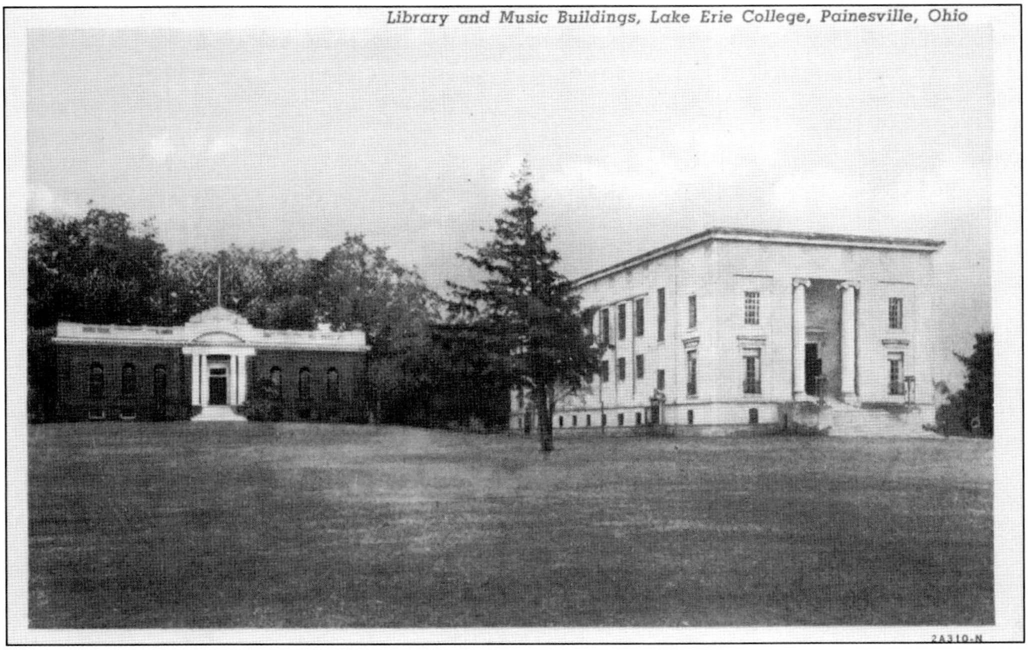

LIBRARY AND MUSIC BUILDINGS, LAKE ERIE COLLEGE, PAINESVILLE. The two college buildings on this postcard both face Route 20. The Murray Library (left) was dedicated in 1908. The Helen Rockwell Morley Memorial Music Hall (right) opened in 1927. It seats 800 people and is considered one of the best small concert halls in the world.

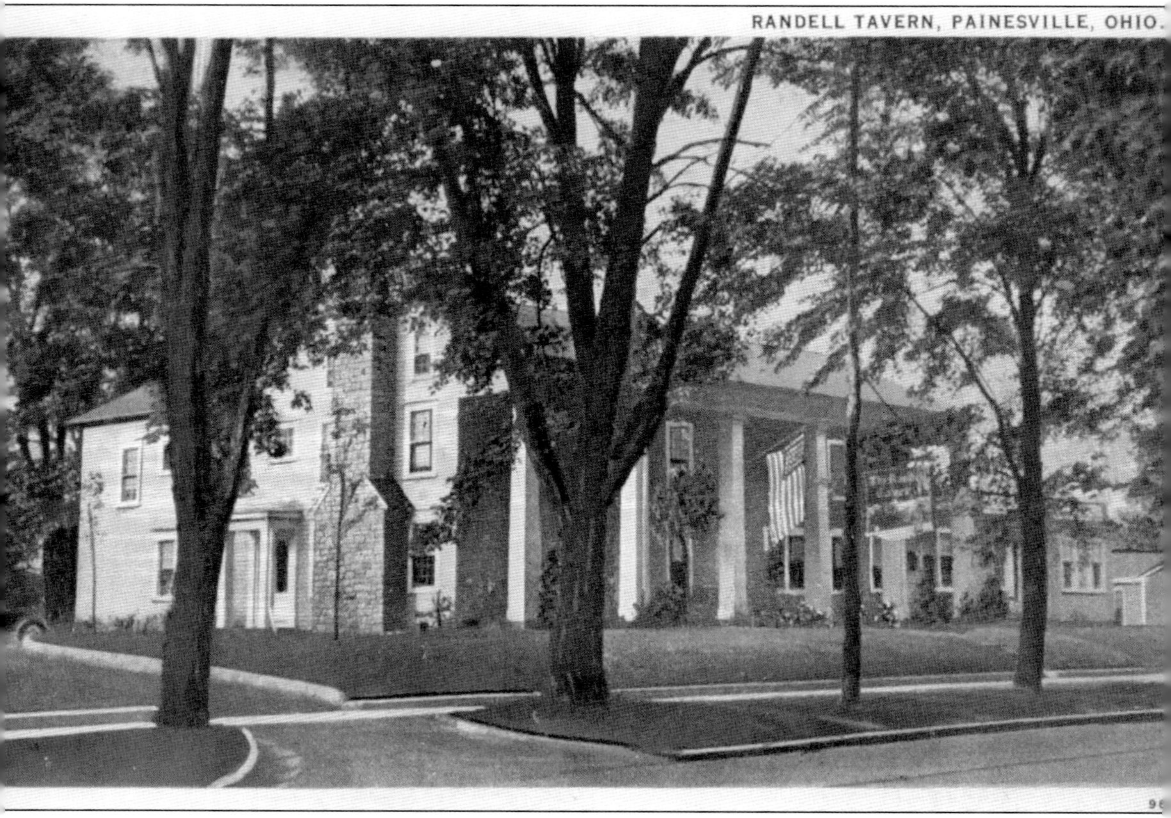

RANDELL TAVERN, 792 MENTOR AVENUE, PAINESVILLE. This tavern, originally called Rider's Inn, was established in 1812 by Revolutionary War veteran Joseph Rider. It was a stagecoach stop on the road between Buffalo and Cleveland and was a preferred shelter for travelers heading for the open lands to the west. Rider had four wives, the third of whom, Suzanne, came from a wealthy family. Within six weeks of their wedding, she died under mysterious circumstances, leaving Rider in control of her large dowry. He married his fourth wife a short time later. The inn was purchased in 1922 by George Randall, who enlarged the property by adding a dining room and a speakeasy. He changed the name to Randell Tavern and served travelers during the early years of Route 20. Later owners changed the name back to Rider's Inn, which it is still called today. The inn is listed in the National Register of Historic Places.

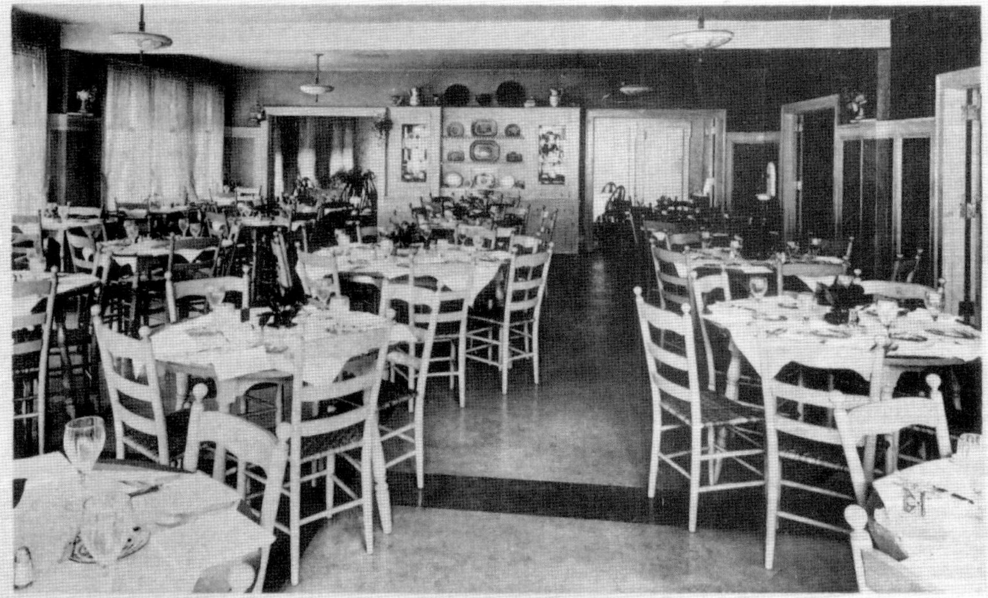

"Sun Dining Room" The Randell Tavern, Painesville, Ohio. A Tavern since 1810.

RANDELL TAVERN DINING ROOM AND BEDROOM, PAINESVILLE. Colorful names were attached to the various rooms at Randell Tavern. The large and popular Sun Dining Room is seen above, comfortably furnished in early American style. It has served both the local citizenry and the traveling public for more than 200 years. The Curly Maple bedroom below was named for the wood used for the four-poster bed and other furniture in the room. Note the step stool beside the bed. Legend has it that the inn is haunted by Joseph Rider's third wife, Suzanne. Her job during her life was to warmly welcome guests, and she has reportedly been seen near the front door and also in the corridor among the guest rooms on the upper floors.

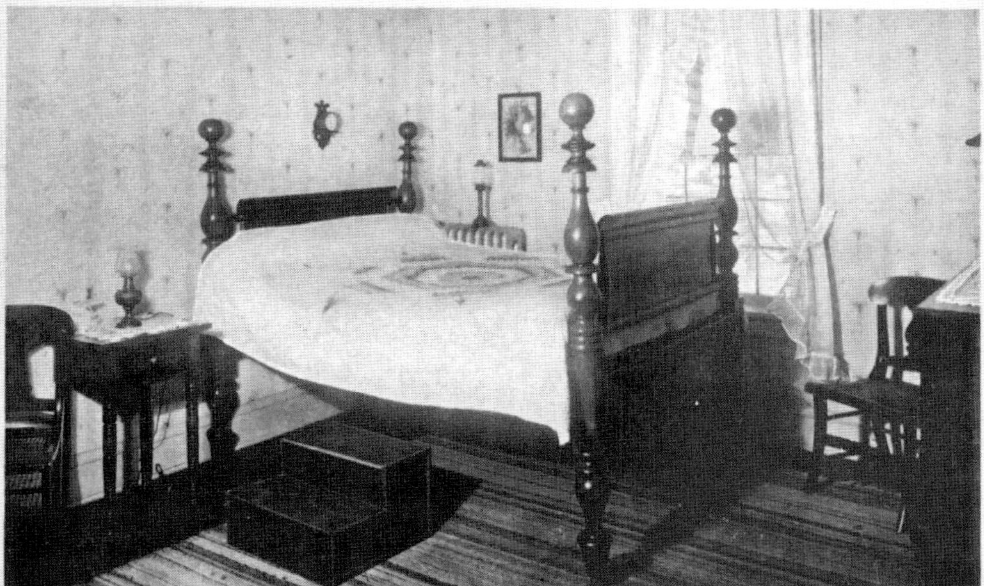

"Curly Maple Room" The Randell Tavern, Painesville, Ohio. A Tavern since 1810.

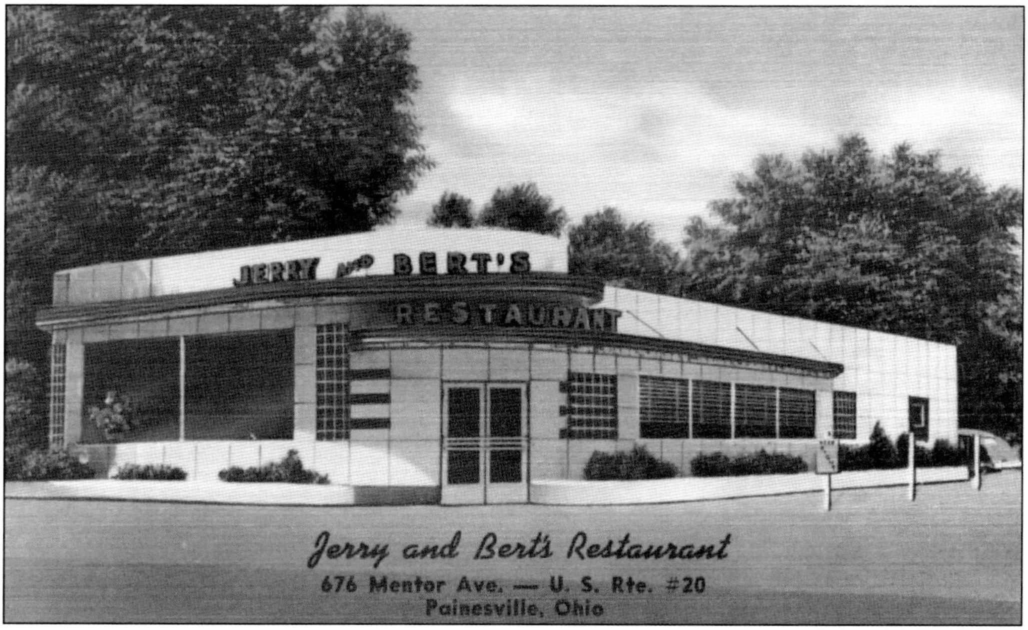

JERRY AND BERT'S COSMOPOLITAN RESTAURANT, 676 MENTOR AVENUE, PAINESVILLE. "Quality Food at Moderate Prices. Anything from sandwiches to full course dinners" was the slogan of this 1940s restaurant. These two linen postcards illustrate the popular Art Deco style of the time in both exterior and interior decor. The restaurant eventually went out of business and was replaced first by a store called Home Decorating and later by a Goodwill retail store. A resolution was eventually passed to enable the demolition of this and other older buildings so that a new building could be erected, thus bringing the Jerry and Bert's era to a close.

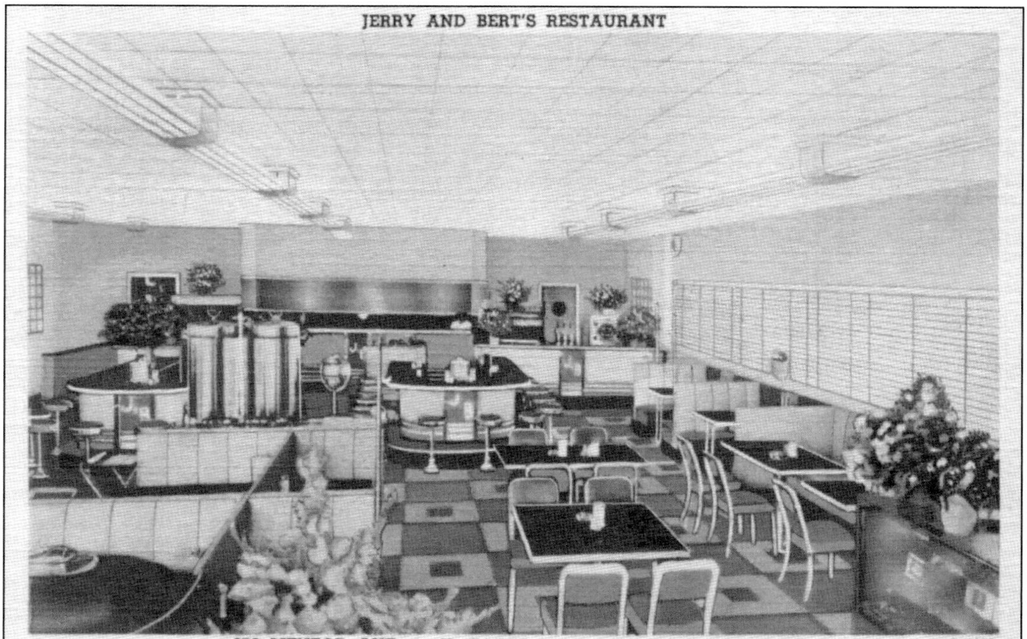

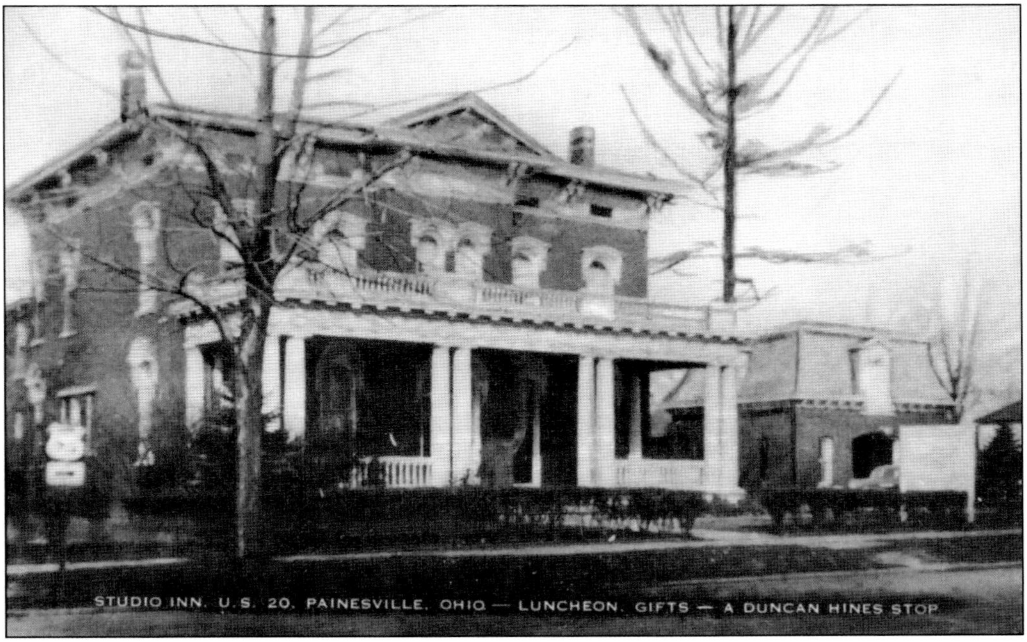

STUDIO INN, ROUTE 20, PAINESVILLE. This large house, with its adjacent coach house, was a private home at one time before being transformed into a restaurant and gift shop. Guests could be sure of quality food and service, as the Studio Inn was recommended by Duncan Hines. Note the Route 20 shield on the left.

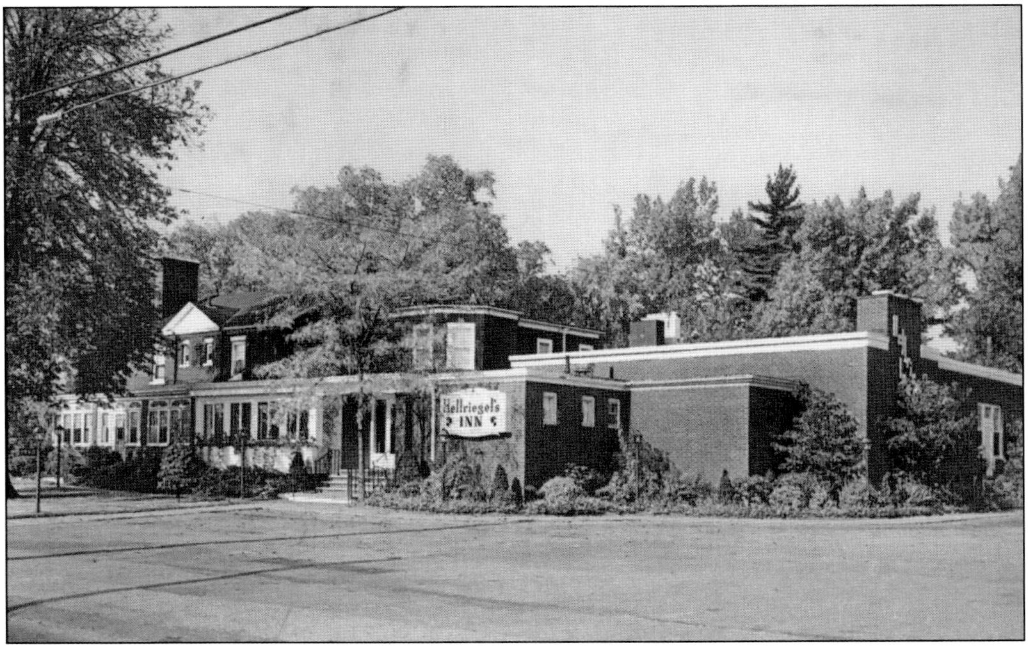

HELLRIEGLE'S INN, 1840 MENTOR AVENUE, PAINESVILLE. Hellriegle's Inn has a history of fine dining at this location since 1928. It hosted distinctive and elegant events, including a breakfast rally for Sen. John F. Kennedy during his run for president in September 1960. Formal and informal affairs could be accommodated in the indoor dining facilities as well as outdoors to take advantage of the inn's seven-acre estate.

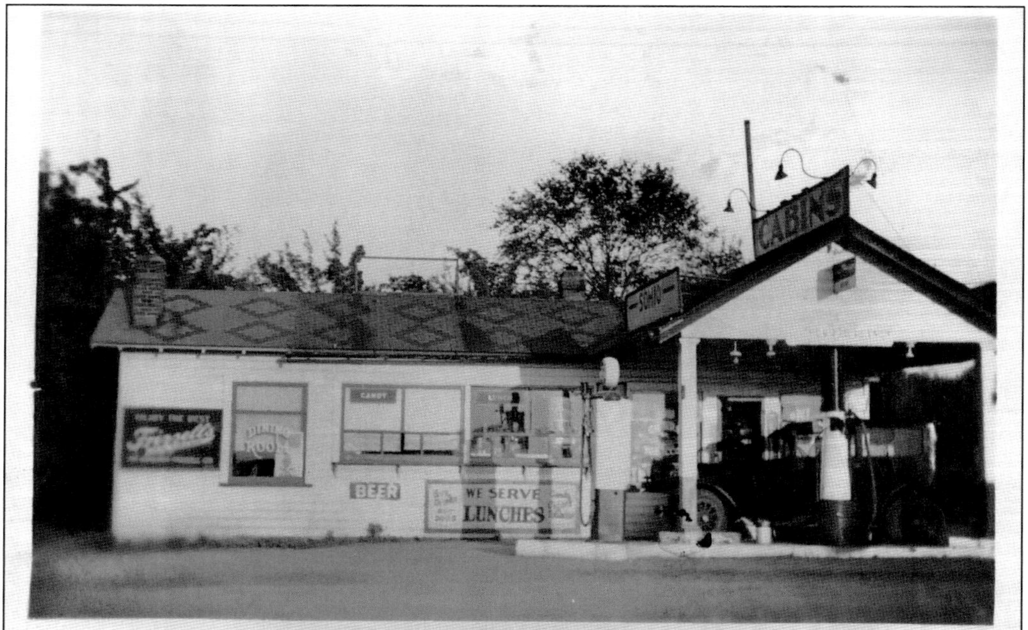

TIP TOP CABINS, U. S. HIGHWAY 20, PAINESVILLE, OHIO

TIP TOP CABINS, HIGHWAY 20, PAINESVILLE. Above, an early-1930s automobile is being serviced at the station. The tall pump on the left of the service island was characteristic of many gas stations during this era. Gasoline was pumped by hand into a large cylinder at the top of the pump, which was marked with lines so the customer could see how much was being purchased. It then flowed by gravity into the car's tank. It took several cycles for a complete fill-up. The Tip Top was a full-service facility, also offering food and overnight accommodations. The dining room is seen above on the left. Judging from the number of cars parked near the cabins in the photograph below, it was a popular place to stop.

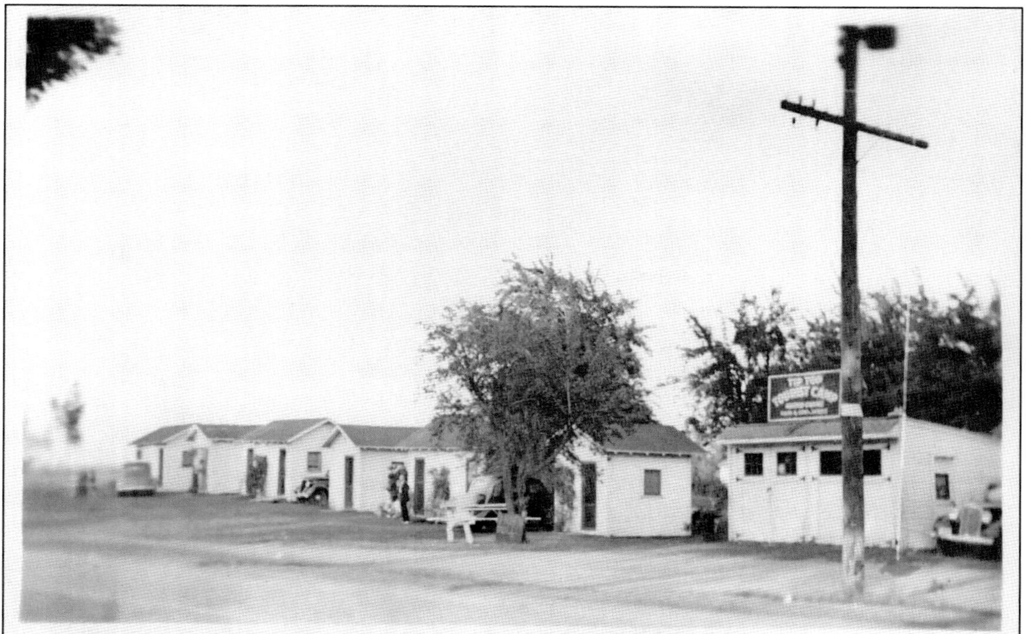

TIP TOP CABINS, U. S. HIGHWAY 20, PAINESVILLE, OHIO

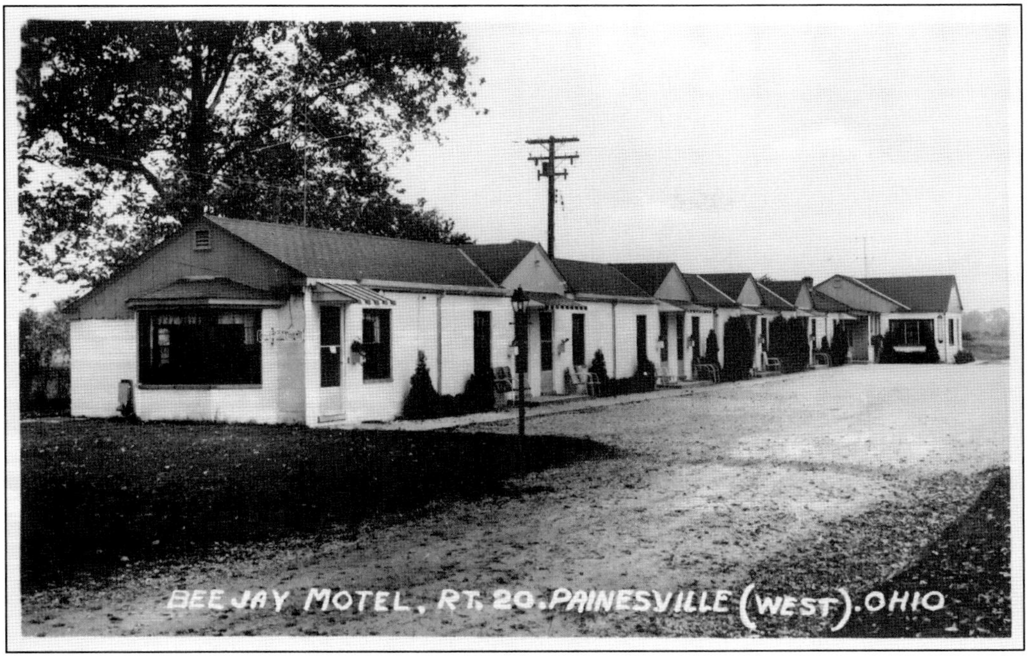

Bee Jay Motel, 2184 Mentor Avenue, Painesville. Guests could park directly in front of their unit at this motel, although the driveway and parking lot were still gravel when this card was produced in the 1940s. The motel was made more inviting by attractive shrubbery. Another novel idea was mounting potted plants on the wall by every door.

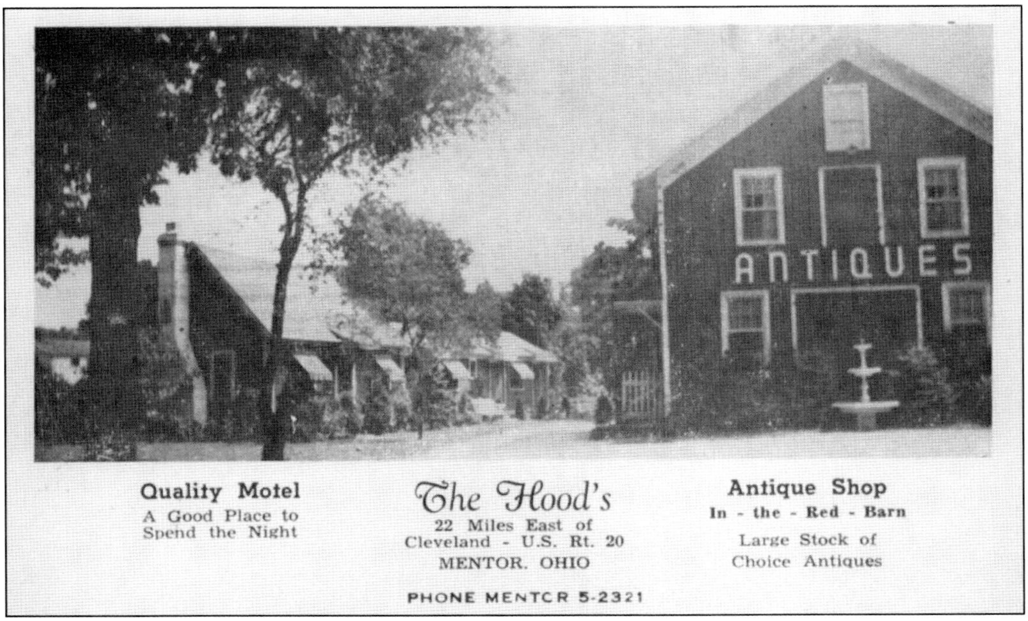

The Hood's, Route 20, Mentor. Tourists who stopped at The Hood's could take advantage of the "Quality Motel" that was "A Good Place to Spend the Night" and visit the antique shop in the red barn. The latter building had likely been a vital structure for the farm that originally occupied the property.

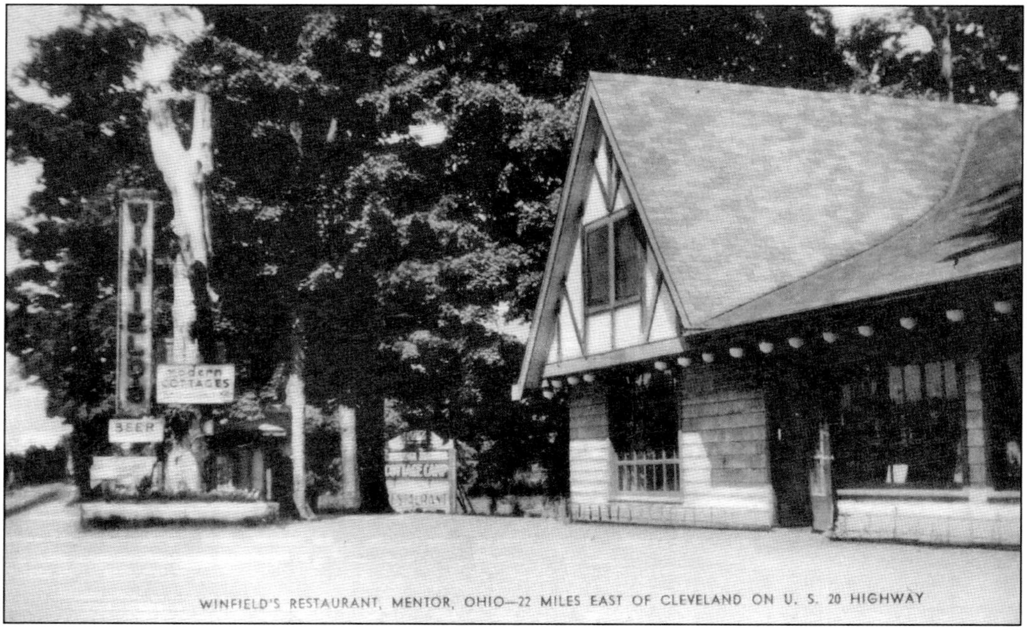

WINFIELD'S TOURIST CAMP, MENTOR. The English Tudor facade added attractiveness to Winfield's restaurant and cottage camp, located 22 miles east of Cleveland. The accommodations were basic, with only beds, hot water, private showers, and toilets provided.

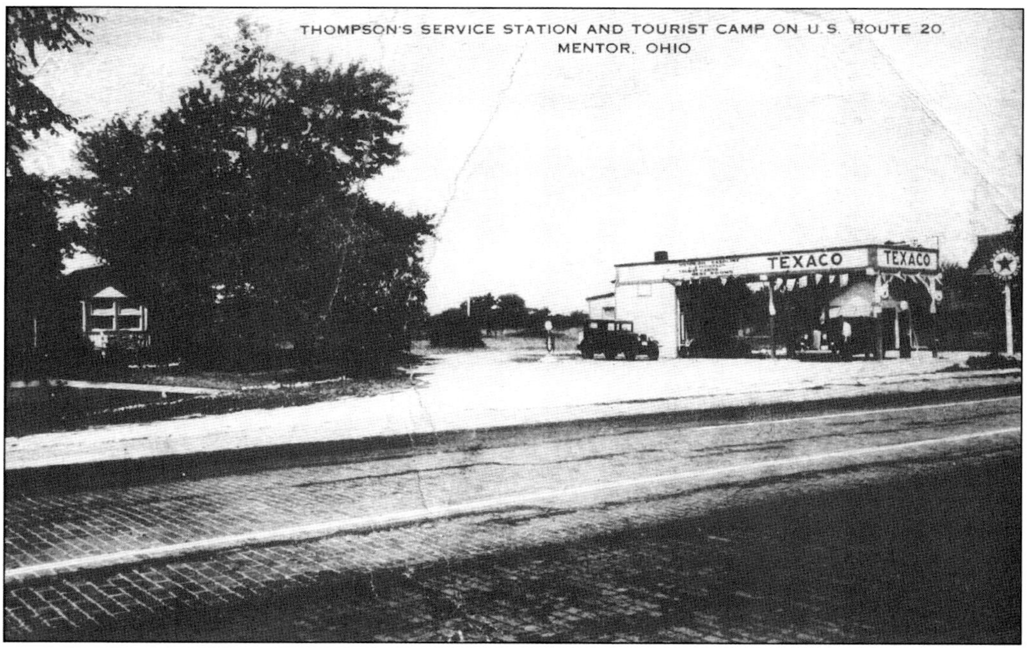

THOMPSON'S SERVICE STATION AND TOURIST CAMP, ROUTE 20, MENTOR. The road surface on this stretch of Route 20 was still brick when this photograph was taken in the 1930s. Thompson's Service Station featured Texaco products. It was ahead of its time, with two service lanes and a canopy to provide protection from the weather.

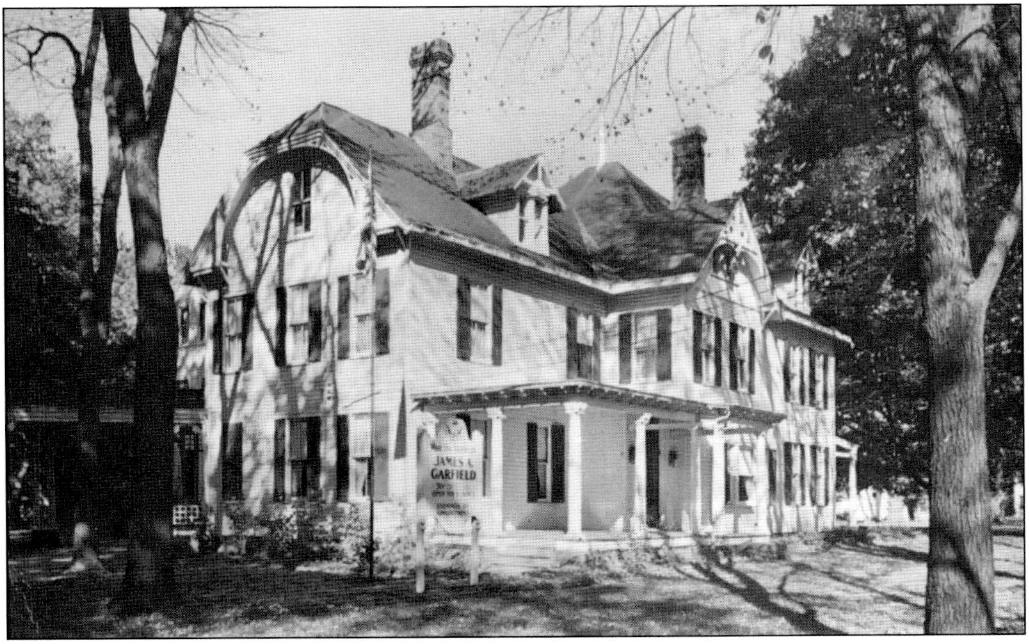

LAWNFIELD, 8095 MENTOR AVENUE, MENTOR. Ohio congressman James A. Garfield acquired the original farmhouse on this site in 1876, and he built an addition (above) to accommodate his wife, his five children, and his mother. In 1880, he did much of his campaigning for the presidency from his front porch, giving speeches that were reported by newspapers, giving rise to the term "front porch campaign." The property's name, Lawnfield, was coined by reporters to describe their location on his front lawn, which was later adopted by the Garfield family. President Garfield is known as "the last of the log cabin presidents." A replica of his humble cabin (below) is located on the grounds of the Lake County Historical Society in nearby Painesville.

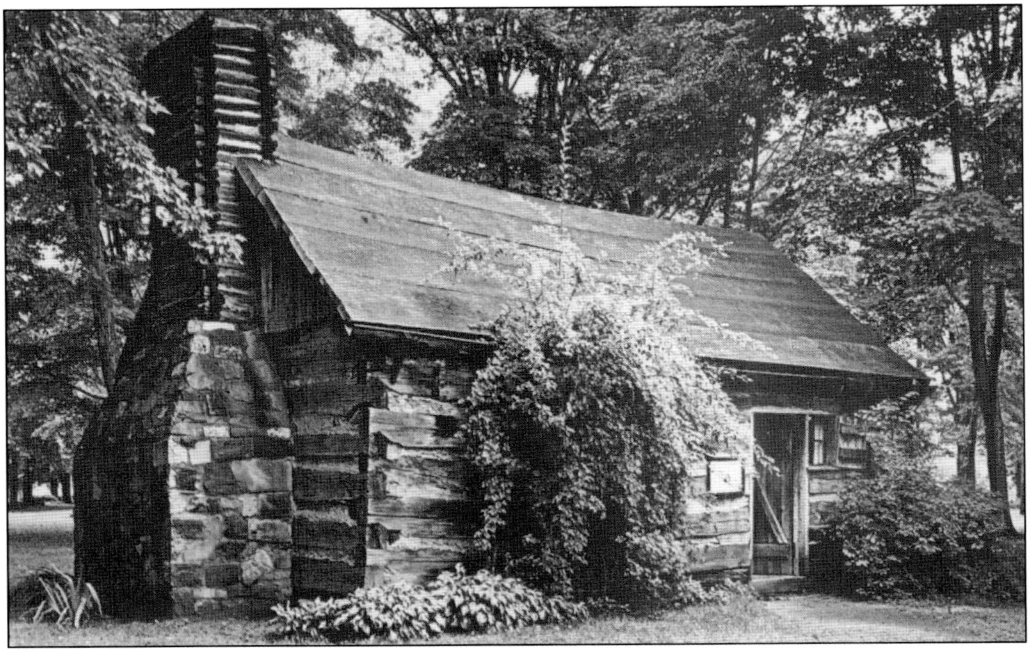

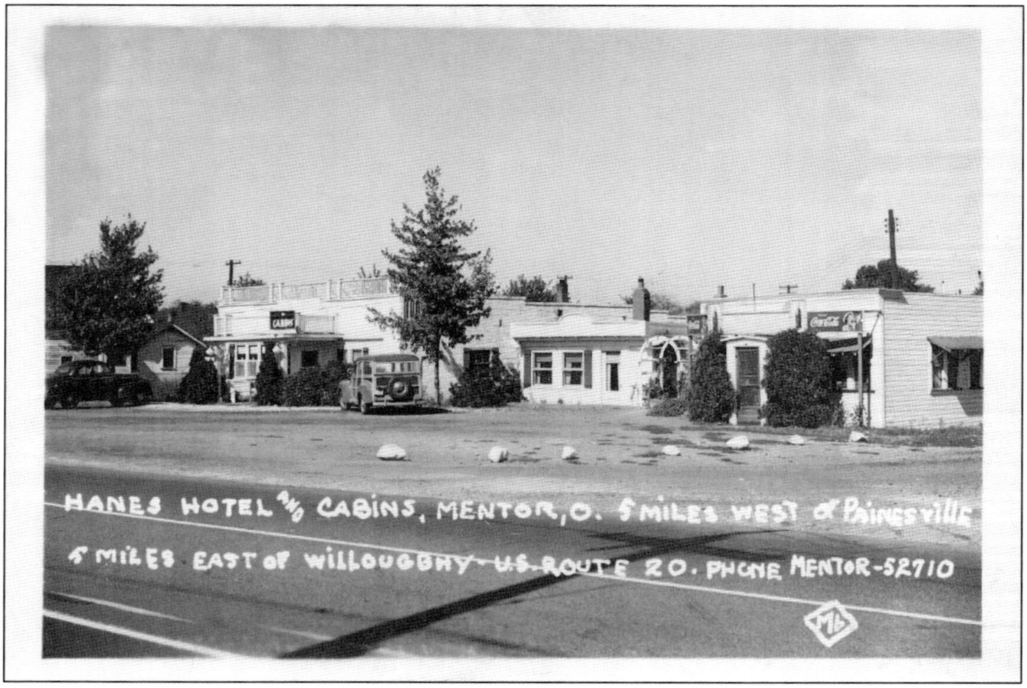

Hanes Hotel and Cabins, Route 20, Mentor. The owners of this quaint roadside establishment still used the term "hotel" rather than the more up-to-date "motel." Here, a classic 1940s woodie is parked in front of the hotel, which was halfway between Painesville and Willoughby.

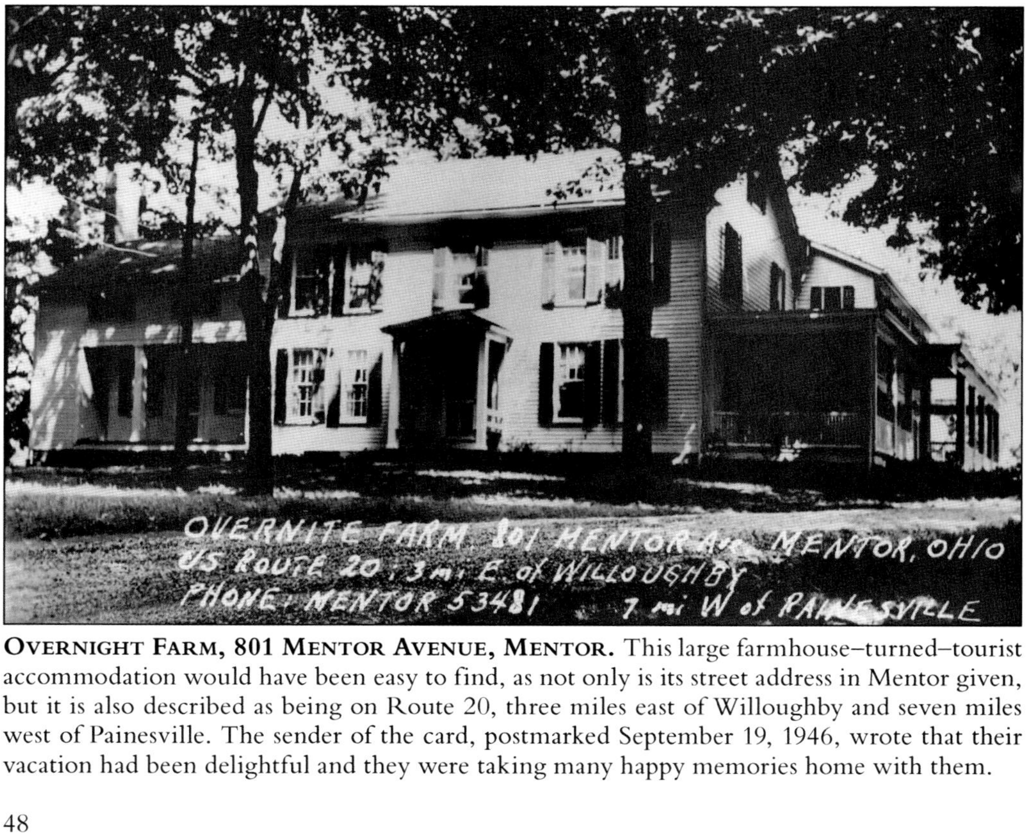

Overnight Farm, 801 Mentor Avenue, Mentor. This large farmhouse–turned–tourist accommodation would have been easy to find, as not only is its street address in Mentor given, but it is also described as being on Route 20, three miles east of Willoughby and seven miles west of Painesville. The sender of the card, postmarked September 19, 1946, wrote that their vacation had been delightful and they were taking many happy memories home with them.

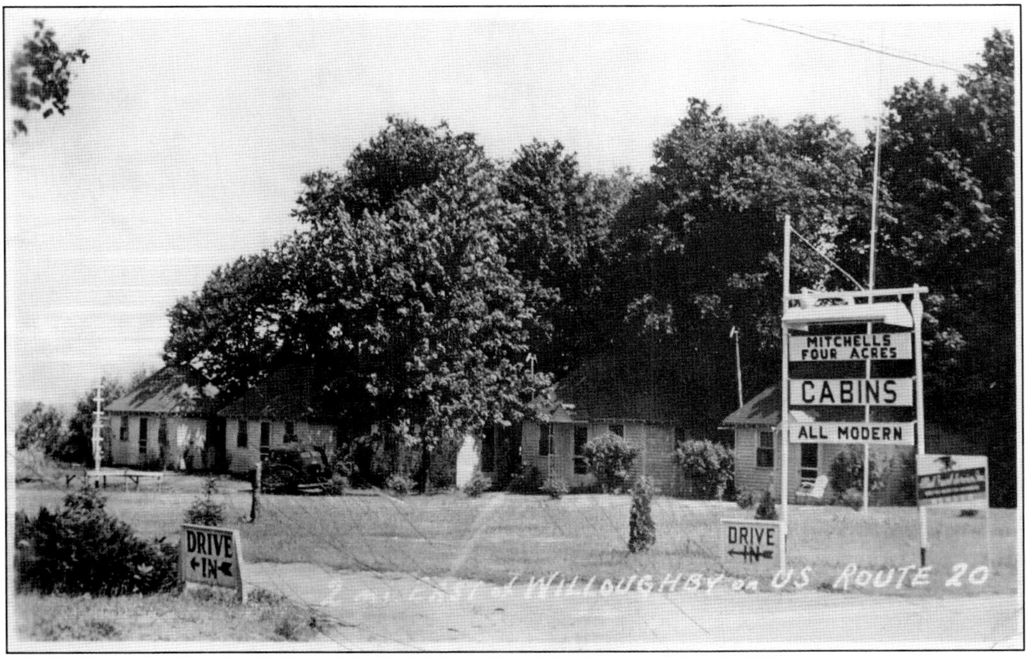

Mitchell's Four Acres Cabins, Route 20, Willoughby. Mitchell's 1940s tourist camp offered five "all modern" cabins in a pleasant wooded setting where tourists could stretch their legs after a long day's drive by strolling among the trees on the property. Restaurants and service stations offering automobile repair were available in the nearby communities.

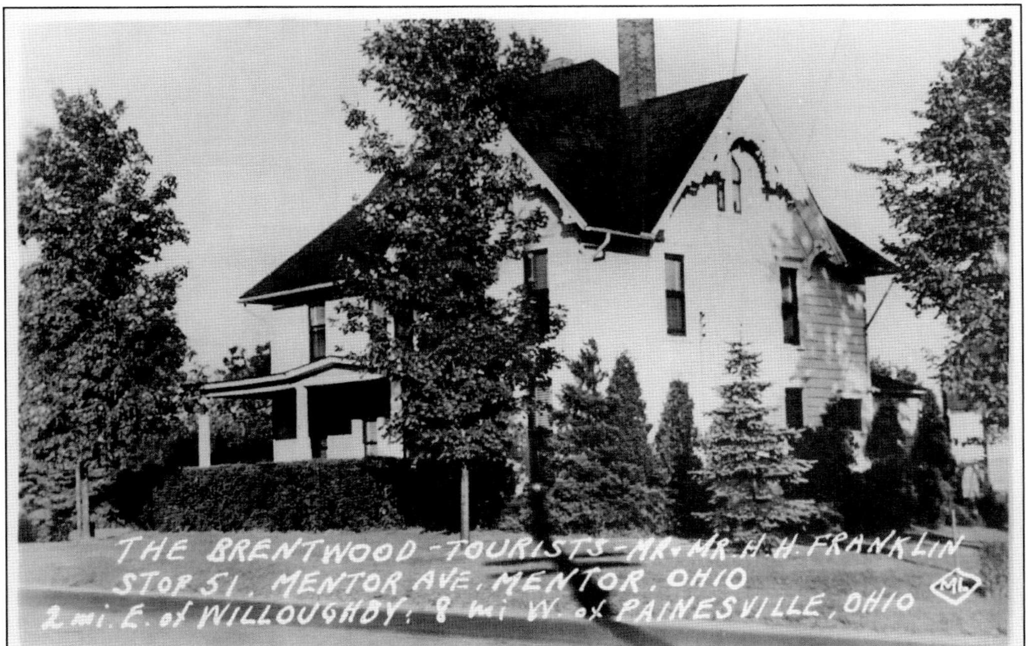

The Brentwood, Willoughby. That Route 20 was nearing Cleveland is evident in the address given for this tourist home, "Stop 51," which most likely indicated a station on the interurban public transportation system of the time.

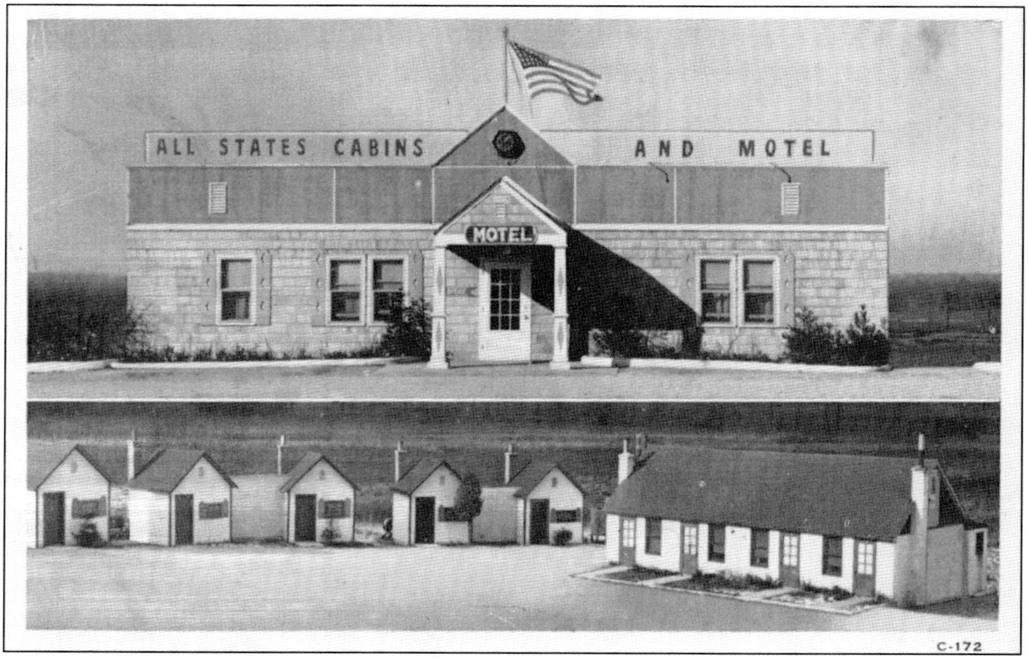

ALL STATES CABINS AND MOTEL, WILLOUGHBY. The original address of this motel was 39131 Mentor Avenue in Willoughby, but it later moved to 7231 Mentor Avenue. Regardless of the specific address, it was advertised as being in the "Heart of Lake Erie's Vacationland."

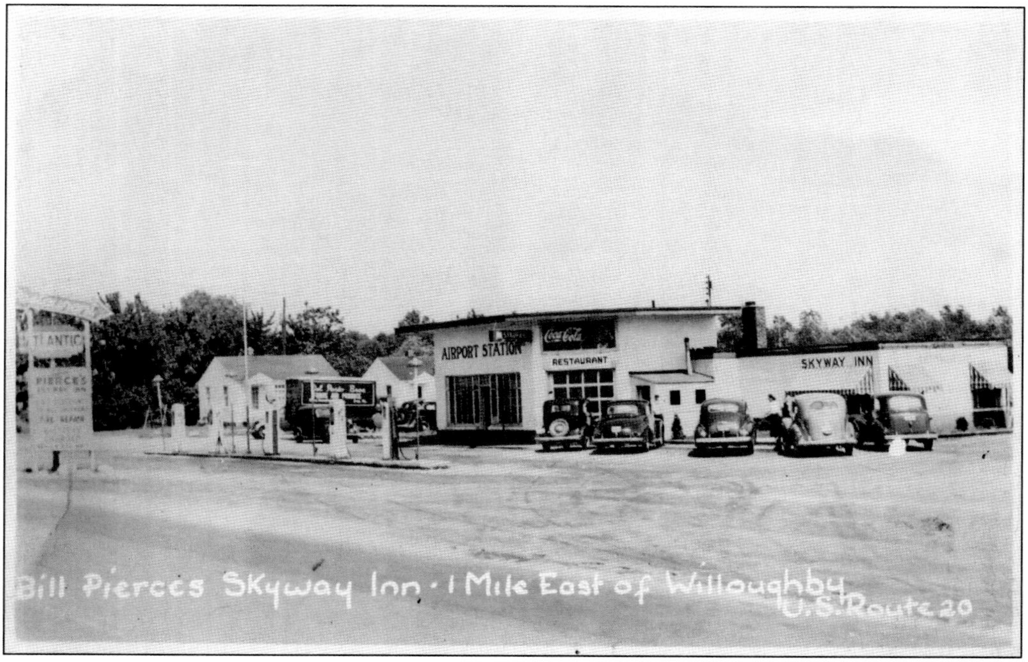

BILL PIERCE'S SKYWAY INN, ROUTE 20, WILLOUGHBY. The Skyway Inn and adjacent Airport Station were located near an airport. On the day this photograph was taken, there appears to be more diners than travelers.

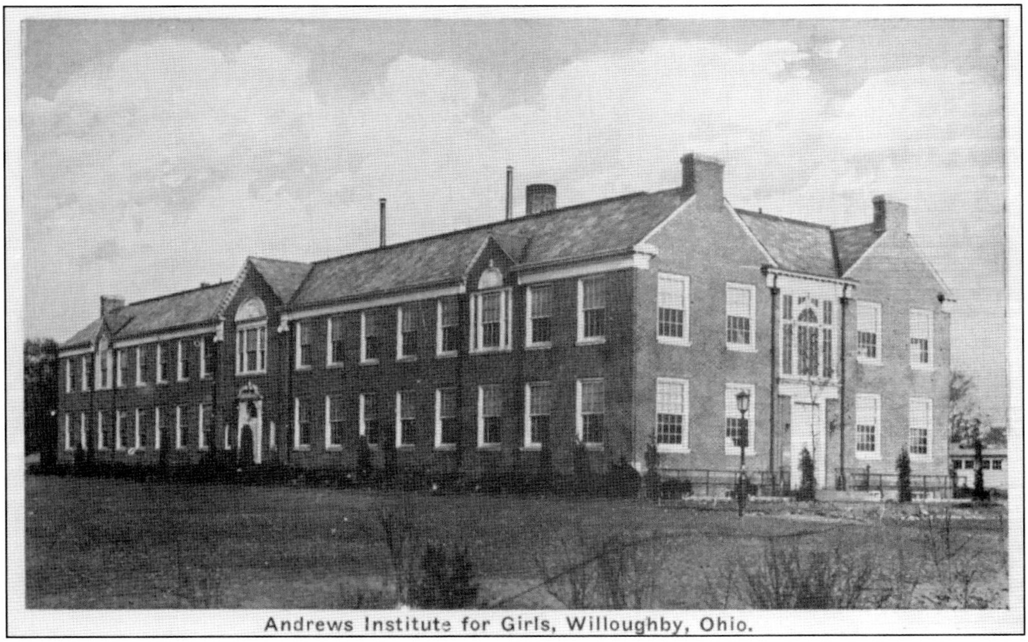

ANDREWS INSTITUTE FOR GIRLS, 38559 MENTOR AVENUE, WILLOUGHBY. Founded in 1910 by philanthropists Wallace and Margaret Andrews in their home, the land for the present school was purchased in 1913. The building seen here was dedicated in 1924, and in 1931 the name Andrews School for Girls was adopted. Tragically, Mr. and Mrs. Andrews died in a house fire before they could see their dream fulfilled.

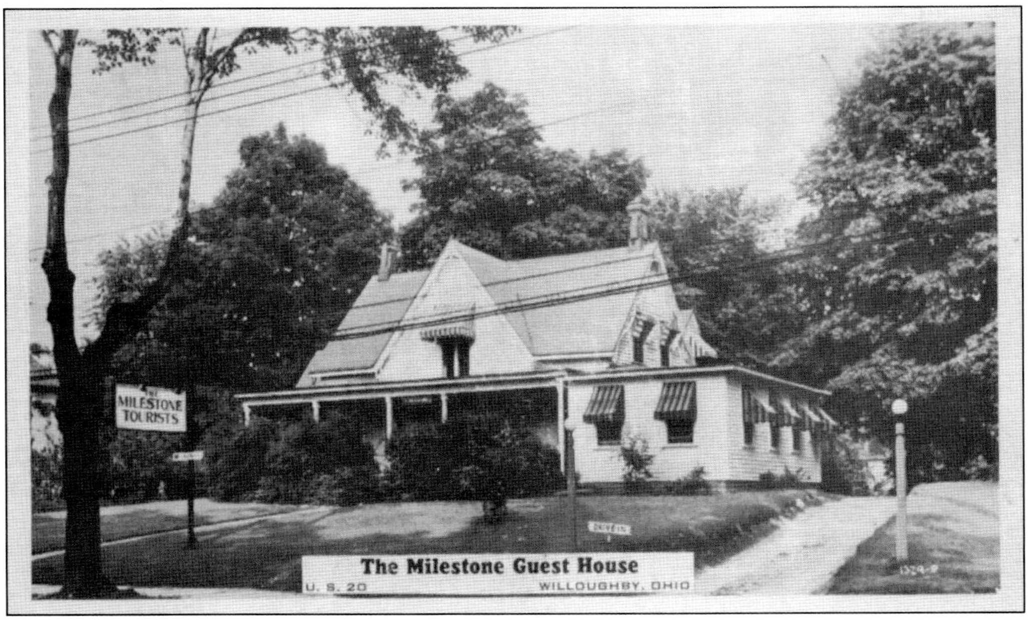

THE MILESTONE GUEST HOUSE, 38016 EUCLID AVENUE, WILLOUGHBY. It could be assumed that the name Milestone referred to the location of this tourist home along the highway, but it was actually the name of the owners, Omar and Erma Milestone. In 1924, this house was used as a dormitory for students from the nearby Andrews Institute for Girls, but the Milestones operated it as a tourist home throughout the 1930s and 1940s.

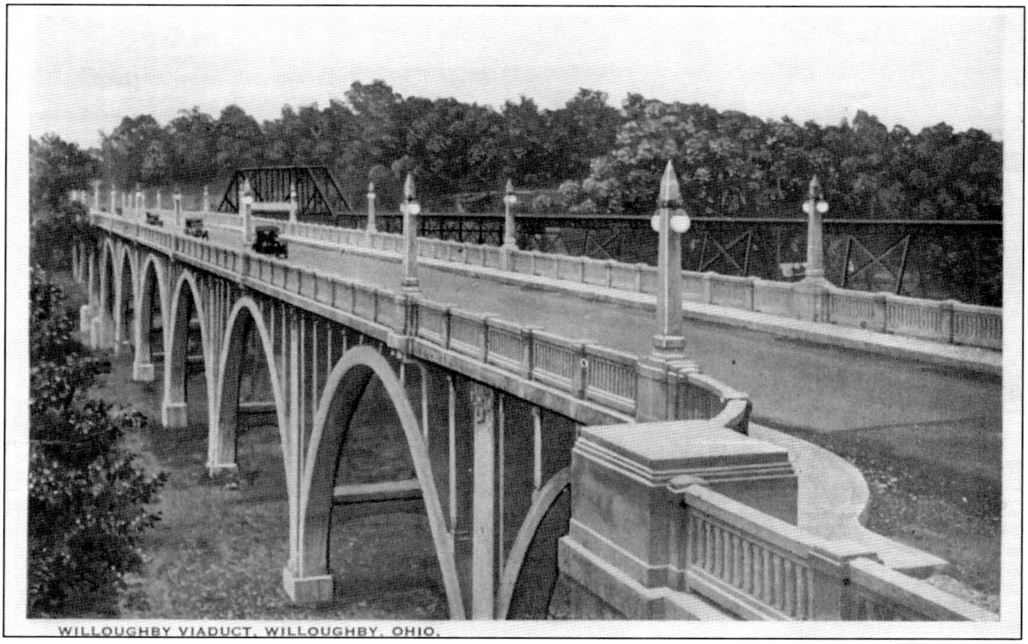

WILLOUGHBY VIADUCT, ROUTE 20, WILLOUGHBY. Concrete-arch bridges were popular in the early years of Route 20. They were practical, but the grace and beauty of the design were also important. This bridge over the Chagrin River was just east of Willoughby's business district. The Cleveland, Painesville & Eastern (CP&E) Railroad bridge ran parallel in the right background.

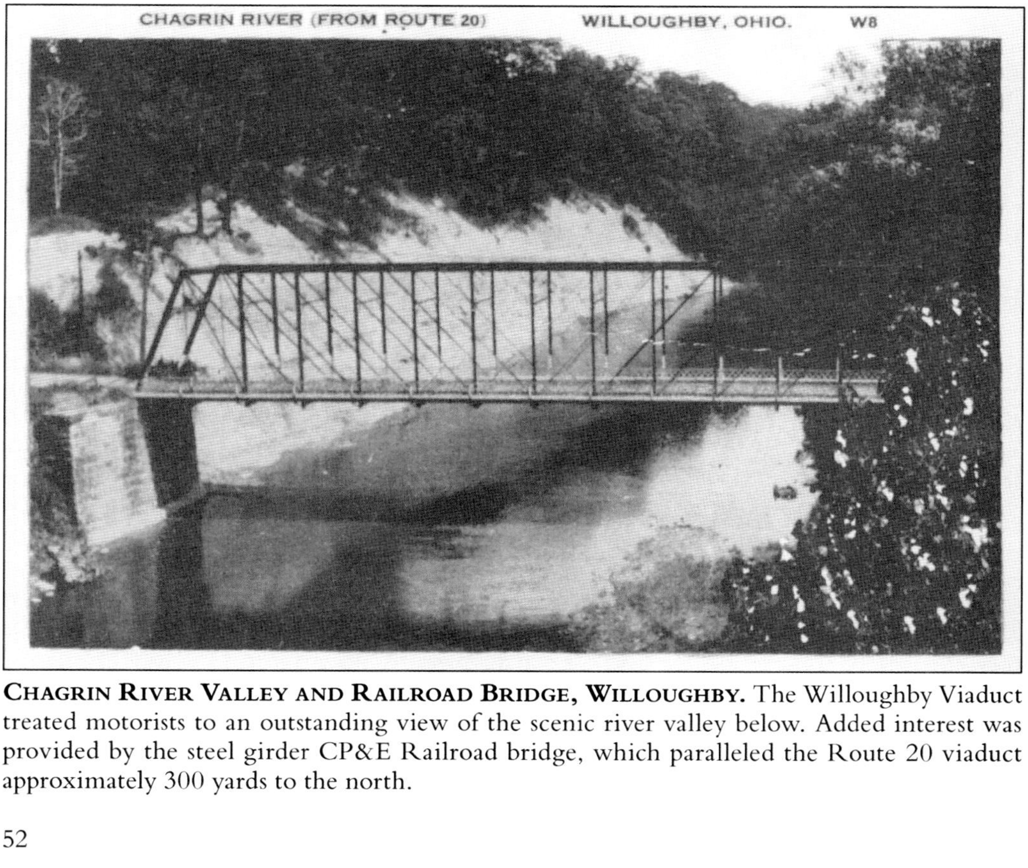

CHAGRIN RIVER VALLEY AND RAILROAD BRIDGE, WILLOUGHBY. The Willoughby Viaduct treated motorists to an outstanding view of the scenic river valley below. Added interest was provided by the steel girder CP&E Railroad bridge, which paralleled the Route 20 viaduct approximately 300 yards to the north.

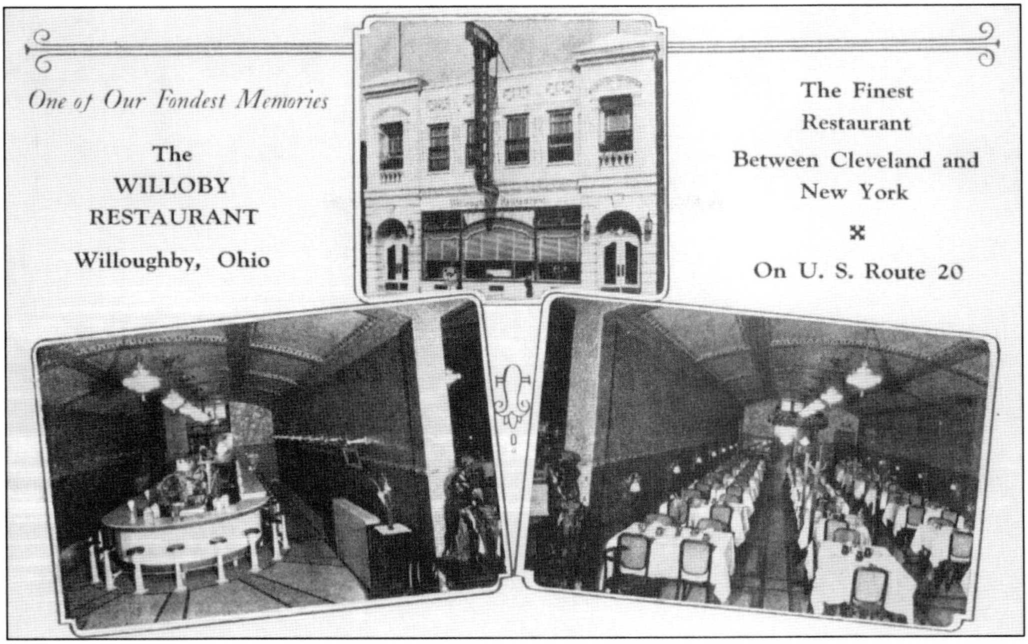

WILLOBY RESTAURANT, ROUTE 20, WILLOUGHBY. This main street restaurant was confident in the quality of its food and service, proclaiming to be "the finest restaurant between Cleveland and New York." It is possible that the unique spelling of "Willoby" on the card was an intentional variation of Willoughby, or it may have been an editing mistake. "Willoughby Restaurant," spelled correctly, appears on the sign above the door in the center image.

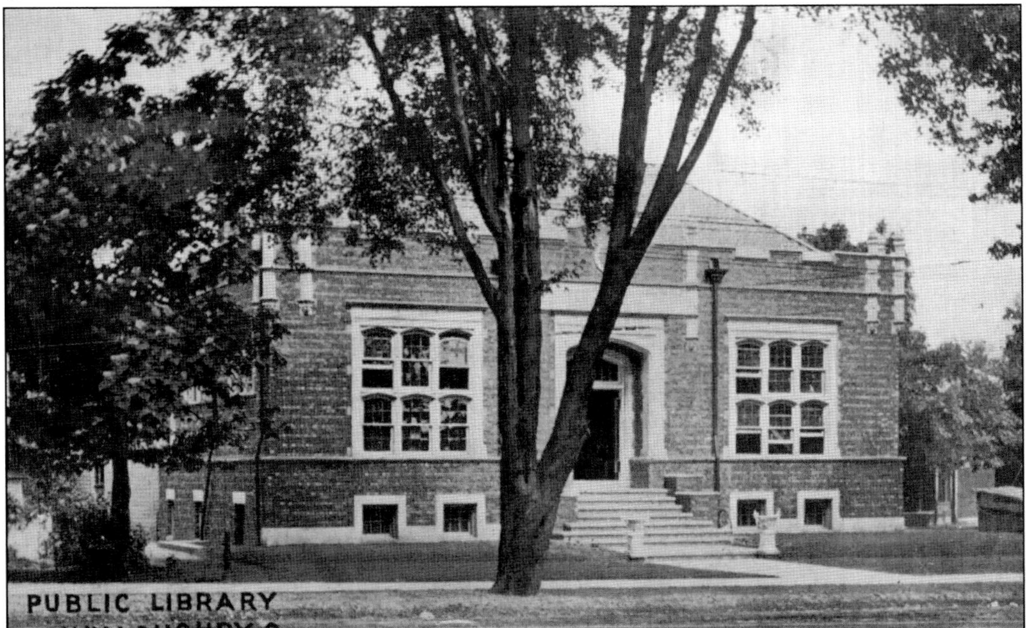

WILLOUGHBY PUBLIC LIBRARY, WILLOUGHBY. With only minor variations, the architectural style of many smaller public libraries was similar throughout the country, and Willoughby Public Library was no exception. Located prominently on the Public Square, the symmetrical brick building with a formal yet welcoming front entrance is still a centerpiece of the city.

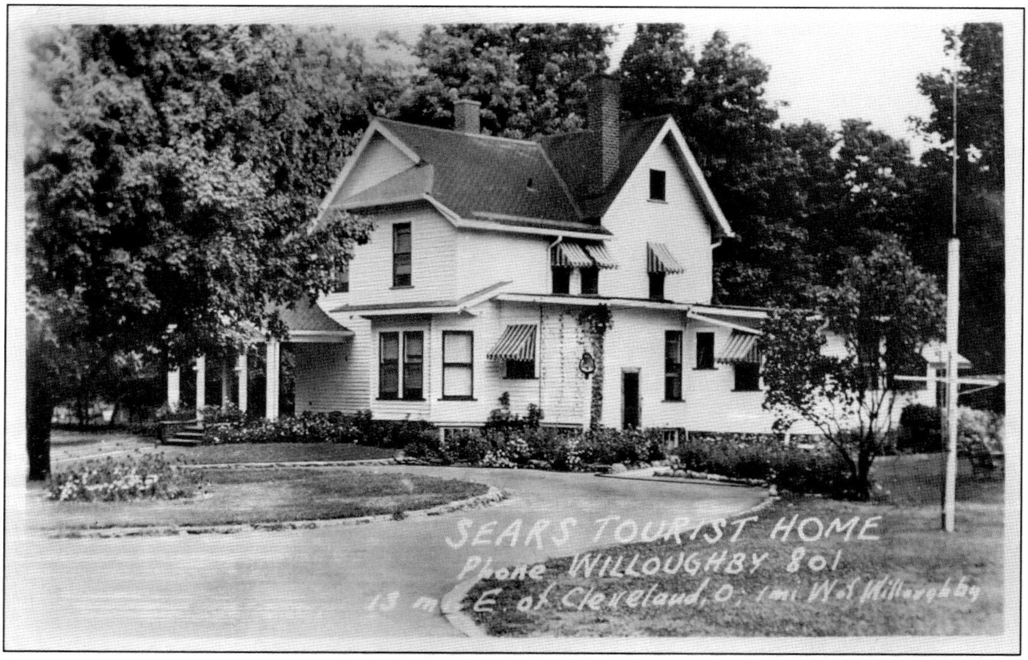

SEARS TOURIST HOME, WILLOUGHBY. This tourist home, only a short distance from Cleveland, would have been a convenient place for westbound travelers to spend the night before tackling Route 20's inevitable downtown traffic congestion. For those driving east, it was a place to relax after successfully negotiating the metropolitan area.

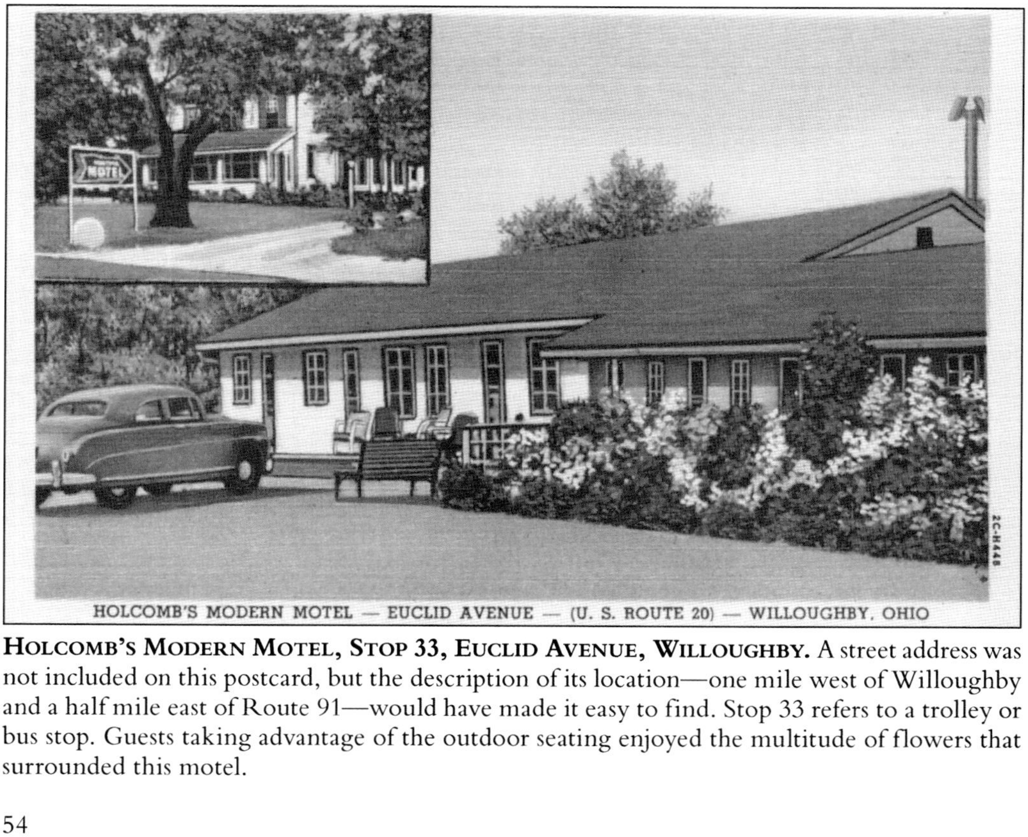

HOLCOMB'S MODERN MOTEL — EUCLID AVENUE — (U. S. ROUTE 20) — WILLOUGHBY, OHIO

HOLCOMB'S MODERN MOTEL, STOP 33, EUCLID AVENUE, WILLOUGHBY. A street address was not included on this postcard, but the description of its location—one mile west of Willoughby and a half mile east of Route 91—would have made it easy to find. Stop 33 refers to a trolley or bus stop. Guests taking advantage of the outdoor seating enjoyed the multitude of flowers that surrounded this motel.

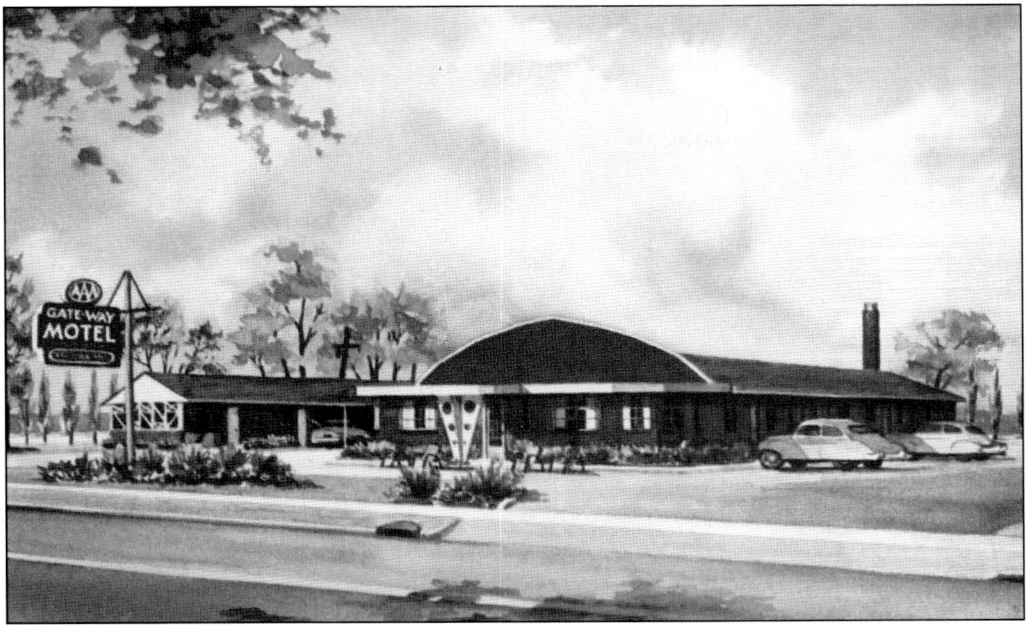

GATEWAY MOTEL, 29865 EUCLID AVENUE, WICKLIFFE. The design of the main building of the Gateway Motel was reminiscent of a World War II Quonset hut. Located 15 miles east of downtown Cleveland on Route 20, this motel offered 22 fully carpeted, smartly furnished, soundproof rooms with ceramic tile baths. Guests could choose to protect their cars from the weather in covered carports.

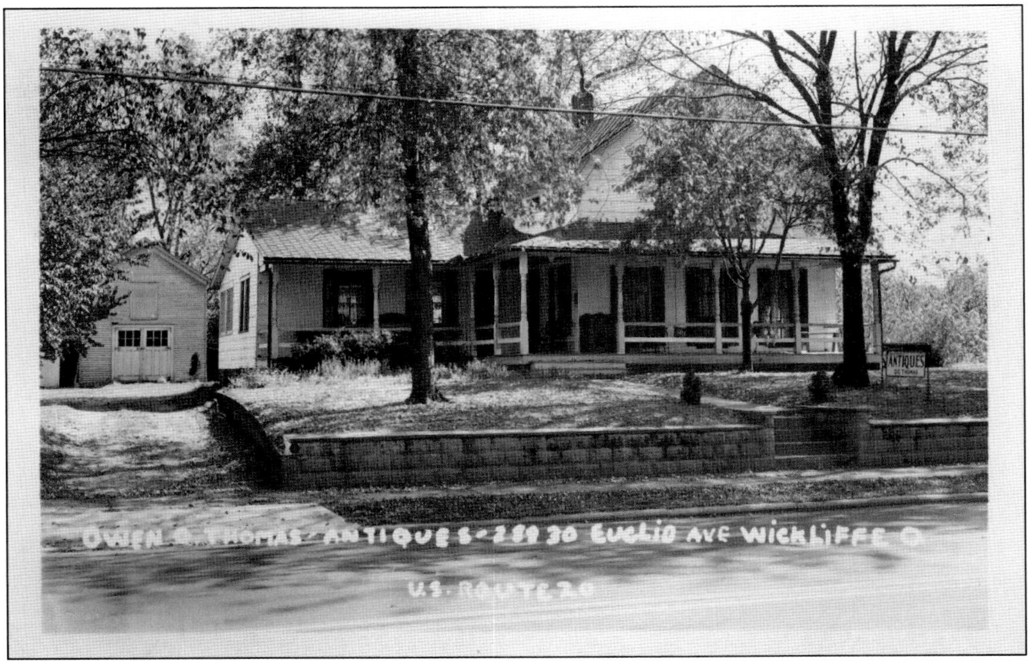

OWEN G. THOMAS ANTIQUES, 28930 EUCLID AVENUE, WICKLIFFE. Small roadside businesses such as this antique shop were found in many communities along Route 20. Although most catered to a local clientele, tourists also found them interesting places to take a break from driving and possibly land a bargain.

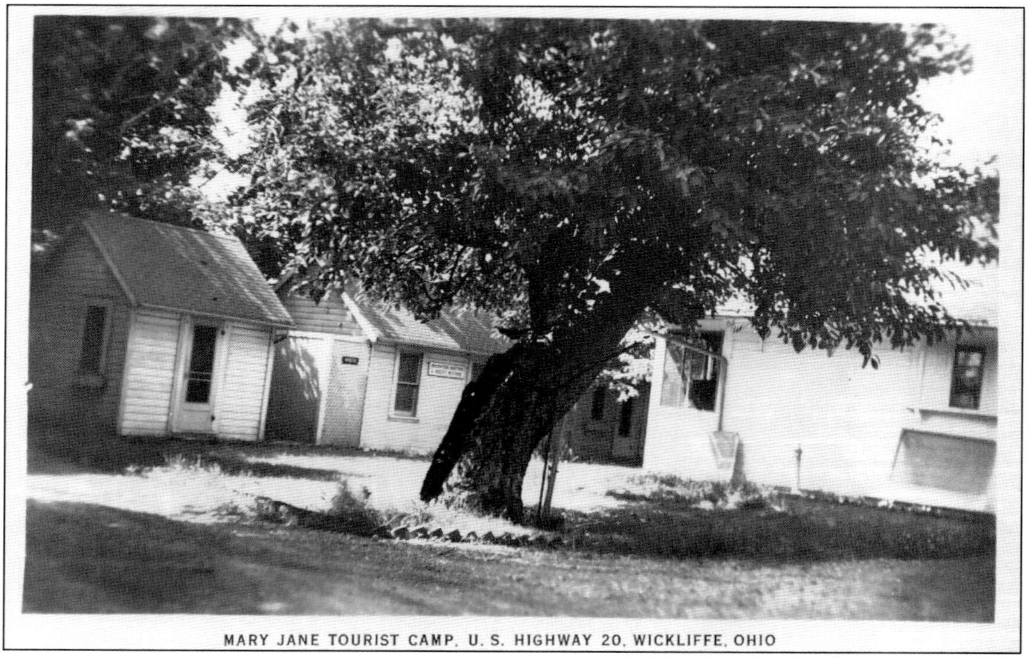

MARY JANE TOURIST CAMP, STOP 26½, EUCLID AVENUE, WICKLIFFE. This card was mailed on June 1, 1939. The writer, Joe, reported, "The race was good and we expect to be on the road a couple more days." Given the date and location, he was probably returning home after attending the 1939 Indianapolis 500, which was won that year by the famous driver Wilbur Shaw.

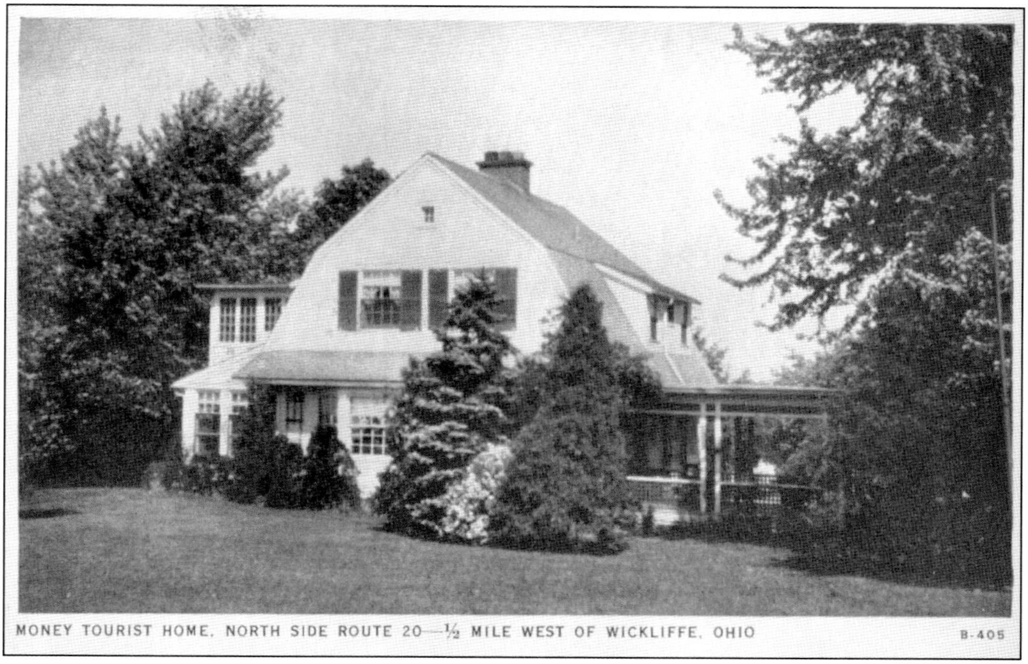

MONEY TOURIST HOME, ROUTE 20, WICKLIFFE. The proprietors of this tourist home, located close to Cleveland's eastern city limits, relied on its pleasant suburban setting and proximity to the city to attract clients. There is no information on this card to indicate amenities, but as was typical of the time, bathrooms were shared with other guests and possibly with the owner's family.

Three

Cleveland

Route 20 holds the unique distinction of only passing through three large cities—Boston, Cleveland, and Chicago—on its cross-country journey. Over the years, Cleveland proved to be a wonderful host to the travelers who plied its route. Entering the city from the east on Euclid Avenue, Route 20 added another unusual feature by following two different streets simultaneously as it progressed toward the city center. From 1926 until 1968, official Route 20, together with Route 6, followed Superior Avenue, and Alternate Route 20 continued on Euclid Avenue, a few blocks to the south. This configuration continued until 1968, when Euclid Avenue became exclusively Route 20, and Route 6 remained on Superior Avenue.

Irrespective of its designation as Alternate Route 20, Euclid Avenue was the more dominant of the two streets, and much of Cleveland's early history can be traced to it. Cleveland State University and the world-famous Cleveland Clinic are both located on Euclid Avenue. The Cleveland Museum of Natural History, the Cleveland Institute of Art, Severance Hall (the home of the Cleveland Orchestra), and Case Western Reserve University all border this important thoroughfare at University Circle.

Euclid Avenue was also the location of Cleveland's Millionaires' Row, which was home to the city's elite in the late 1800s. Unfortunately, most of those ornate mansions have succumbed to urban renewal. Nearer the downtown business district, Euclid Avenue passed through Playhouse Square, which was once home to opulent playhouses. Closer to the Public Square, both Superior and Euclid Avenues housed Cleveland's most prestigious hotels, some of which are shown in this chapter.

Superior and Euclid Avenues converged at the Public Square, the four-square-block focal point of downtown Cleveland. Surrounding the square are some of Cleveland's most historical structures, including the Old Stone Church, Terminal Tower, and the Soldiers and Sailors Monument. West of the Public Square, historic Route 20 followed West Superior Avenue across the spectacular High Bridge. It then proceeded west through affluent neighborhoods along Clifton Avenue, near Lake Erie, before crossing the Rocky River into the western suburbs.

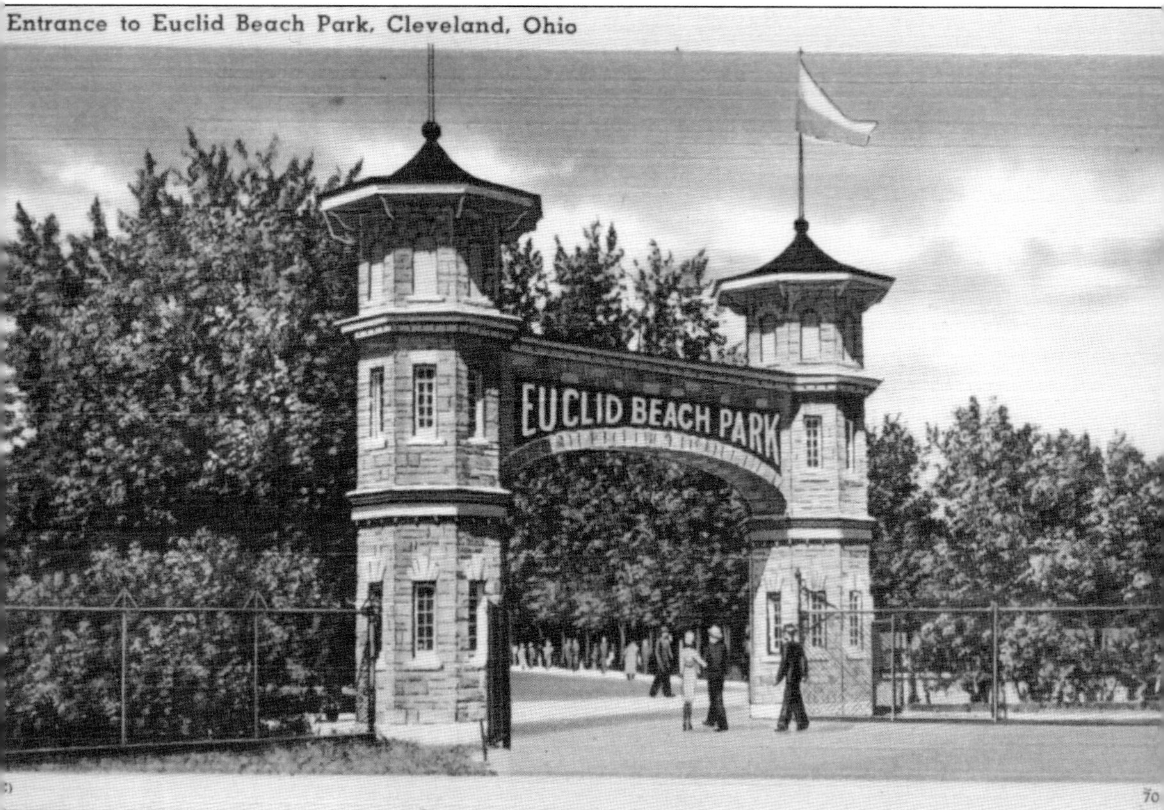

EUCLID BEACH PARK, CLEVELAND. Euclid Beach Park, established in 1895 on the Lake Erie shore, was one of Cleveland's most popular destinations for over 70 years. Located only a short distance north of Euclid Avenue in eastern Cleveland, the park's entrance gate led to its more than 100 amusement attractions, including the beach, a dance pavilion, a carousel, seven wooden roller coasters, and picnic grounds. The park's family friendly philosophy banned the sale of alcoholic beverages, and patrons were required to conform to the park's strict dress code. Sadly, racial discrimination was prevalent; African Americans were allowed access only on certain days, and intermingling of the races was forbidden. This led to a series of protests and eventually to riots in 1946. The result was legislation requiring licensure for amusement parks and a provision for revocation if discrimination was practiced. Euclid Beach Park survived this incident and continued in operation, but the changing tastes of the populace eventually brought about its closure in 1969.

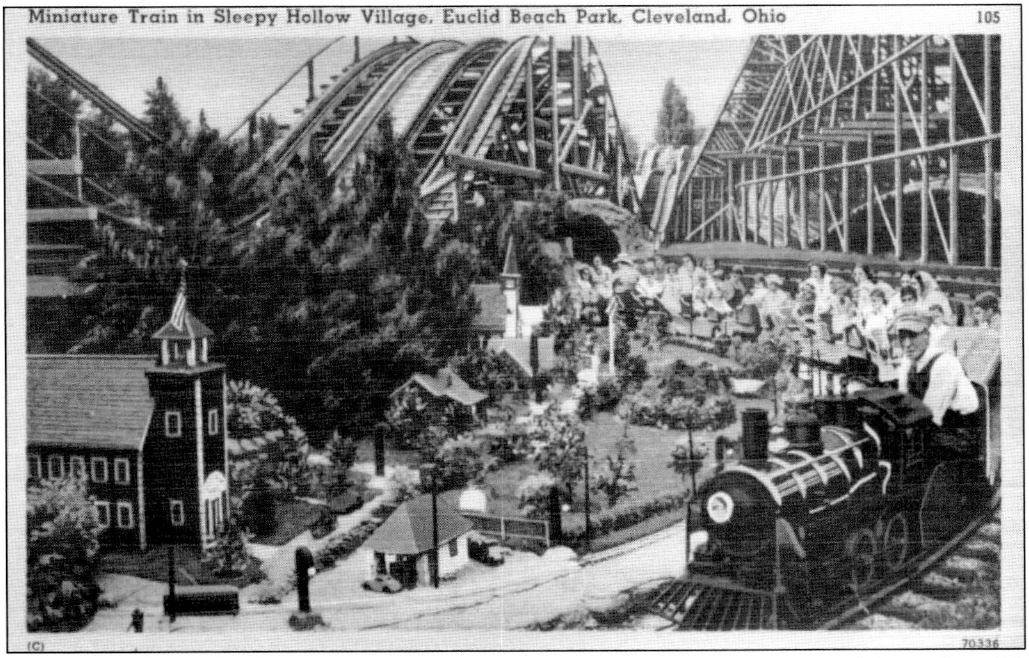

SLEEPY HOLLOW VILLAGE, EUCLID BEACH PARK, CLEVELAND. Two of Euclid Beach Park's most popular attractions are seen in this postcard. Sleepy Hollow Village included a miniature working train that was a favorite of younger children. The wooden roller coasters in the background provided excitement for teenagers and adults. The grounds throughout the park featured exceptional landscaping and floral gardens.

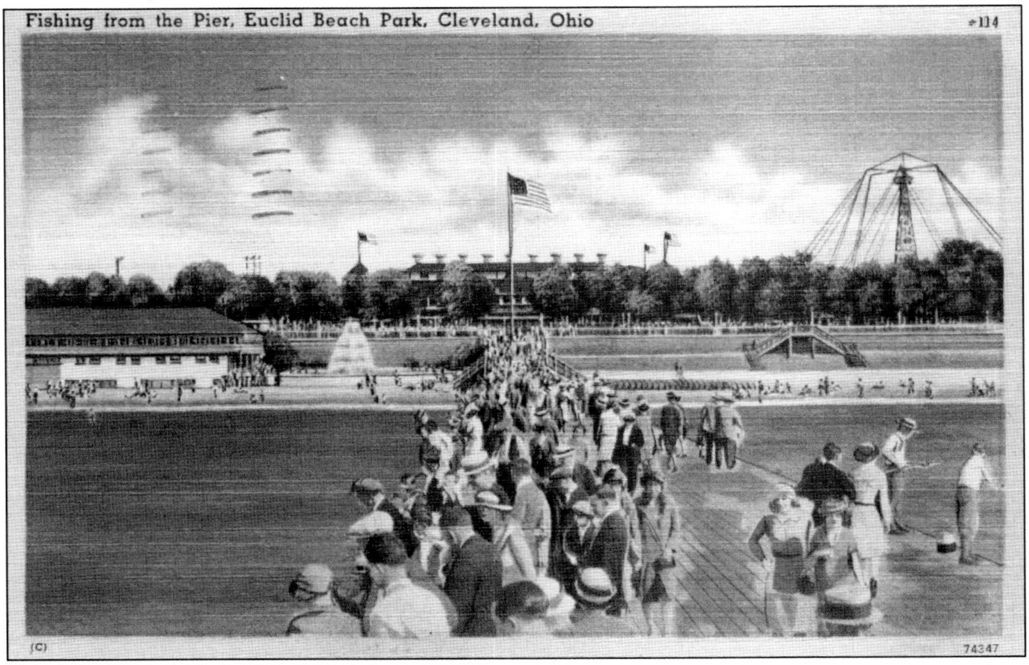

FISHING FROM THE PIER, EUCLID BEACH PARK, CLEVELAND. Fishing was a popular pastime at Euclid Beach. The background of this postcard shows a panorama of the park, including the beach, the pavilions, and the giant swings.

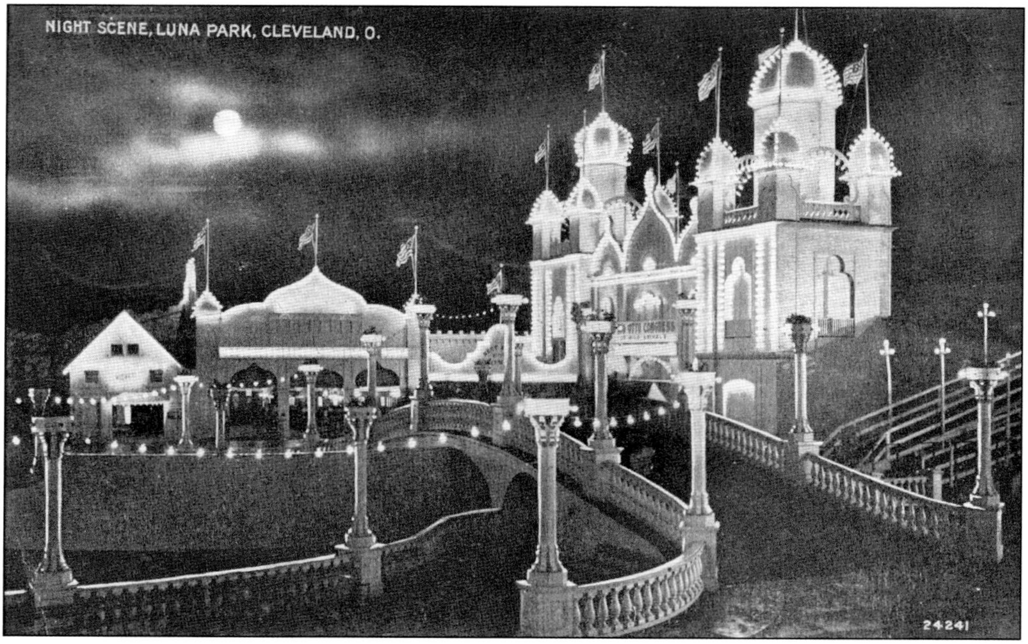

LUNA PARK, EAST CLEVELAND. Luna Park was another East Cleveland landmark located near Route 20. It was the country's second electrified amusement park and presented a spectacular nightly light display. Luna Park derived considerable income from alcohol sales. The passing of the 18th Amendment in 1919, prohibiting the manufacture and sale of alcohol, greatly reduced Luna Park's revenue, and the Great Depression dealt a final blow. The park closed in 1929.

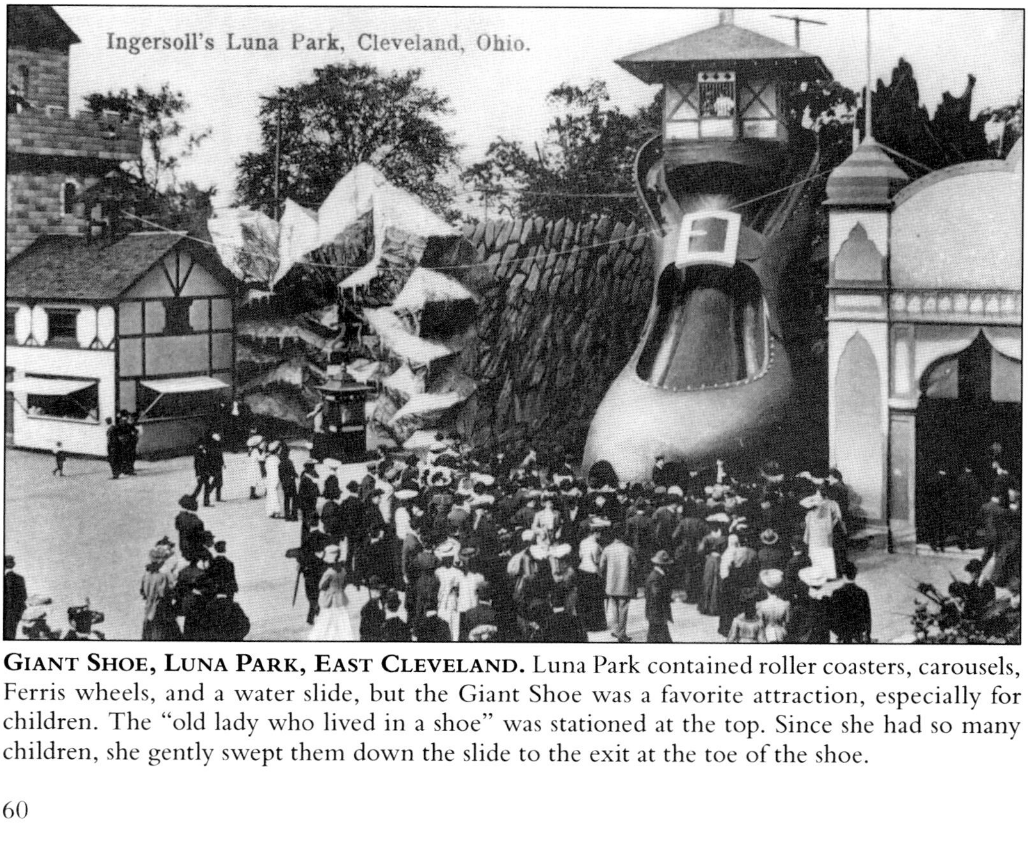

GIANT SHOE, LUNA PARK, EAST CLEVELAND. Luna Park contained roller coasters, carousels, Ferris wheels, and a water slide, but the Giant Shoe was a favorite attraction, especially for children. The "old lady who lived in a shoe" was stationed at the top. Since she had so many children, she gently swept them down the slide to the exit at the toe of the shoe.

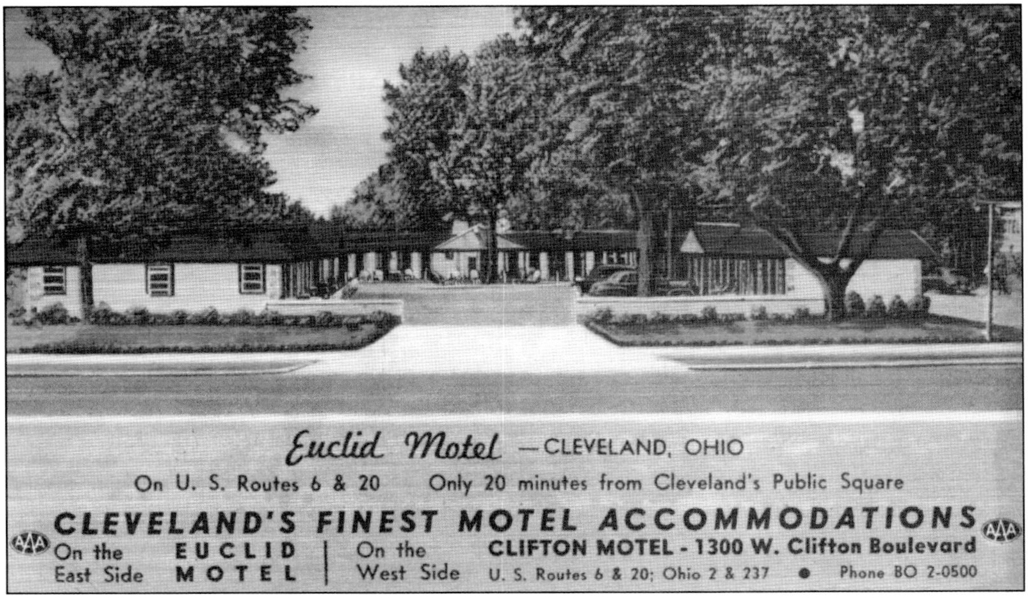

EUCLID MOTEL, 18327 EUCLID AVENUE, CLEVELAND. Route 20 followed Euclid Avenue from the eastern suburbs into Cleveland proper. The Euclid Motel was one of the first motels within city limits that a traveler would have encountered. It was one of two motels under the same ownership, which were both billed as having "Cleveland's finest motel accommodations." The second motel, in western Cleveland, is seen on page 82.

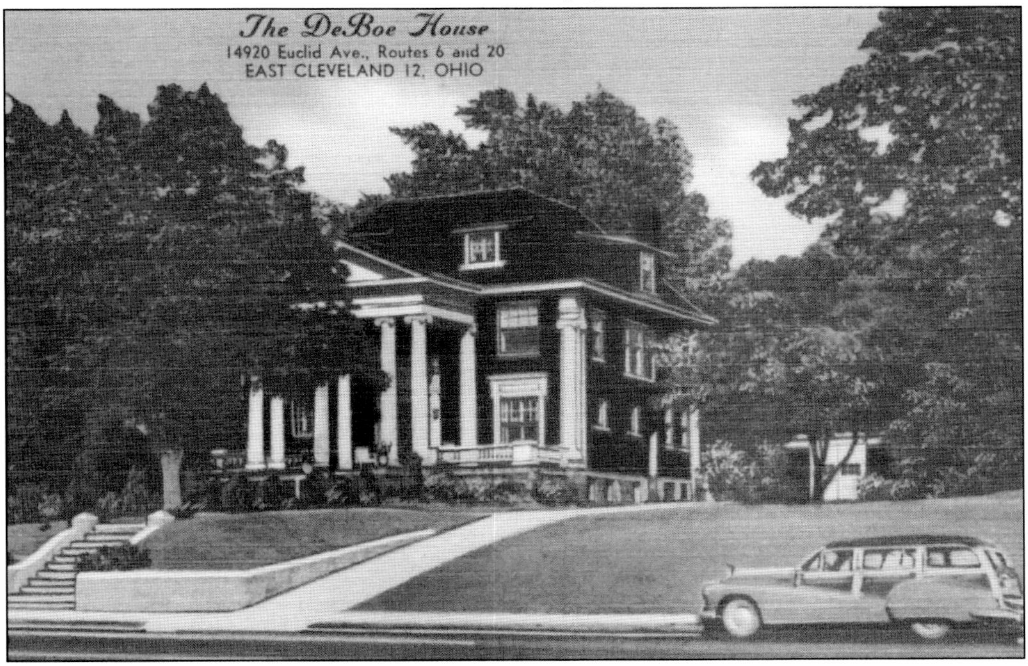

DEBOE HOUSE, 14920 EUCLID AVENUE, EAST CLEVELAND. This stately tourists' home was well placed on Routes 6 and 20. It advertised itself as "Your Home Away From Home." Mildred DeBoe, the home's proprietor, ensured her guests modern, clean, well-furnished rooms, some of them with private baths, as well as free parking. The owner of the sleek late-1940s Buick woodie parked at the curb may have been a guest.

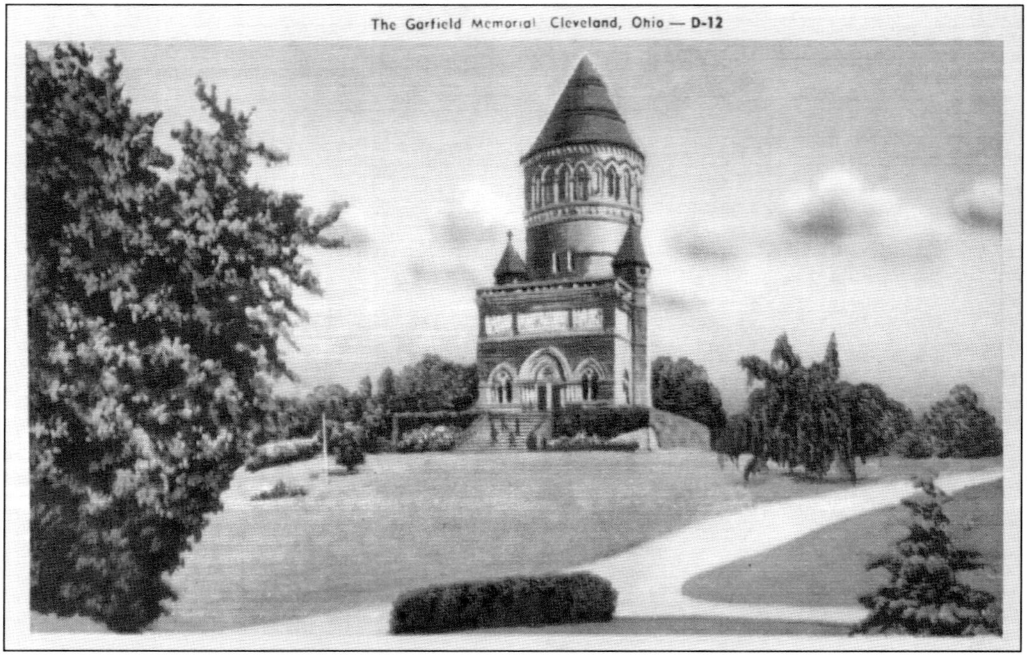

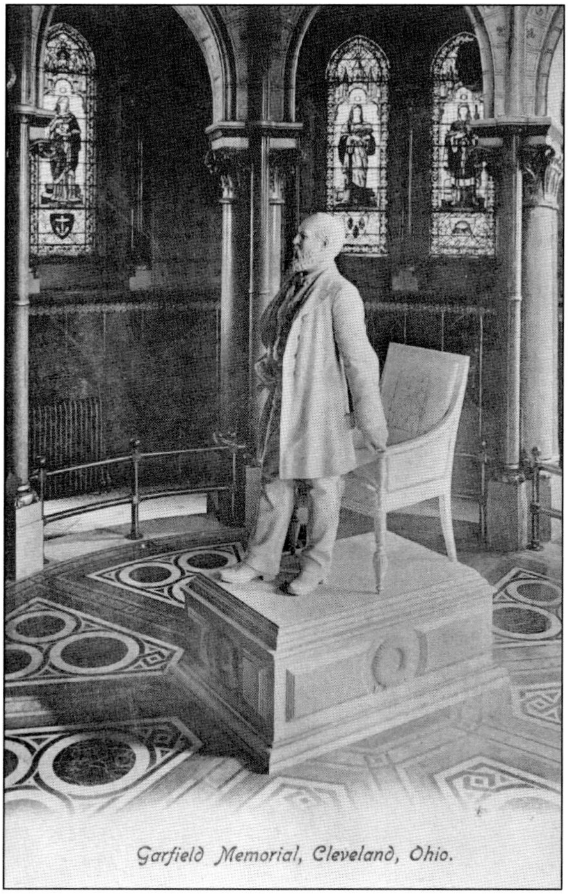

GARFIELD MEMORIAL, LAKEVIEW CEMETERY, CLEVELAND. Lakeview Cemetery is directly along Route 20 in Cleveland. It is the burial site of Pres. James Garfield, whose monument is seen in these two postcards. The tower (above) was designed by architect George Keller and erected two years after Garfield's death. It is 180 feet high and 50 feet in diameter. The exterior walls contain five bas-relief panels, representing Garfield as teacher, soldier, orator, president, and lying in state. The centerpiece of the ornate interior (left) is an oversized statue of the president, sculpted by Alexander Doyle. There are also 14 stained-glass windows representing the 13 original colonies and Ohio. Other prominent Ohioans buried in Lakewood Cemetery include John D. Rockefeller; John Hay, diplomat and secretary to Abraham Lincoln; famous crime fighter Eliot Ness; and former Cleveland mayors Tom Johnson and Carl Stokes.

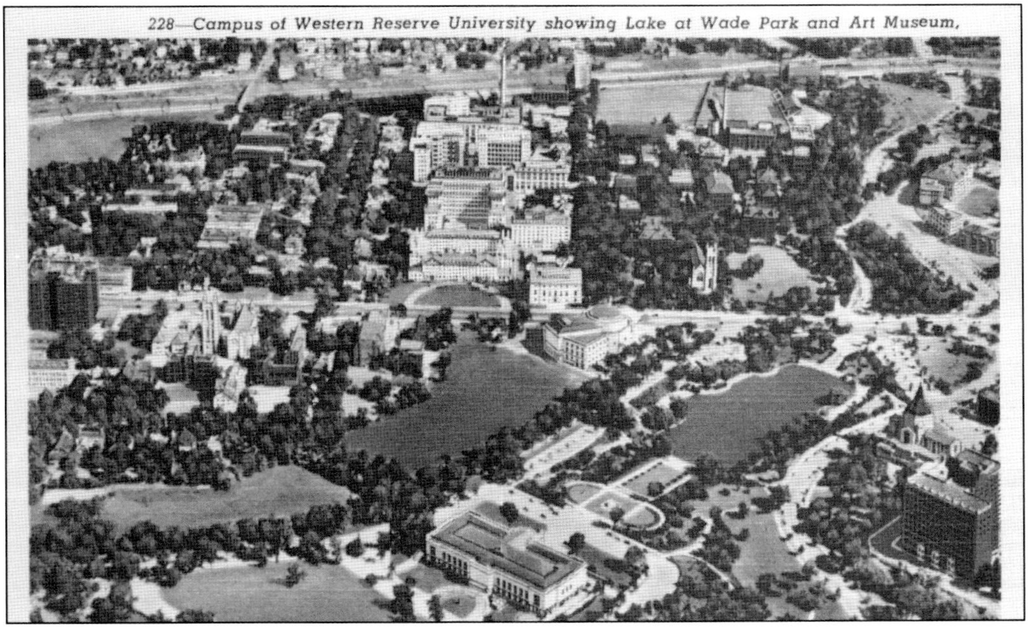

CASE WESTERN RESERVE UNIVERSITY, CLEVELAND. Euclid Avenue, seen in the center of this postcard, carried Route 20 through Cleveland's cultural district. Case Western Reserve University, one of the oldest universities west of the Allegheny Mountains, is at the top of the card. Severance Hall, the home of the Cleveland Orchestra, is the domed building in the center, and the Cleveland Art Museum is the rectangular building in the lower center.

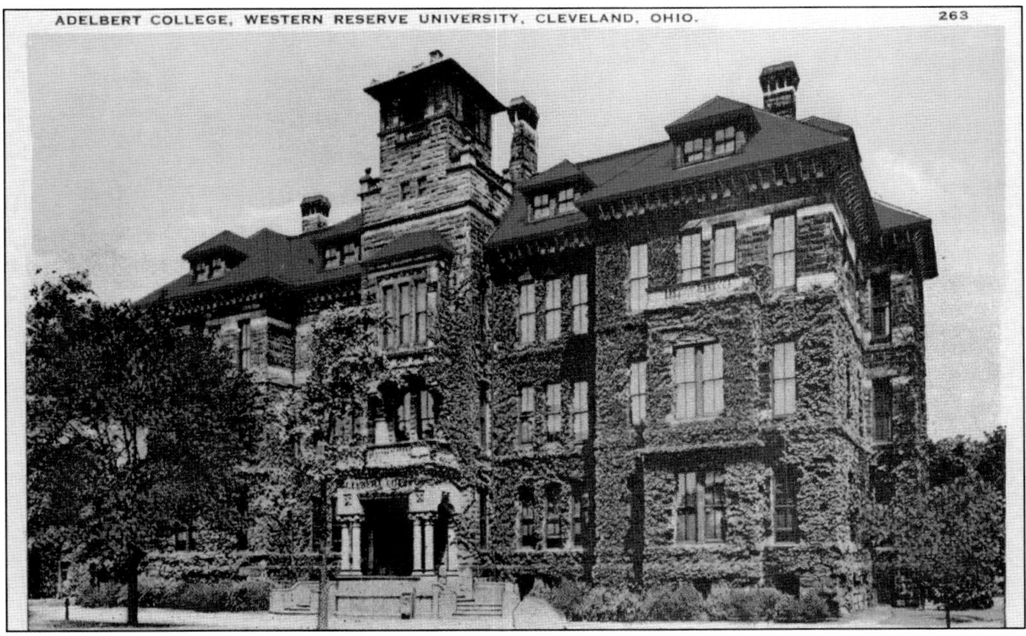

ADELBERT COLLEGE, CASE WESTERN RESERVE UNIVERSITY, CLEVELAND. Western Reserve College opened in 1826 in Hudson, Ohio. In 1882, it was moved to Cleveland, and in 1892 the name was changed to Adelbert College of Western Reserve University following a donation from Amasa Stone in honor of his son. This building was among the first on the Cleveland campus and has occupied its prominent position ever since.

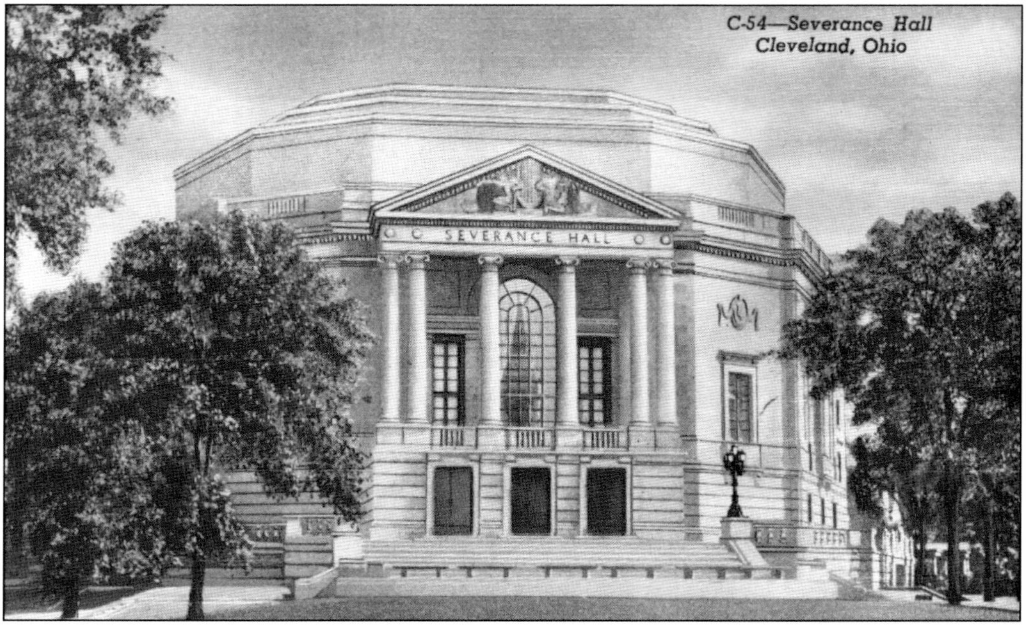

SEVERANCE HALL, 11001 EUCLID AVENUE, CLEVELAND. Severance Hall is one of the world's most beautiful concert halls. Completed in 1931, it was endowed through a $1.5 million gift from industrialist and philanthropist John Severance. In 1930, he gave an additional $1 million in honor of his wife, Elisabeth, who had recently passed away. Severance Hall is listed in the National Register of Historic Places.

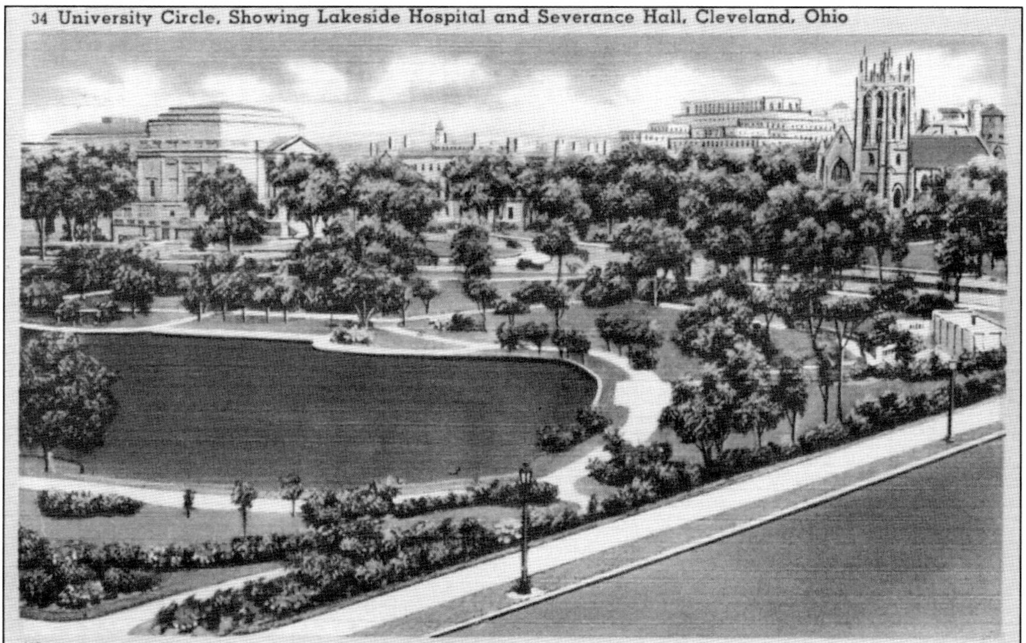

UNIVERSITY CIRCLE, CLEVELAND. Beautifully landscaped Wade Park, with its placid lagoon, was a popular site on Euclid Avenue to stroll and picnic. It was especially enjoyed by people who lived and worked in the surrounding buildings. Severance Hall is on the left, and Lakeside Hospital occupied the white buildings in the center right. The Amasa Stone Chapel's gothic tower is on the far right.

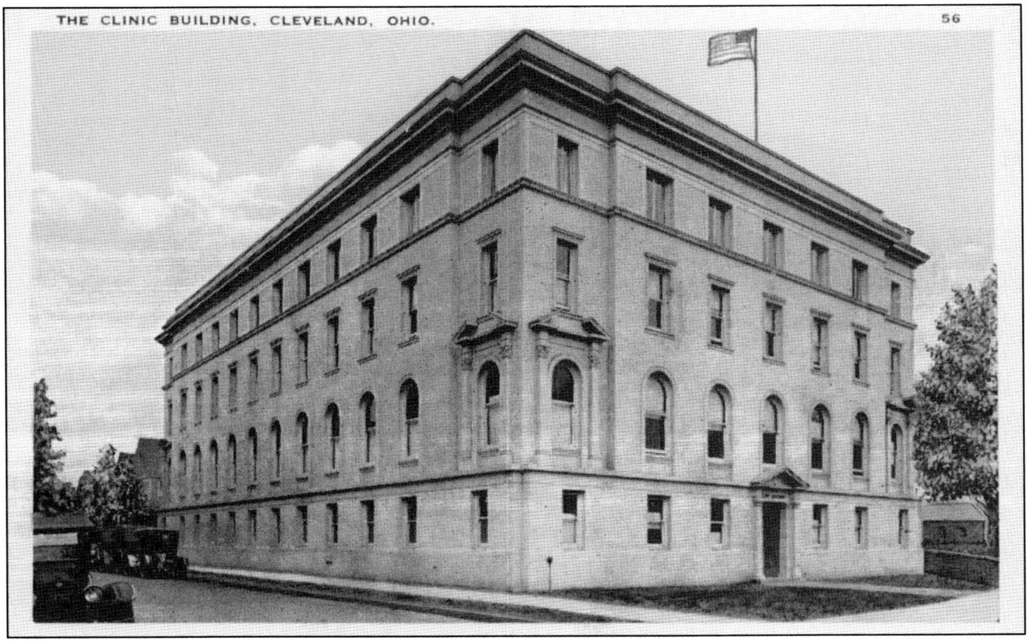

CLEVELAND CLINIC, EUCLID AVENUE AT NINETY-THIRD STREET, CLEVELAND. In February 1921, the Cleveland Clinic admitted its first patients in the building above. The clinic was started by four physicians who had served together in World War I and were dedicated to, in their words, "better care for the sick, investigation into their problems, and further education of those who serve." Their objective was realized, and the Cleveland Clinic has become one of the most advanced medical centers in the country. The photograph below shows the expansion during the early decades of the clinic. A second building was added in 1924. In 1929, a disastrous fire that killed 123 people, followed by the stock market crash, curtailed progress, but the clinic survived. The research buildings on the far left were added throughout the ensuing years.

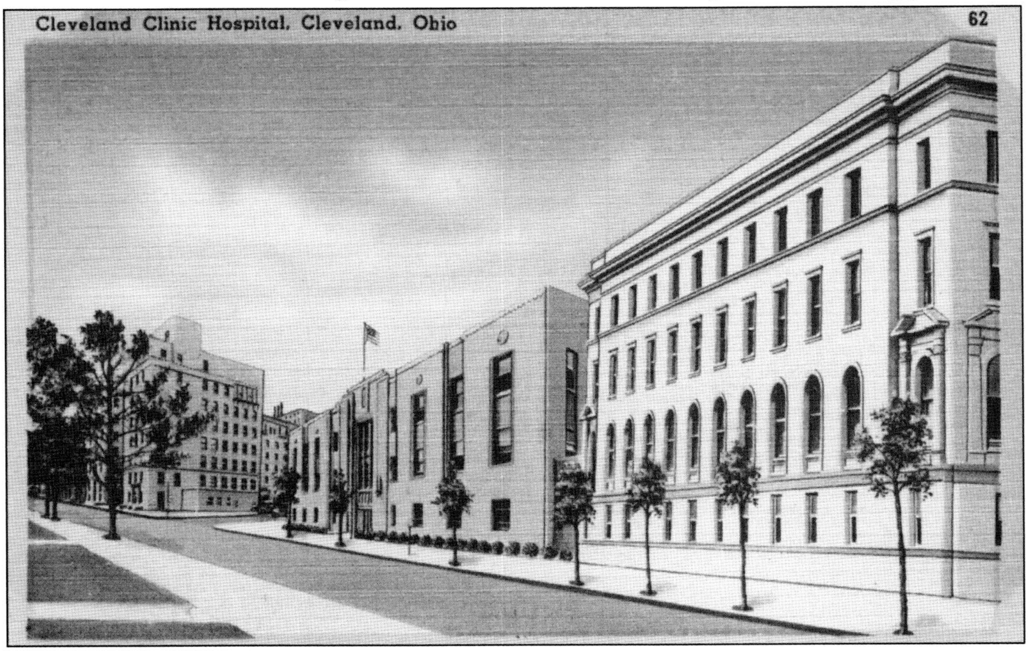

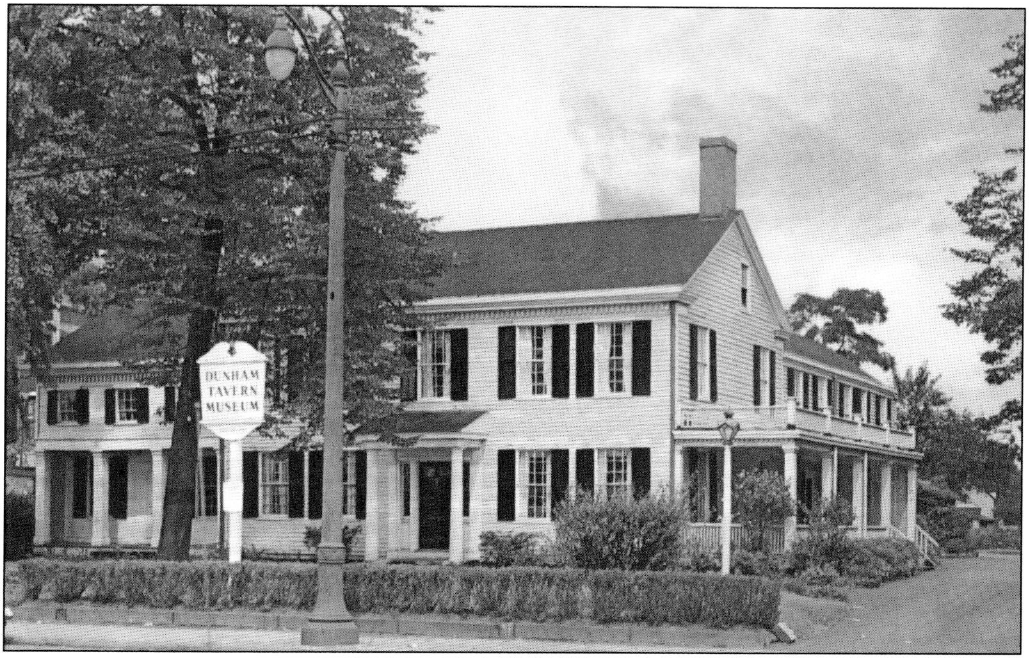

DUNHAM TAVERN MUSEUM, 6709 EUCLID AVENUE, CLEVELAND. This former stagecoach stop was completed in 1832 and is the oldest building in Cleveland that still occupies its original site. In 1857, it was purchased by a Cleveland family to be a country home. During the Great Depression, it became a studio for Works Progress Administration (WPA) artists. Dunham Tavern has been a museum and a National Historic site since 1941.

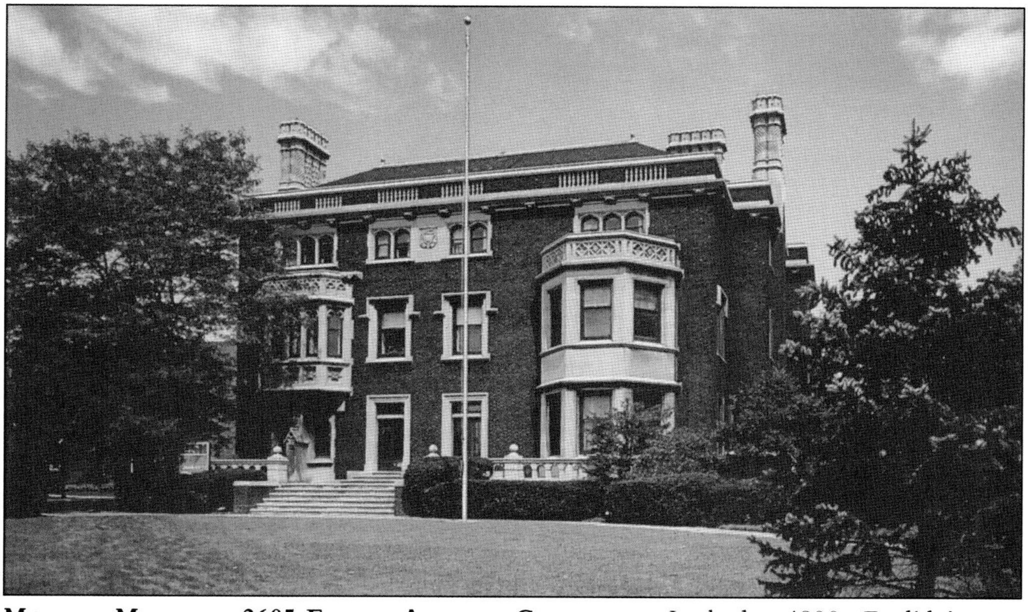

MATHER MANSION, 2605 EUCLID AVENUE, CLEVELAND. In the late 1800s, Euclid Avenue was home to Millionaires' Row, featuring the mansions of the city's elite. The Mather mansion is one of only three of the palatial homes remaining. The 45-room mansion, now owned by Cleveland State University, is in the National Register of Historic Places and is a designated Ohio Historical Site and Cleveland Landmark.

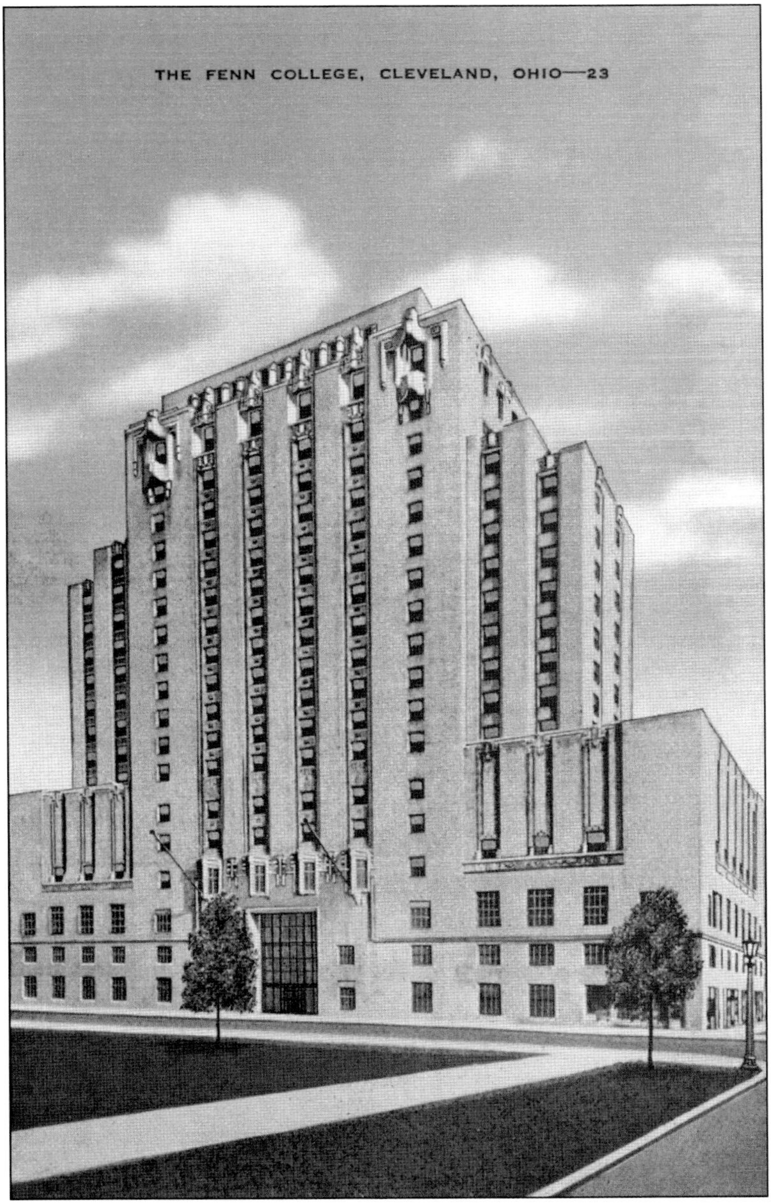

FENN COLLEGE, 2401 EUCLID AVENUE, CLEVELAND. Fenn College evolved out of free evening classes offered by the YMCA in the 1870s. It was named in honor of Sereno Peck Fenn, a founder of the Sherwin-Williams paint company, the longtime president of Cleveland's YMCA, and a generous donor to the college. This building, Fenn Tower, was constructed in 1930 by the National Town and Country Club as a clubhouse. It was acquired by the YMCA in 1937 and converted into a multipurpose college facility. Fenn College eventually became Cleveland State University. The inscription on the back of this card reads, "Fenn College, Cleveland's 'Skyscraper Schoolhouse' 22 stories high. With an enrollment of 3,000 this typically urban college is on the cooperative plan, each student alternating three months of college with a similar period at a job. This collegiate skyscraper is three buildings in one—the first four floors for administration and classrooms, the next two for gymnasium, swimming pool, handball courts, and from there up for dormitory."

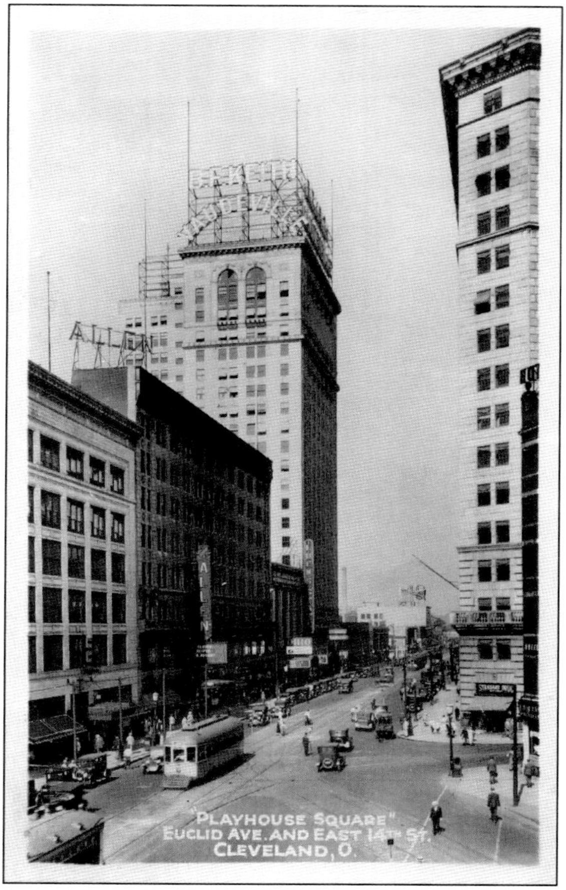

PLAYHOUSE SQUARE, EUCLID AVENUE, CLEVELAND. Since the early 1920s, Playhouse Square has been Cleveland's theater district and, in conjunction with the nearby hotels and restaurants, a center for the city's social activities. Five theaters, the Allen, the Palace, the Ohio, the State, and the Hanna, all opened between 1921 and 1922. Their collective seating capacity of approximately 10,000 made Playhouse Square one of the largest entertainment complexes in the country. Silent films, vaudeville, movies, touring Broadway shows, and legitimate theater were presented. The district is seen at left in the 1920s and below in the early 1950s. The Allen Theater featured the film *Fabiola*, which is described on the marquee as "the most fabulous film spectacular ever made." The entire district is listed in the National Register of Historic Places under the name Playhouse Square Group.

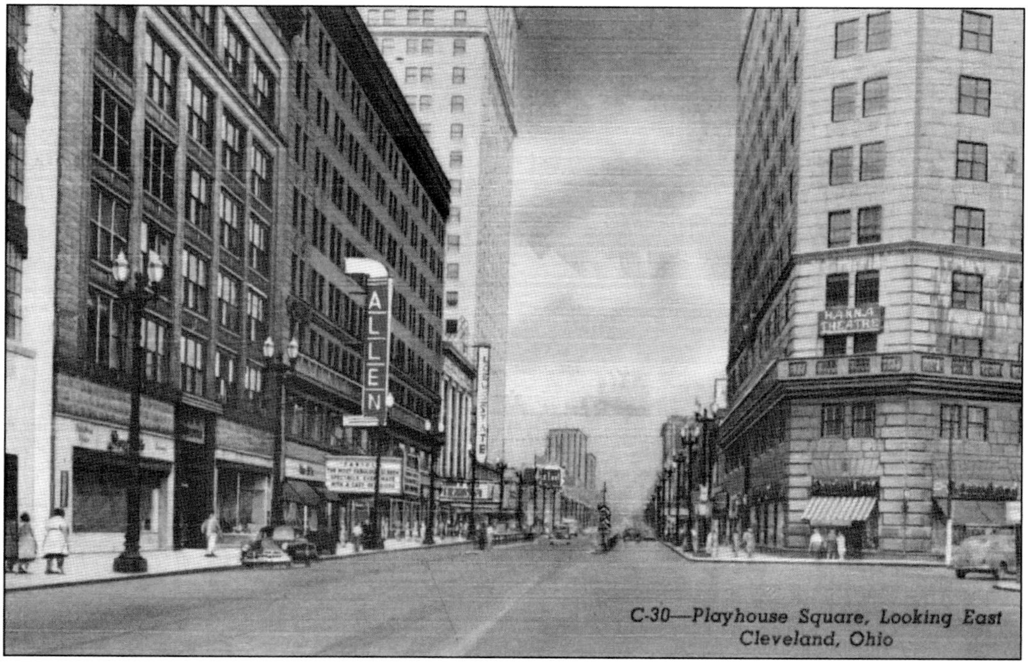

HOTEL STATLER, EUCLID AVENUE AND EAST TWELFTH STREET, CLEVELAND. The Hotel Statler opened in 1912 and was a center of activity in Cleveland in the first half of the 1900s. The original 700 rooms were expanded to 1,000 in the 1930s, and ornate dining, entertainment, and conference rooms were added. Its central location and proximity to garages offering complete automotive services were attractive to motorists on Route 20.

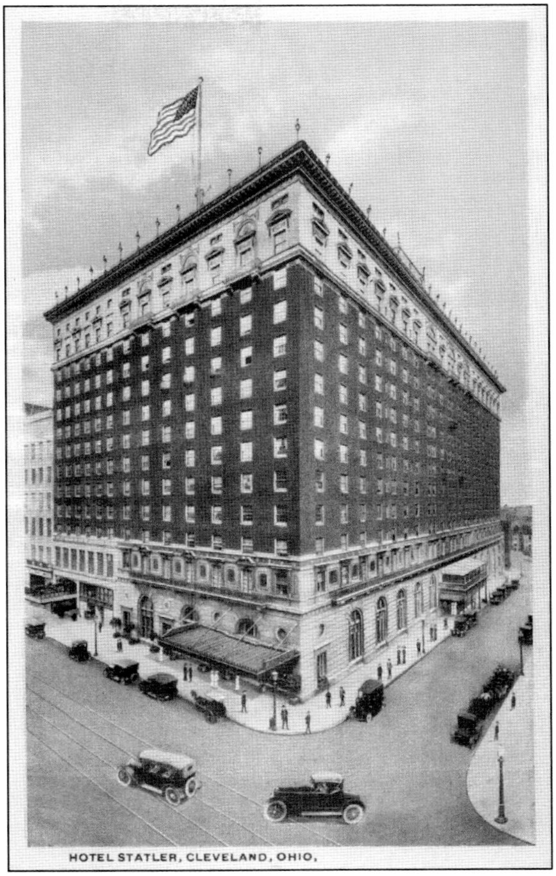

COLONIAL HOTEL, EUCLID AVENUE, CLEVELAND. Located in the heart of Cleveland's shopping and business district, the Colonial was one of the city's most prominent hotels throughout the early decades of the 1900s. Its advertising slogan was "The Pathway of Welcome Leads to Our Doors." The hotel was fireproof and offered accommodations to its guests on the European plan at a cost of $2 and up.

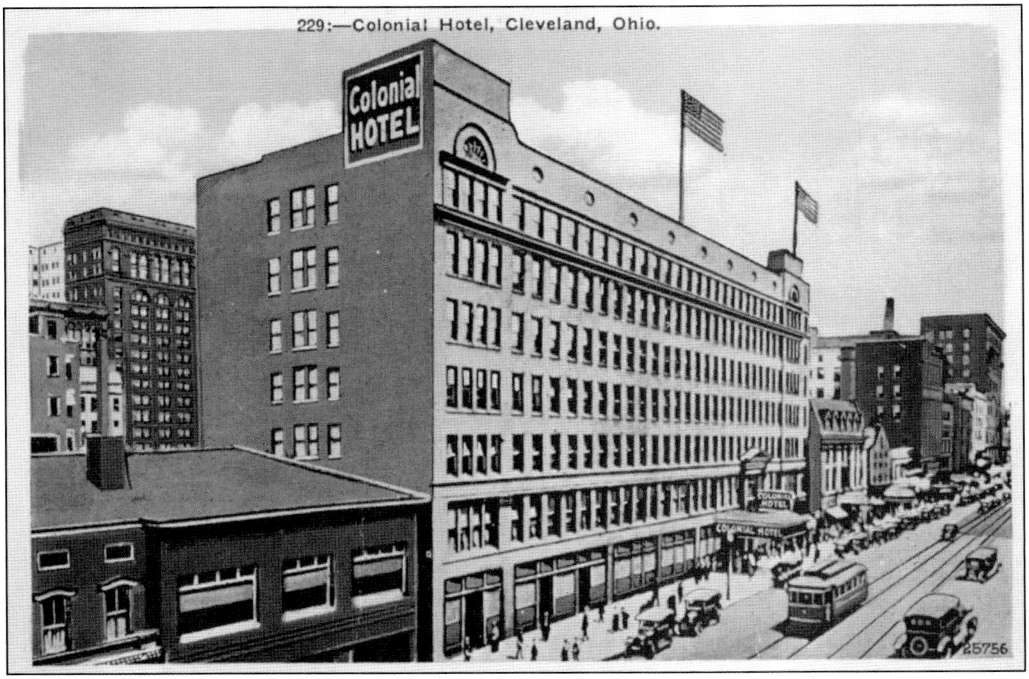

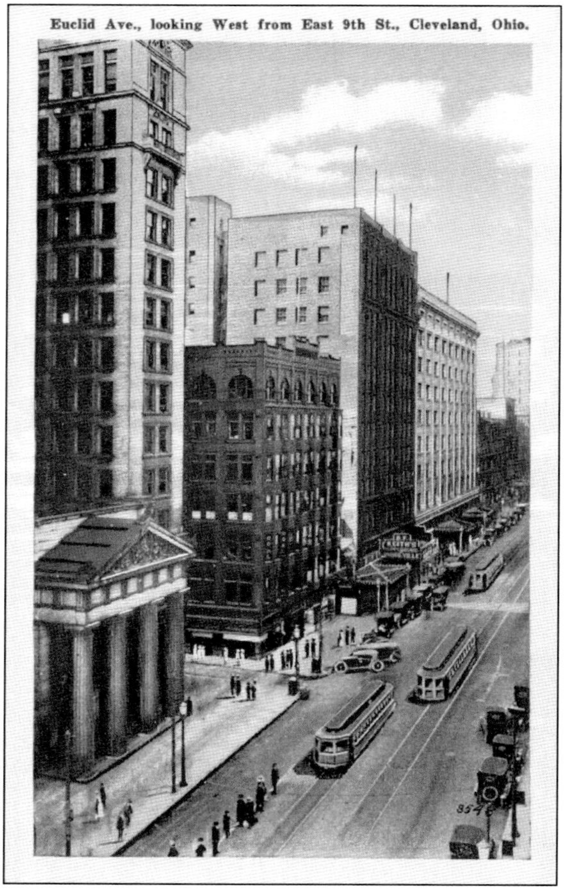

EUCLID AND SUPERIOR AVENUES, LOOKING WEST FROM NINTH STREET, CLEVELAND. From 1926 to 1936, Route 20 entered downtown Cleveland from the east via Superior Avenue. In 1936, Alternate Route 20 via Euclid Avenue was designated, and in 1967 the Alternate designation was discontinued in favor of the Euclid Avenue route, thus ending Superior Avenue's claim to the highway. Irrespective of the designation, both streets played an important role in Route 20's course through Cleveland. The images on this and the following page show the two streets at a time when both Euclid and Superior Avenues were part of Route 20. These first two images were taken from the their respective junctions with Ninth Street. The photograph at left shows the view motorists had when approaching the Public Square on Euclid Avenue, and the photograph below gives the perspective from Superior Avenue.

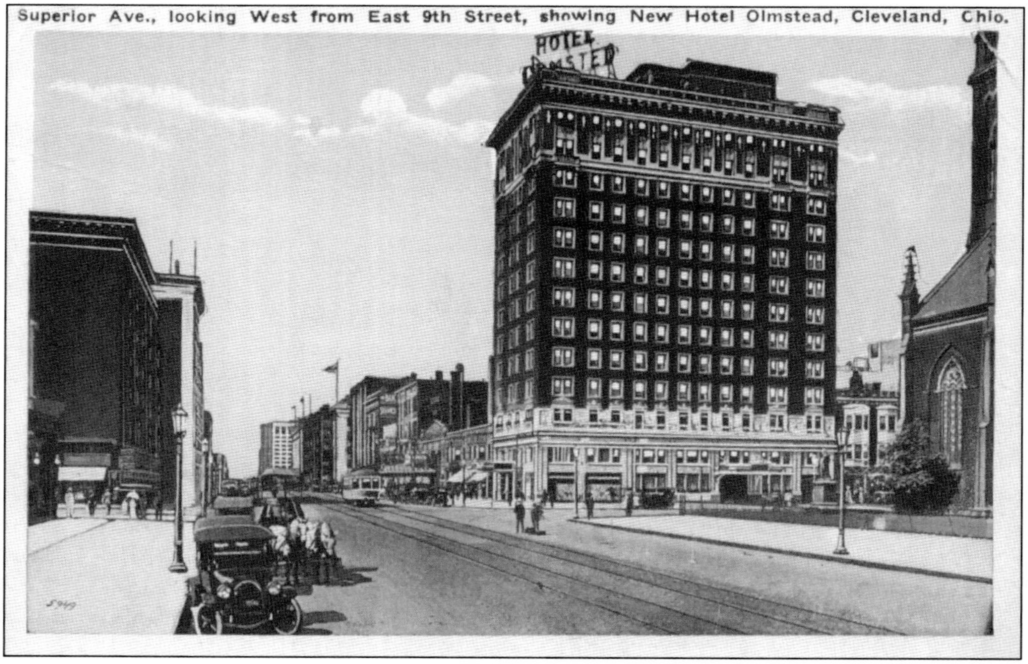

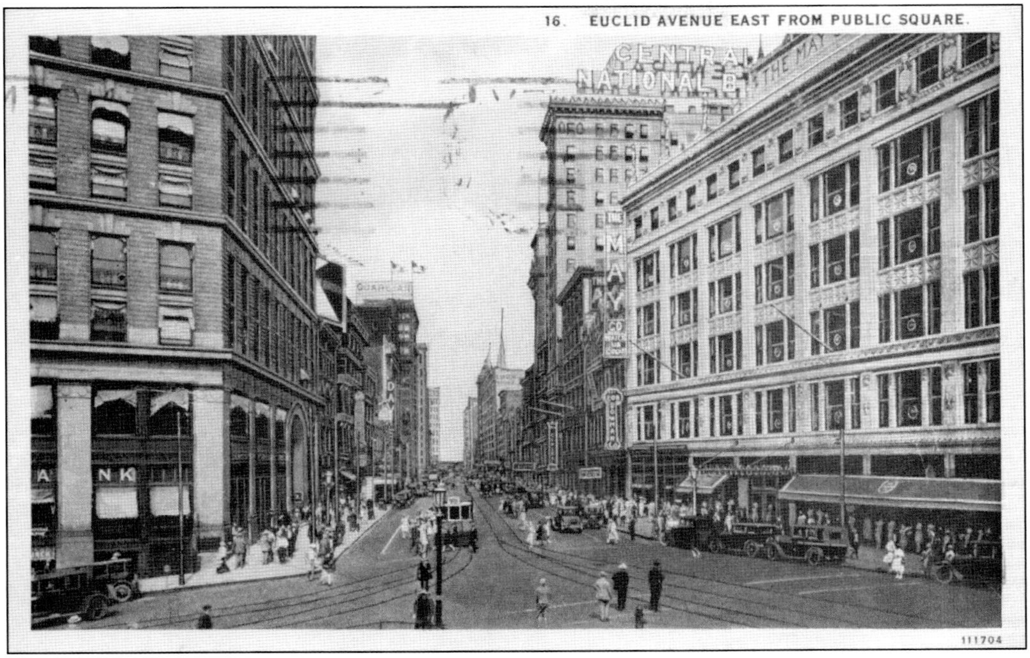

EUCLID AND SUPERIOR AVENUES, LOOKING EAST FROM THE PUBLIC SQUARE, CLEVELAND. Euclid and Superior Avenues merged at Cleveland's Public Square and continued west as a single street. The postcard above shows Euclid Avenue bustling with automobile, trolley, and pedestrian traffic. The May Company, an early department store, occupied the grey building on the right. The postcard below shows Superior Avenue, also looking east from the Public Square. The building in the left foreground is the Old Federal Building. Immediately behind it is the Cleveland Public Library, and the Cleveland Discount Building is in the distance. Both buildings are listed in the National Register of Historic Places.

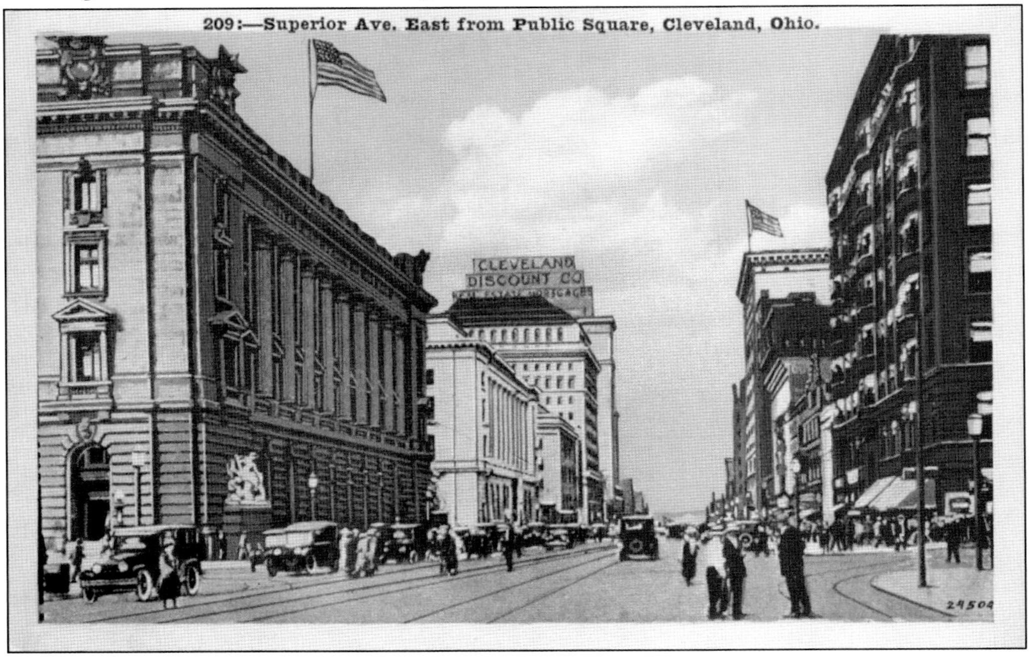

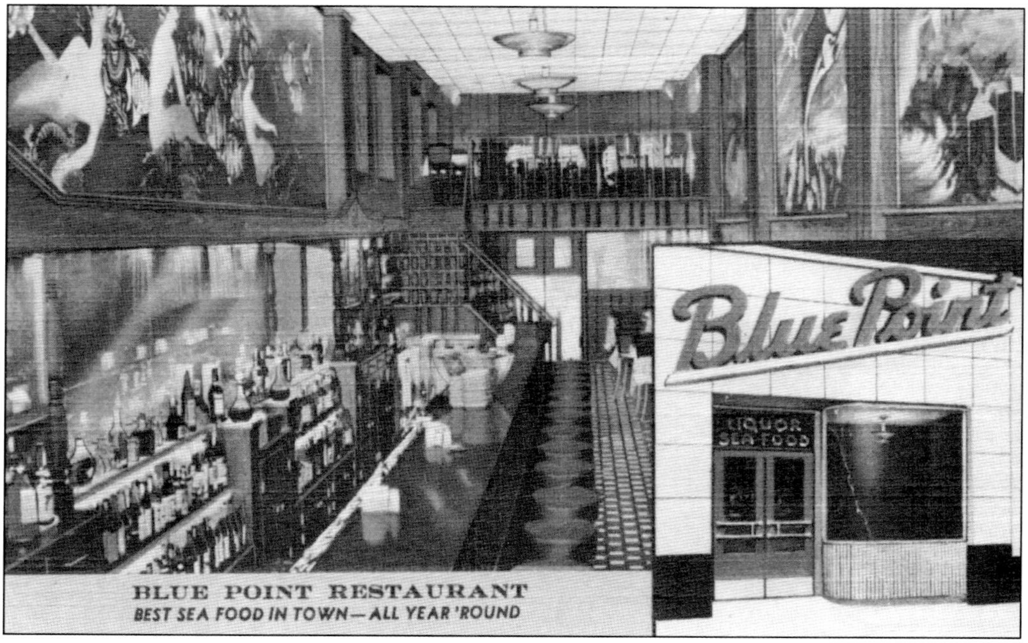

Blue Point Restaurant, Ninth Street, Cleveland. Several fine restaurants were located along Route 20 in downtown Cleveland. The Blue Point proudly proclaimed that it served "the finest in seafood." This card was mailed on March 24 (year unknown), and the sender complained that the weather was lousy, writing that it was snowing and the wind was blowing.

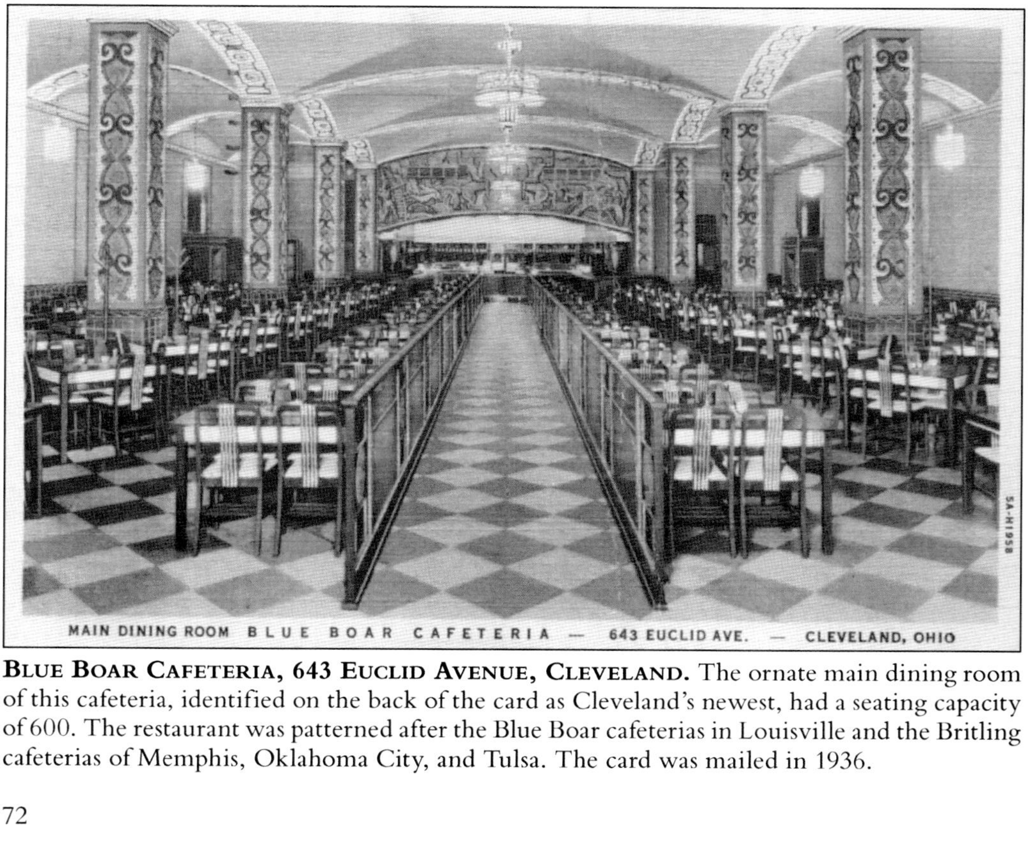

Blue Boar Cafeteria, 643 Euclid Avenue, Cleveland. The ornate main dining room of this cafeteria, identified on the back of the card as Cleveland's newest, had a seating capacity of 600. The restaurant was patterned after the Blue Boar cafeterias in Louisville and the Britling cafeterias of Memphis, Oklahoma City, and Tulsa. The card was mailed in 1936.

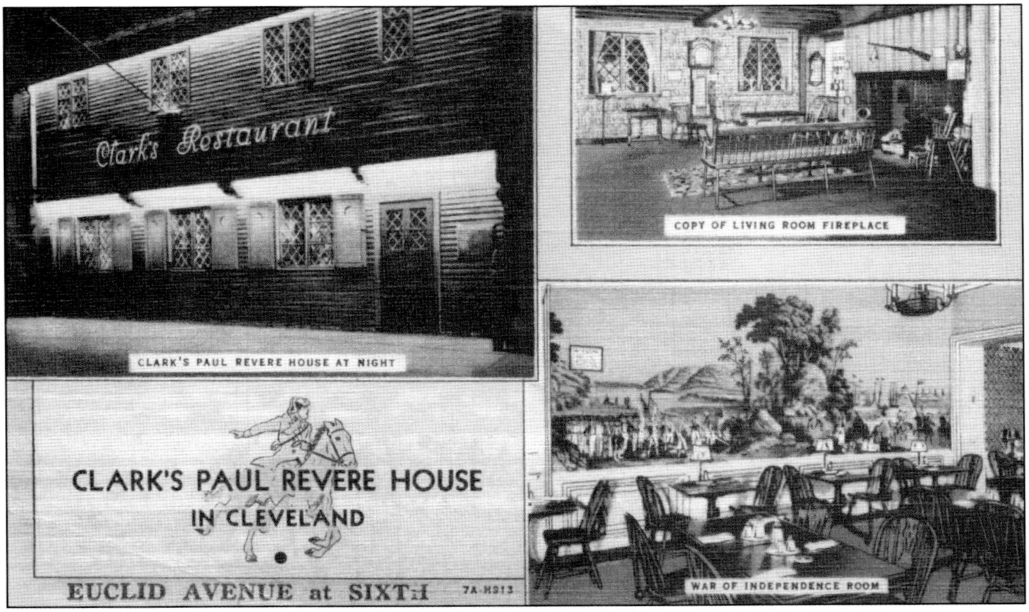

CLARK'S PAUL REVERE HOUSE, EUCLID AVENUE AT SIXTH STREET, CLEVELAND. The following description of this restaurant is printed on the back of the card: "A faithful reproduction of the historic old home of that sturdy patriot of the American Revolution, immortalized by Longfellow's famous poem." The theme rooms within the restaurant duplicated those in the original Paul Revere house in Boston.

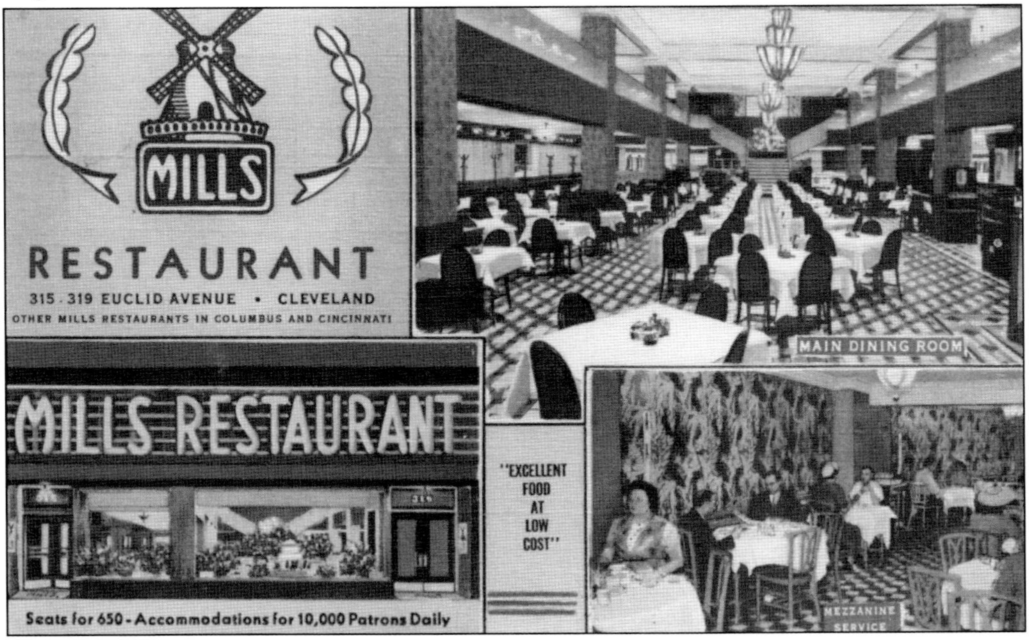

MILLS RESTAURANT, 315–319 EUCLID AVENUE, CLEVELAND. Its location within walking distance of Cleveland's Public Square and the Union Terminal no doubt contributed to the appeal of this large downtown restaurant, with a seating capacity of 650. Mills Restaurants also operated businesses in Columbus and Cincinnati. The company used a windmill logo, and travelers were encouraged to "stop at the sign of Mill's mill."

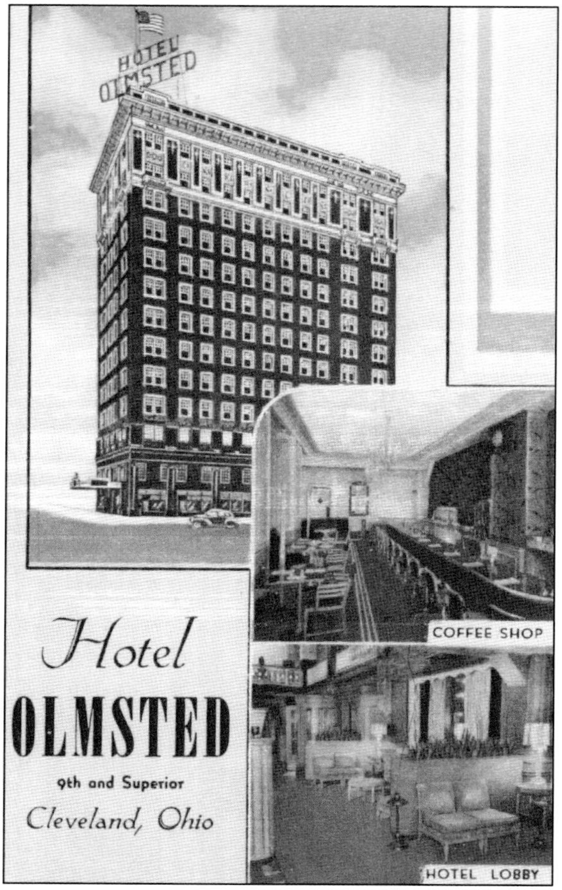

HOTEL OLMSTED, SUPERIOR AVENUE AND NINTH STREET, CLEVELAND. A favorite Superior Avenue hotel, the Olmsted had 250 rooms, with baths and a radio in every room. The Guild Bar and the Bamboo Room were popular gathering points for businessmen from the area and people attending performances at the Playhouse Square theaters, only a short walk away. The Olmsted's coffee shop and bars were air-conditioned for patrons' comfort.

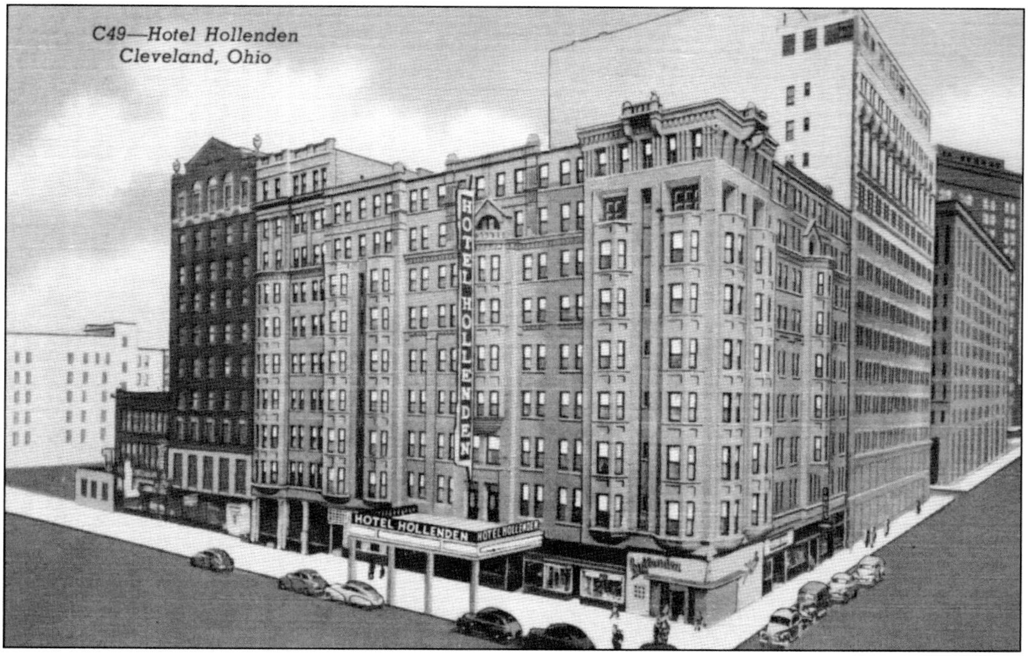

HOTEL HOLLENDEN, SUPERIOR AVENUE AND SIXTH STREET, CLEVELAND. The Hollenden opened in 1885 and was one of Cleveland's finest hotels. In 1926, it was expanded to include more than 1,000 rooms. The hotel's location within walking distance of the Public Square, Playhouse Square, and the Superior Street Arcade made it a center for conferences, receptions, and political events for more than half a century. The building was demolished in 1963.

SUPERIOR STREET ARCADE, 420 SUPERIOR AVENUE, CLEVELAND. The multilevel arcade seen in both of these photographs has been a Cleveland landmark since 1890. It extends for a full city block between Superior and Euclid Avenues. It opened on Memorial Day 1890 and included a nine-story commercial building at either end, connected by the five-story glass and metal atrium that housed retail establishments. The Cleveland Arcade was among the first enclosed shopping malls in the United States. Architect John Eisenmann is said to have modeled the arcade after Milan's famous Galleria Vittorio Emanuele II. The cost of the building was nearly $900,000, and it was financed by several of Cleveland's wealthiest citizens, including John D. Rockefeller. The building was listed in the National Register of Historic Places in 1975.

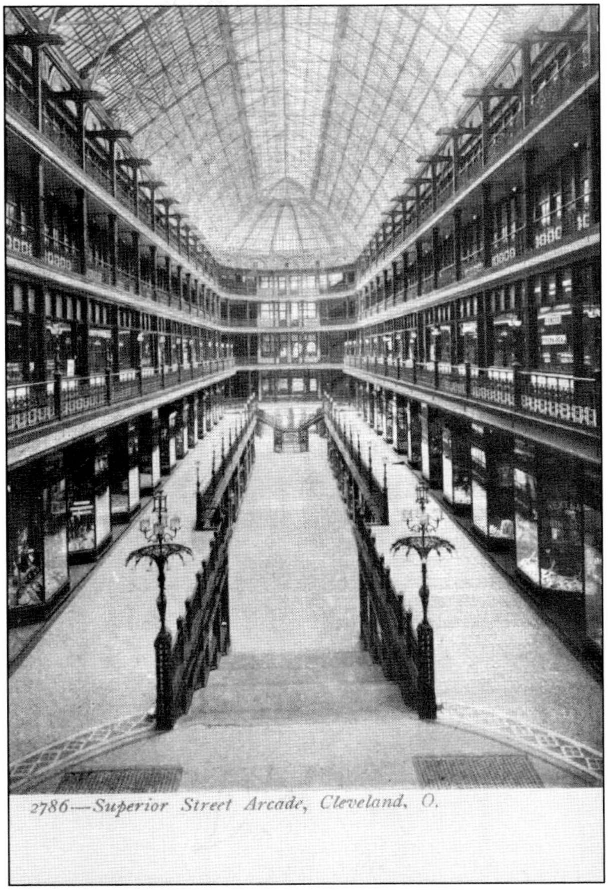

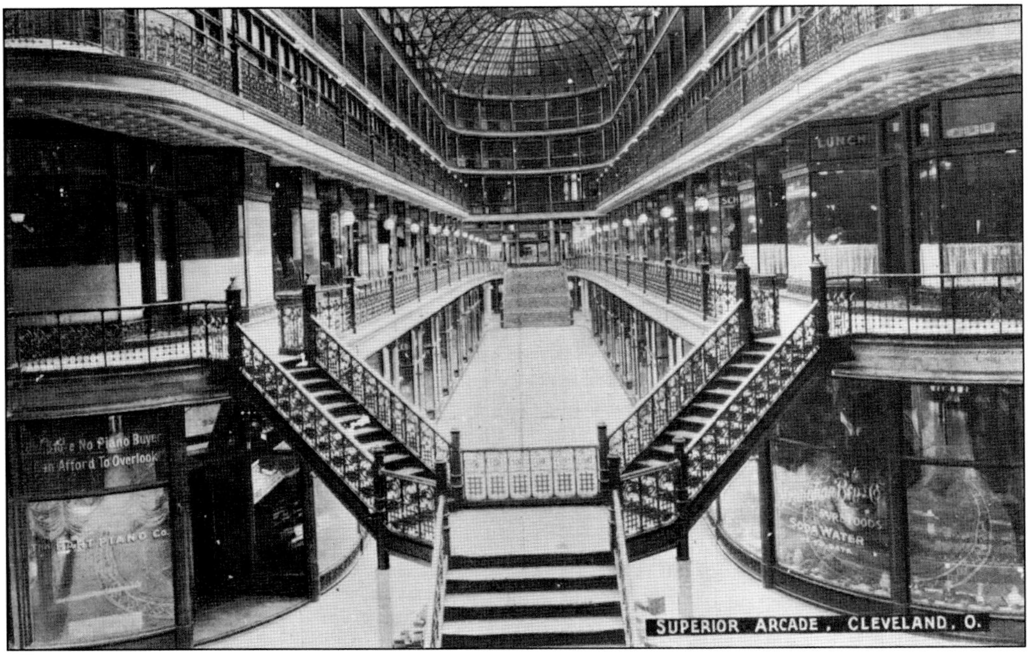

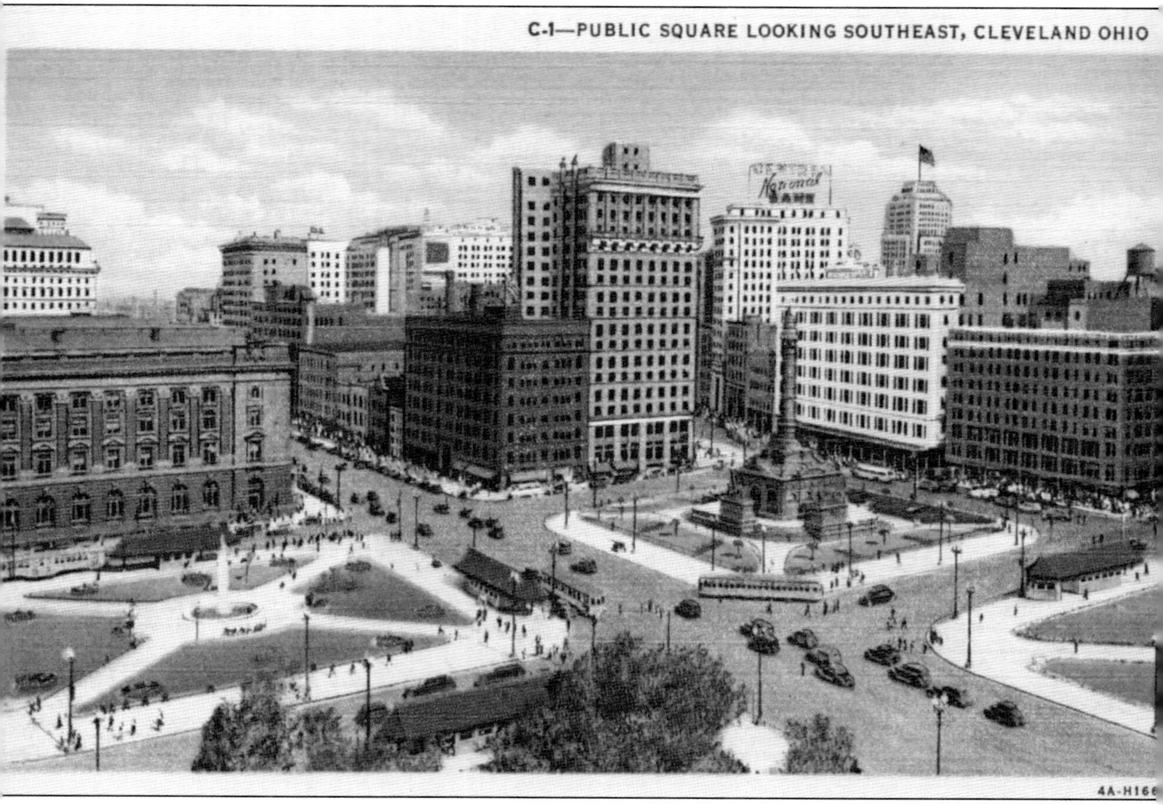

PUBLIC SQUARE, CLEVELAND. Located at the hub of downtown, Cleveland's Public Square in 1879 became the first square in the country illuminated by electric lights. The square's four quadrants, each a city block in size, are often used for public events. The dominant structure in the square is the Soldiers and Sailors Monument, but it also is home to the statues of Gen. Moses Cleveland, the city's founder, and Tom Johnson, the popular Cleveland mayor who espoused fair taxation and social reform. Many of Cleveland's most significant and historical buildings surround the Public Square, including the Terminal Tower complex, the Old Stone Church, and the Old Federal Building. Superior and Euclid Avenues are seen here entering the square. Superior Avenue is in the center left and Euclid Avenue enters in front of the white building in the upper right.

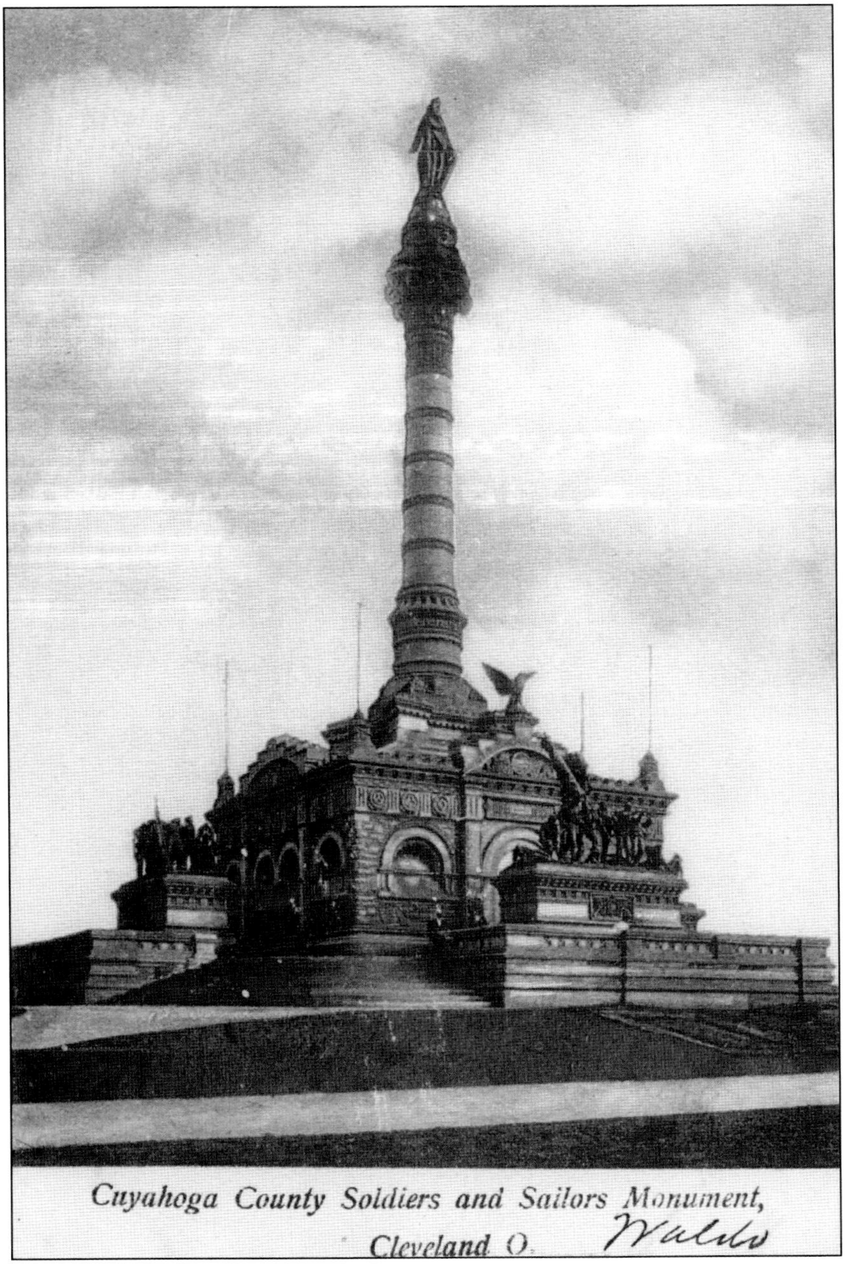

SOLDIERS AND SAILORS MONUMENT, PUBLIC SQUARE, CLEVELAND. This monument has been the focal point of Cleveland's Public Square since its dedication on July 4, 1894. It honors northeastern Ohio's 10,000 Civil War veterans and was designed to be both historical and educational. The monument consists of a Memorial Hall, on top of which sits a 125-foot pedestal complete with a 15-foot statue of the Goddess of Liberty, signifying loyalty to the nation. The four sides of the Memorial Hall represent the four principal branches of military service at the time: infantry, artillery, cavalry, and navy. All are seen in larger-than-life bronze statuary depicting fierce combat scenes. The interior of Memorial Hall displays tablets with the names of Ohio's Civil War veterans, plus reliefs representing the "Emancipation of Slaves," the "Beginning of the War in Ohio," and the "End of the War."

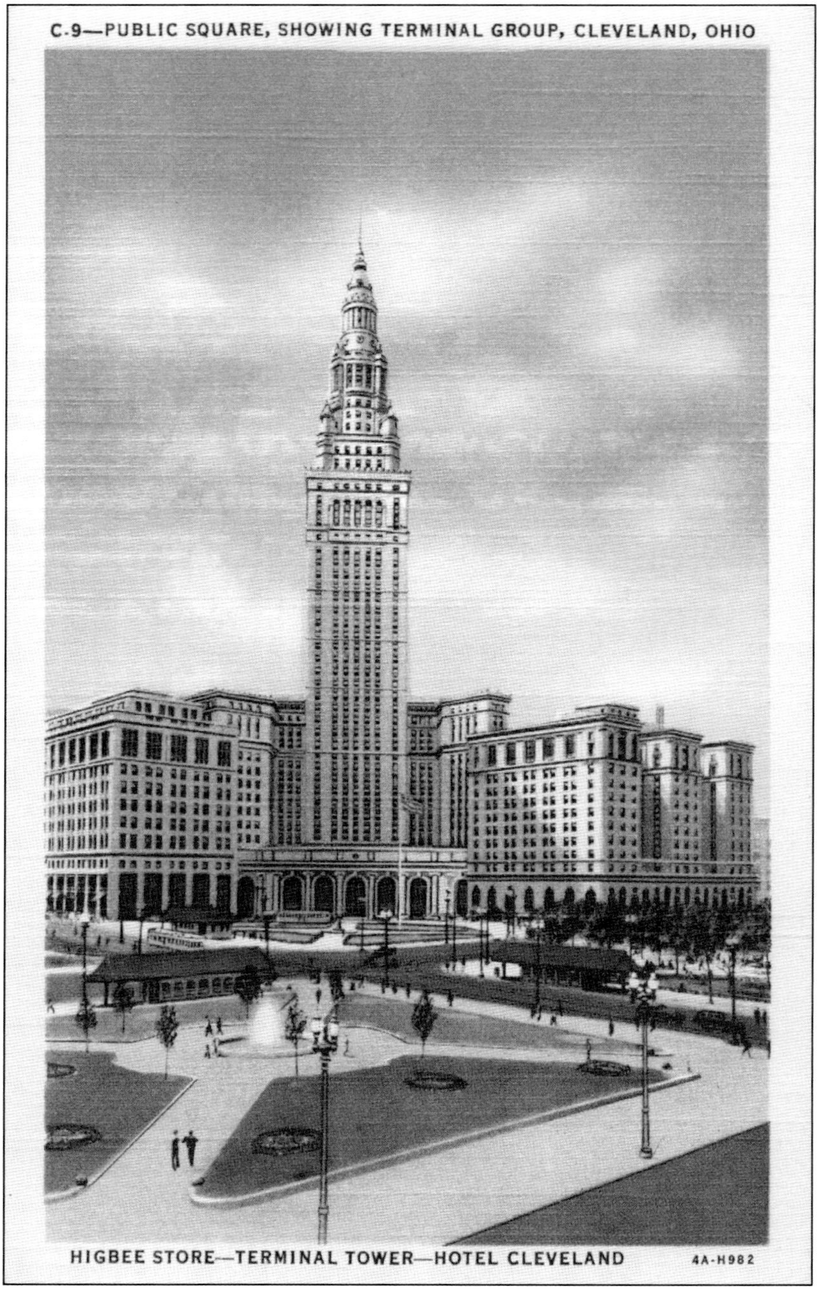

TERMINAL TOWER, PUBLIC SQUARE, CLEVELAND. The 52-story Terminal Tower is the most significant landmark in downtown Cleveland. Located on the Public Square, it was part of the Union Terminal railroad station and is constructed on "air-rights" over railroad tracks. The lower level housed the railroad terminal, which was intended to serve all trains coming into Cleveland. The tower was expanded in August 1927, and when it was completed in 1930, it was the tallest building in the United States outside of New York City, a distinction it held until 1967. The building had a 63-foot-tall flagpole at its top, which brought its total height to 771 feet. Terminal Tower was listed in the National Register of Historic Places in 1976 as part of the Union Terminal Group.

HOTEL CLEVELAND, PUBLIC SQUARE, CLEVELAND. The Hotel Cleveland was built on the original site of Cleveland's first tavern, Mowry's. The luxury hotel opened in 1919 as part of the Terminal Tower complex, a feature that was intended to provide convenience for travelers arriving in Cleveland by train. The hotel contained 1,000 rooms, all with baths, and beautifully appointed public rooms to meet the needs of every business and social occasion.

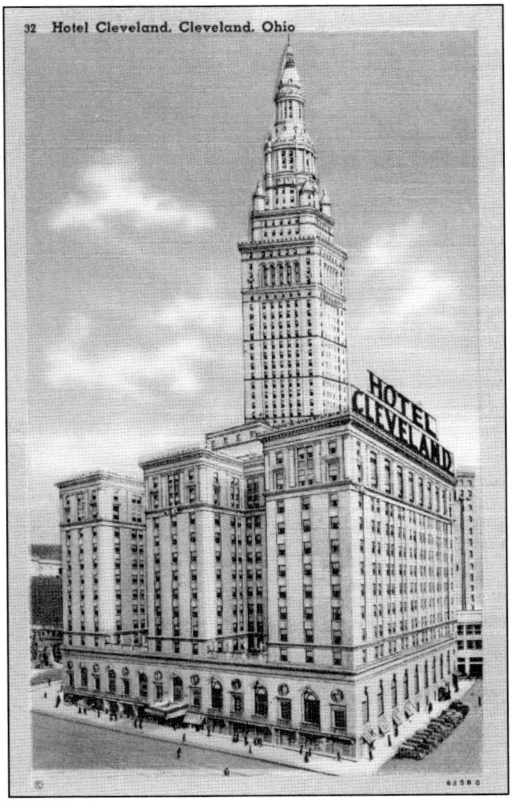

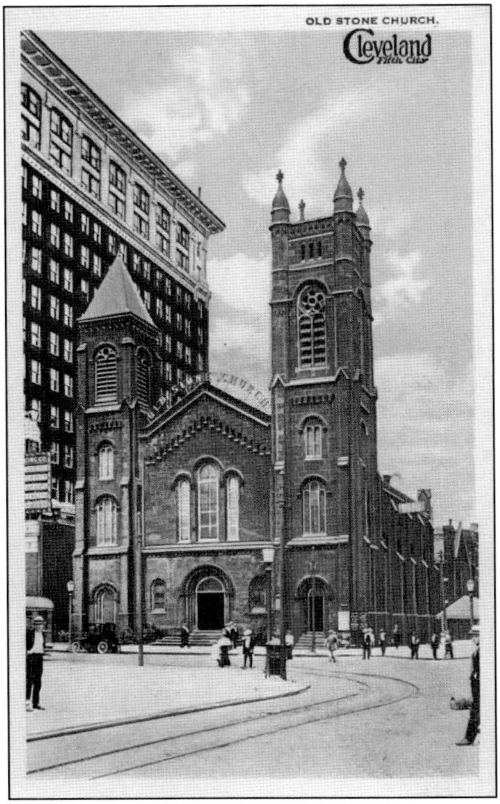

OLD STONE CHURCH, 91 PUBLIC SQUARE, CLEVELAND. The original church on this site was completed in 1833, but the rapidly expanding congregation required its demolition and the construction of the present, larger building, which was completed in 1855. It is the oldest building on the Public Square and is listed in the National Register of Historic Places.

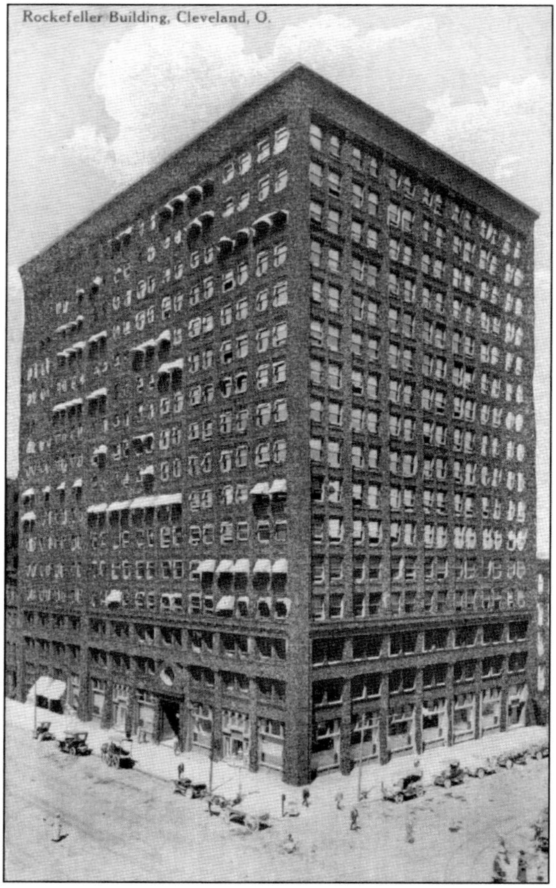

ROCKEFELLER BUILDING, 614 WEST SUPERIOR AVENUE, CLEVELAND. This 17-story building was Cleveland's first skyscraper. It housed John D. Rockefeller's business empire before he moved to New York. The building's design was influenced by the Chicago style promoted by Louis Sullivan. In fact, the Rockefeller Building has been called "one of the finest Louis Sullivan buildings that Sullivan didn't design!" This local landmark is listed in the National Register of Historic Places.

AERIAL VIEW, HIGH LEVEL AND MAIN AVENUE BRIDGES, CLEVELAND. As Route 20 proceeded west from downtown Cleveland, it crossed the Cuyahoga River on the High Level Bridge in the center left of this postcard. The many railroads in the lower-left corner all led toward Cleveland's central railroad station, located below Terminal Tower. Cleveland's Main Avenue Bridge and Lake Erie are in the distance.

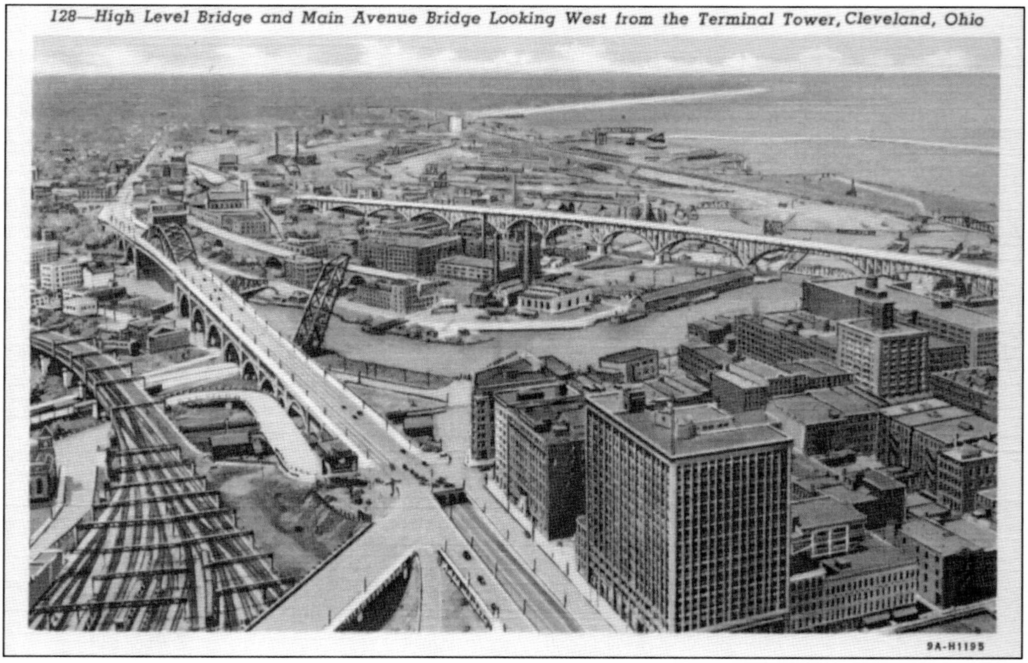

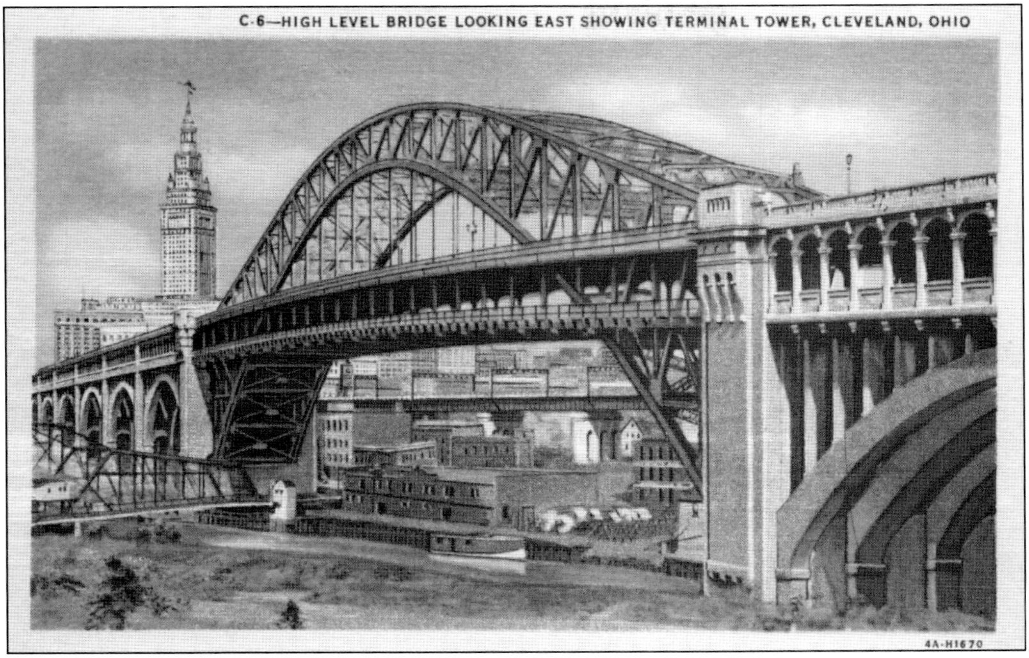

HIGH LEVEL BRIDGE, CUYAHOGA RIVER, CLEVELAND. At the time of its construction, the official name of the span in these photographs was Detroit-Superior Bridge, indicating the streets it joined on the west and east sides of the Cuyahoga River, respectively. Built from 1914 to 1918, the two-level bridge carried automobiles and pedestrian traffic on the upper level and electric streetcars on the lower level. The photograph above shows the bridge's impressive superstructure. The total length of the bridge, which includes the 12 concrete arches that anchor the massive arched steel span in the center, is 3,112 feet. The central span is 592 feet long, with a total height of 196 feet and 96 feet of clearance above the river. The bridge is listed in the National Register of Historic Places. The photograph below shows the view a driver would have had while crossing the bridge toward downtown Cleveland in the 1920s.

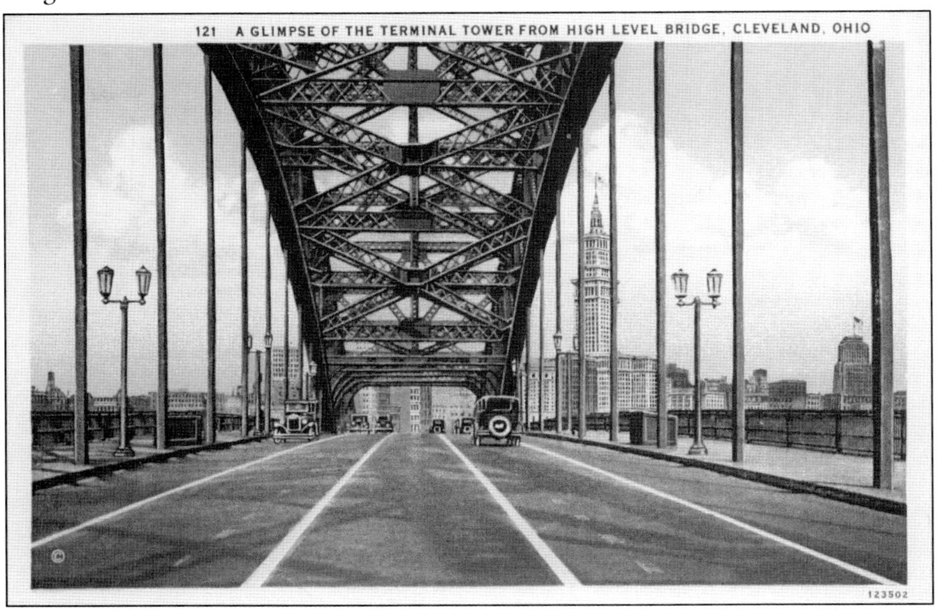

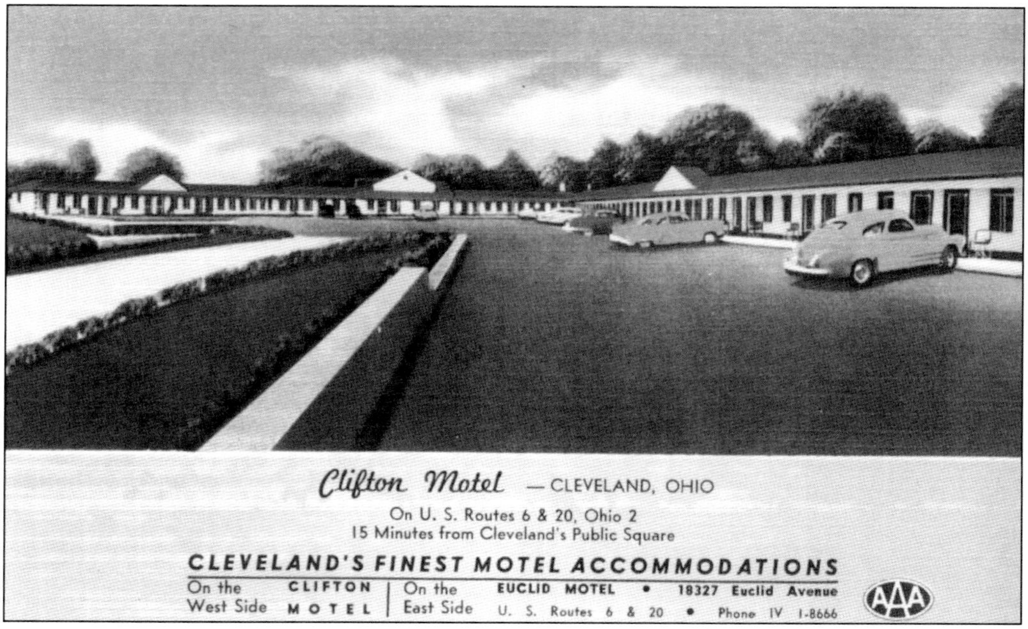

CLIFTON MOTEL, 1300 WEST CLIFTON BOULEVARD, LAKEWOOD. This motel is the counterpart of the Euclid Motel on the east side of Cleveland, which was featured on page 61. The Clifton Motel was prominently located on Route 20 in Lakewood, a western suburb. Both motels were touted as having "Cleveland's finest motel accommodations."

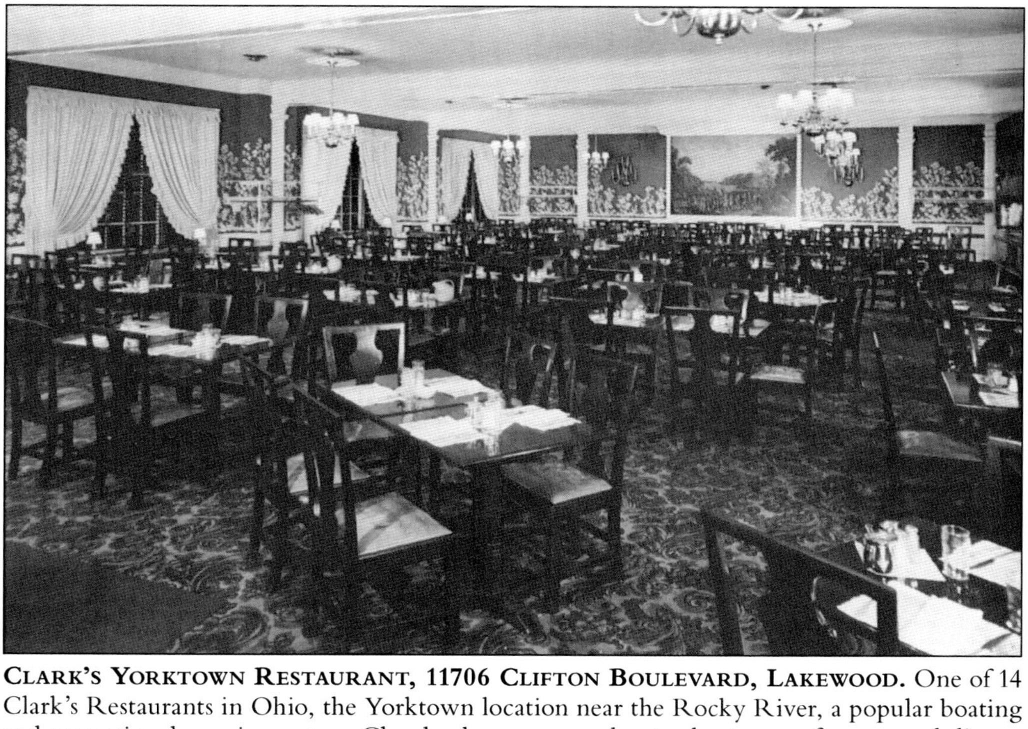

CLARK'S YORKTOWN RESTAURANT, 11706 CLIFTON BOULEVARD, LAKEWOOD. One of 14 Clark's Restaurants in Ohio, the Yorktown location near the Rocky River, a popular boating and recreational area in western Cleveland, was ensured a steady stream of guests and diners. The nautical theme was emphasized in the name of the dining room, the Snug Harbor Room, seen here.

Four

West of Cleveland

The Rocky River is the demarcation between Cleveland and its western suburbs. For the first several years after Route 20 was declared a federal highway, the road crossed the river on the Hilliard Road Bridge. Later, the course was changed to the Rocky River Bridge, a short distance to the north, where it passed the luxurious Westlake Hotel on the river's western bank. Travelers could look from the bridge to the hotel's beautiful gardens and marina below and from there to the mouth of the river at Lake Erie. The Rocky River Bridge, once the world's longest arch-supported concrete bridge, was replaced by a new bridge in 1980, but the superstructure on the west bank was put to unique use; it was incorporated into a new office building appropriately named the Bridge Building.

Both the Hilliard Road and Rocky River Bridges connected with Wooster Road, which continued south and connected with Center Ridge Road. It then went southwest through the towns of Westlake and North Ridgeville before entering Elyria. There, the name changed to Cleveland Street and subsequently to East Bridge Street. At the junction with Broad Street, the road turned west and proceeded through the downtown business district. It turned left (south) at Middle Avenue, passing Ely Park and the historical Lorain County Courthouse.

Route 20 turns 45 degrees to the right at Oberlin Road, which eventually becomes Oberlin-Elyria Road. East of Oberlin, original Route 20 followed the road that is now Route 511, which progresses through Oberlin as East and West Lorain Street. The road goes directly through the Oberlin College campus, leaving the city heading west. Among the notable buildings on the campus is the Anderson Art Institute, designed by architect Cass Gilbert, whose other celebrated buildings include the US Supreme Court and the Minnesota State Capitol.

Oberlin College has long been recognized for its progressive educational and social positions. It was one of the first institutions of higher education to accept women and African American students on an equal basis with white male students. The college is listed as a National Historic Landmark.

34 HILLIARD ROAD BRIDGE, ROCKY RIVER, LAKEWOOD, CLEVELAND'S FASHIONABLE SUBURB

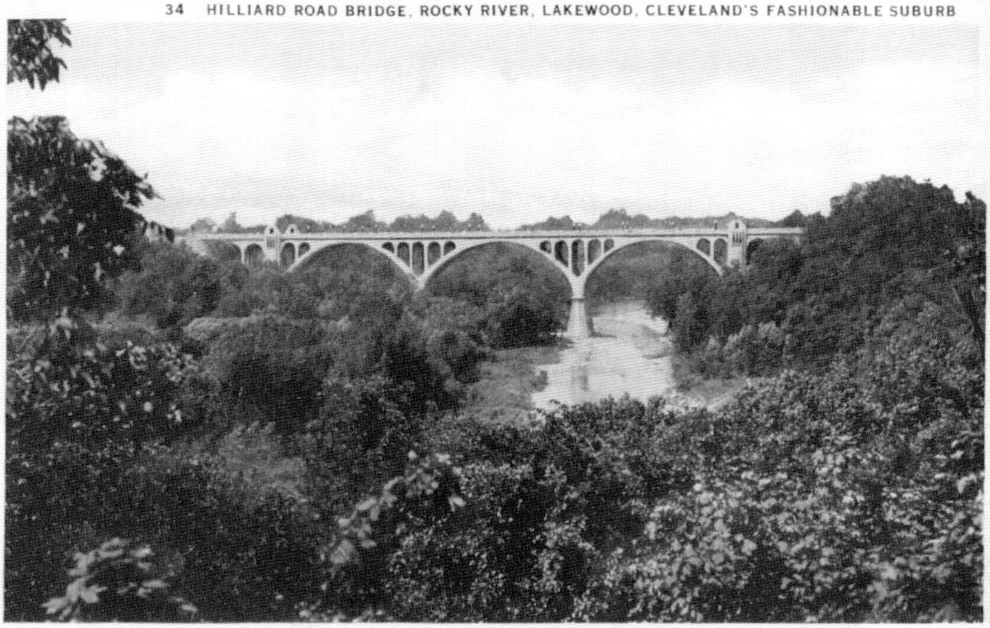

111699

HILLIARD ROAD AND DETROIT AVENUE BRIDGES OVER THE ROCKY RIVER. Originally, Route 20 crossed the Rocky River via the Hilliard Road Bridge (above). Later, the route was changed, and the Detroit Road Bridge (below), also called the Rocky River Bridge, became the designated span. Both bridges were attractive and contributed to the beauty of the valley, as well as improving traffic flow in Cleveland's western suburbs. The Rocky River Bridge opened in 1909 and was notable for its 708-foot unreinforced concrete arch, the world's longest. It continued in service for 70 years until it was razed in 1980. The original bridge piers at the west end remained intact to form the foundation for the Bridge Building. The Hilliard Road Bridge, opened in 1925, is still in use today.

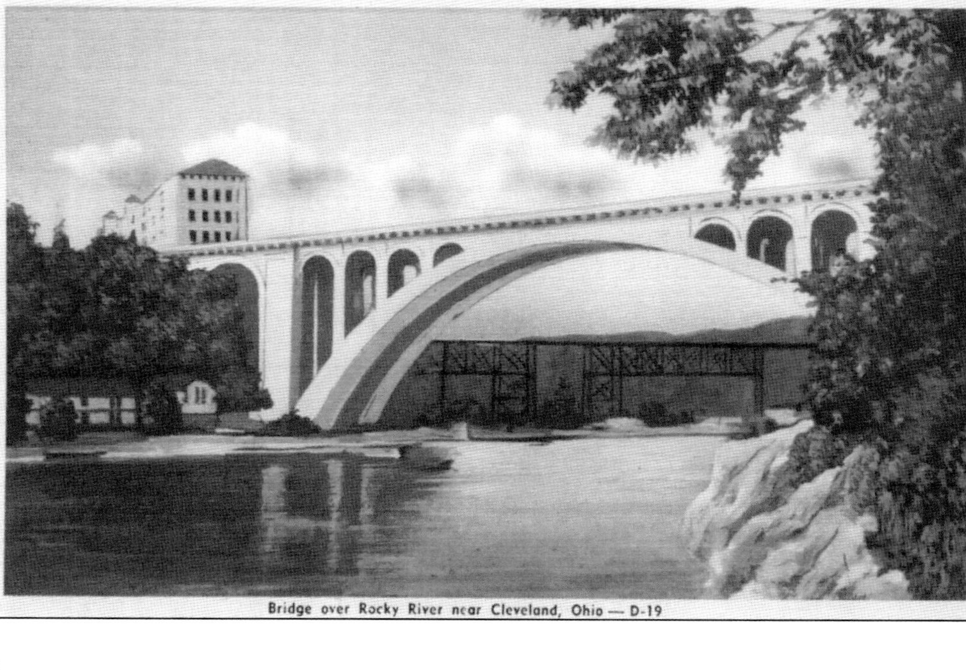

Bridge over Rocky River near Cleveland, Ohio — D-19

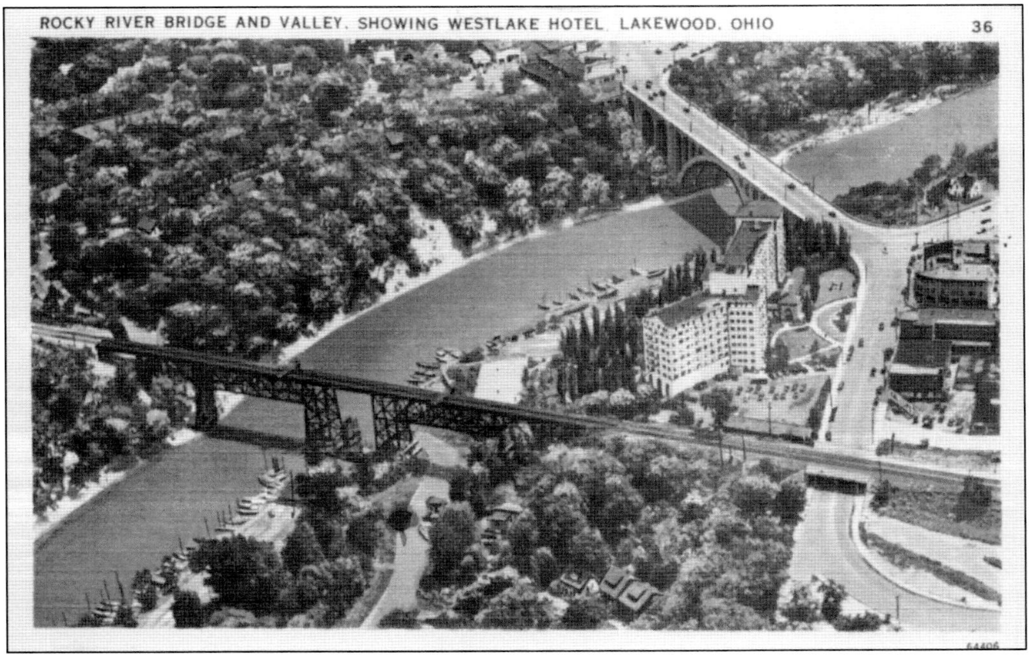

AERIAL VIEW, ROCKY RIVER AND WESTLAKE HOTEL, ROCKY RIVER. This postcard, postmarked 1936, shows Route 20 crossing the Rocky River Bridge adjacent to the 400-room Westlake Hotel, which was affectionately dubbed the "Pink Palace." The view looks east toward Cleveland. Motorists following Route 20 west from Cleveland turned left immediately after crossing the bridge at the intersection in the upper right.

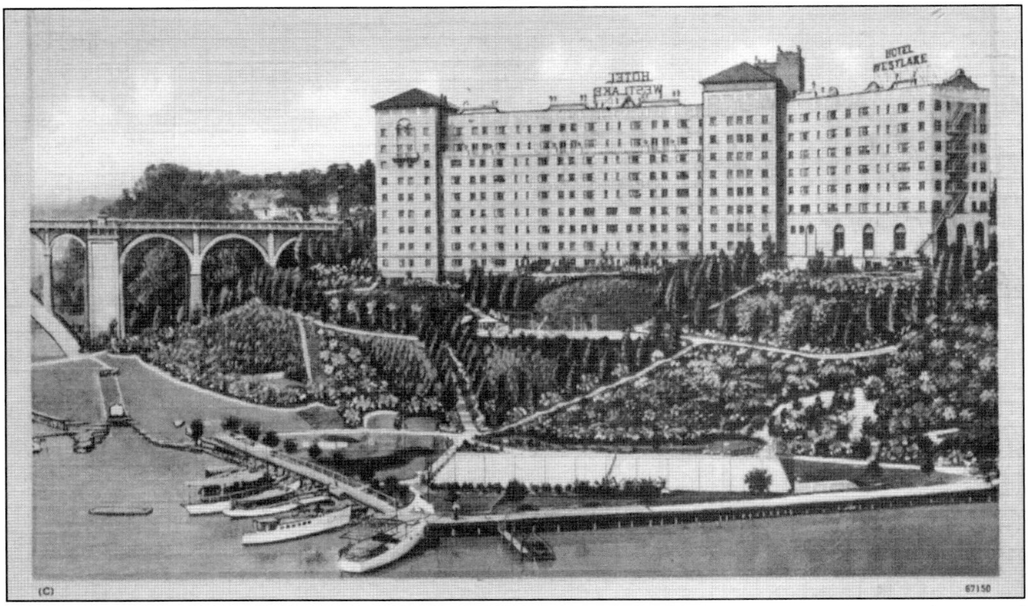

WESTLAKE HOTEL, ROUTES 2, 6, AND 20, ROCKY RIVER. The Westlake Hotel opened in 1925 and quickly ranked with the top luxury hotels in Cleveland. From the river valley, it portrayed a metropolitan hotel amid the charm of lake and stream. The grounds included gardens, playgrounds, tennis courts, stables, and a yacht harbor. Route 20 passed just south of the hotel after crossing the beautiful Rocky River Bridge, seen in the background.

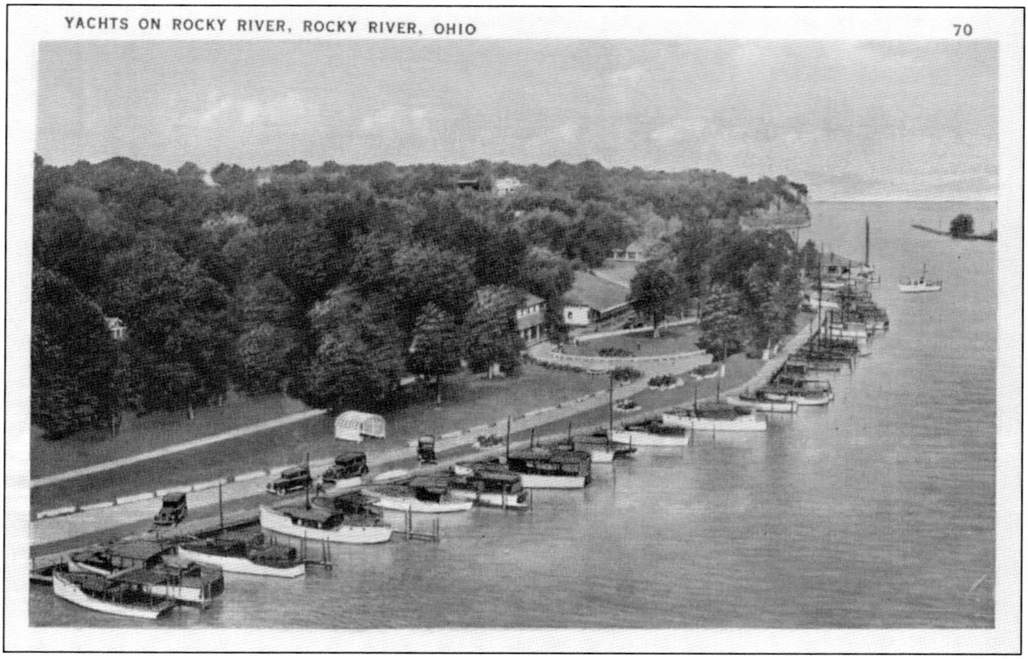

YACHTS AND SAILBOATS ON THE ROCKY RIVER, ROCKY RIVER. The height of the Rocky River Bridge provided travelers with an outstanding view of the river valley below, extending all the way to Lake Erie. The river was a popular site for boating, fishing, and other water sports, as indicated by the large number of pleasure boats moored along the riverbank above. Those who preferred sailing and sailboat racing also had ample opportunity to pursue their sport, as seen below.

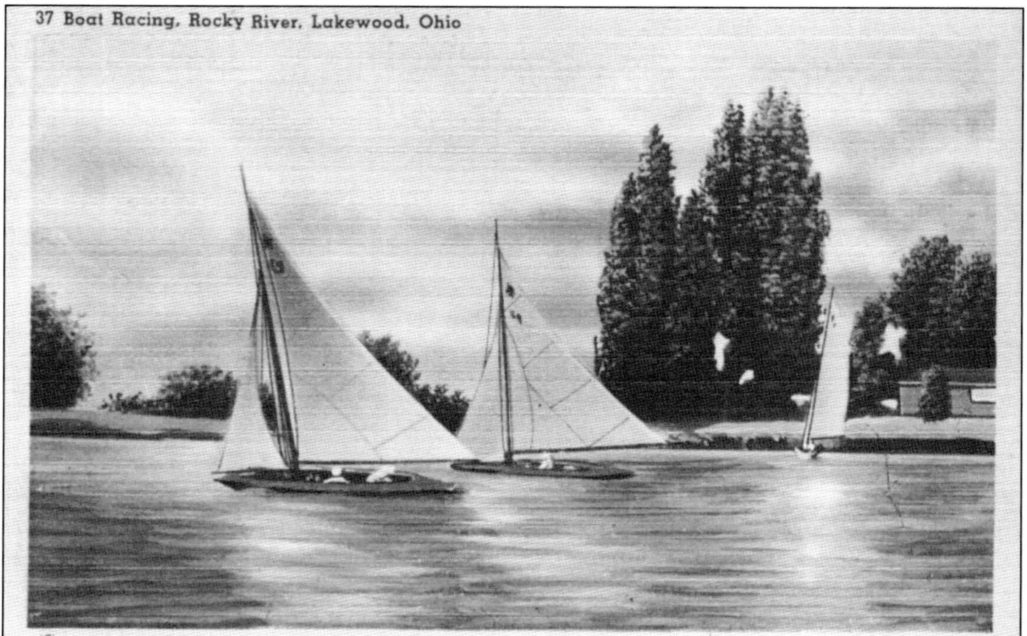

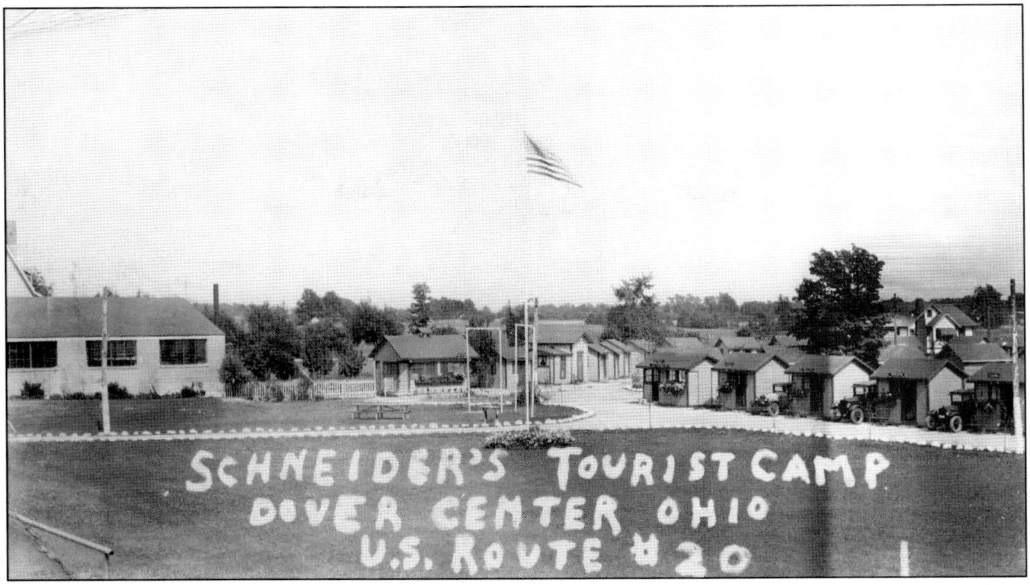

SCHNEIDER'S TOURIST CAMP, DOVER CENTER. Although it no longer appears on modern maps, Dover Center was located on Route 20 approximately 12 miles west of the Rocky River. This card was produced in the 1920s, when the accommodations were primitive. A later card from the 1930s touts several improvements, including running water, private toilets in every cottage, city water, electric lights, and cooking in a community kitchen.

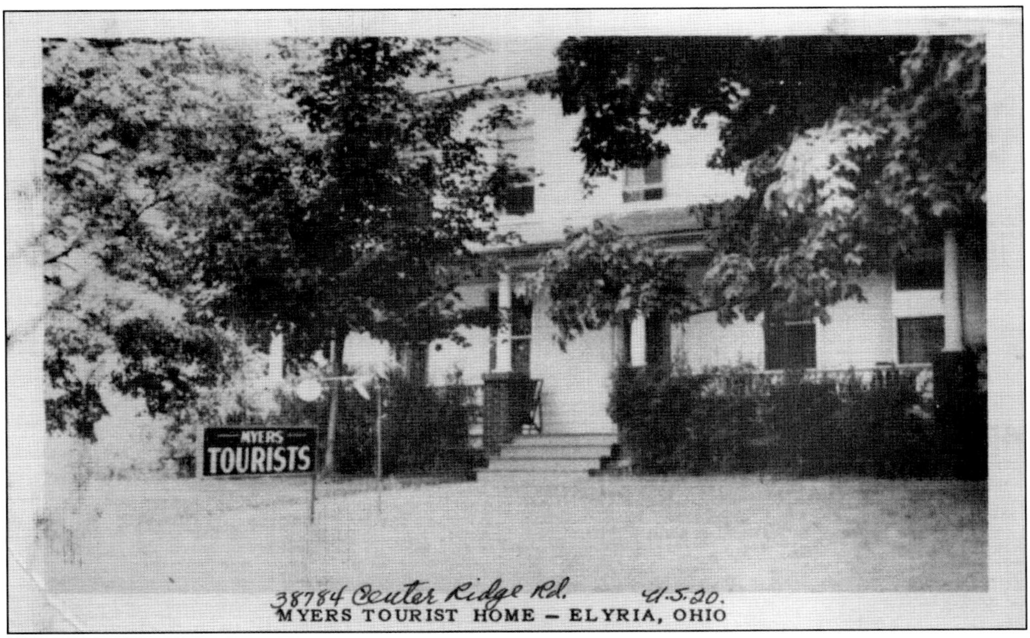

MYERS TOURIST HOME, 38784 CENTER RIDGE ROAD, ELYRIA. The Myers Tourist Home was in a pleasant neighborhood near Elyria's eastern city limits. Guests could relax on the large front porch and the attractive front lawn. Those who craved some exercise could stroll along the tree-lined street into Elyria's business district only a few blocks away.

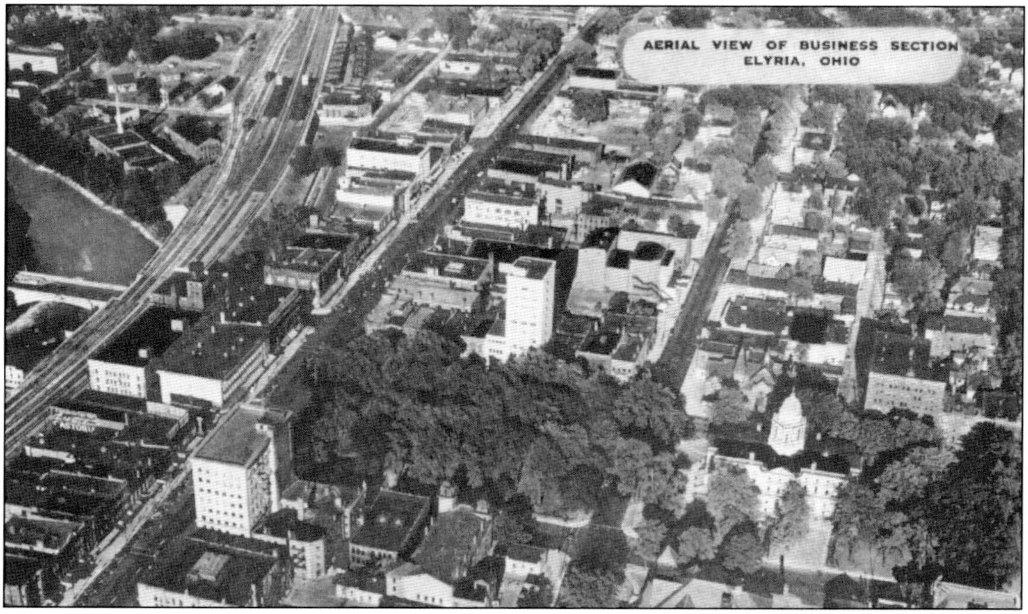

AERIAL VIEW OF BUSINESS SECTION, ELYRIA. Route 20 (Broad Street) is the prominent thoroughfare coming down from the upper center of this postcard. It proceeded through the business district to Ely Park, the green, heavily treed area, where it turned left onto Middle Avenue, extending toward the lower right and passing by the gold-domed Lorain County Courthouse on the left side of the street.

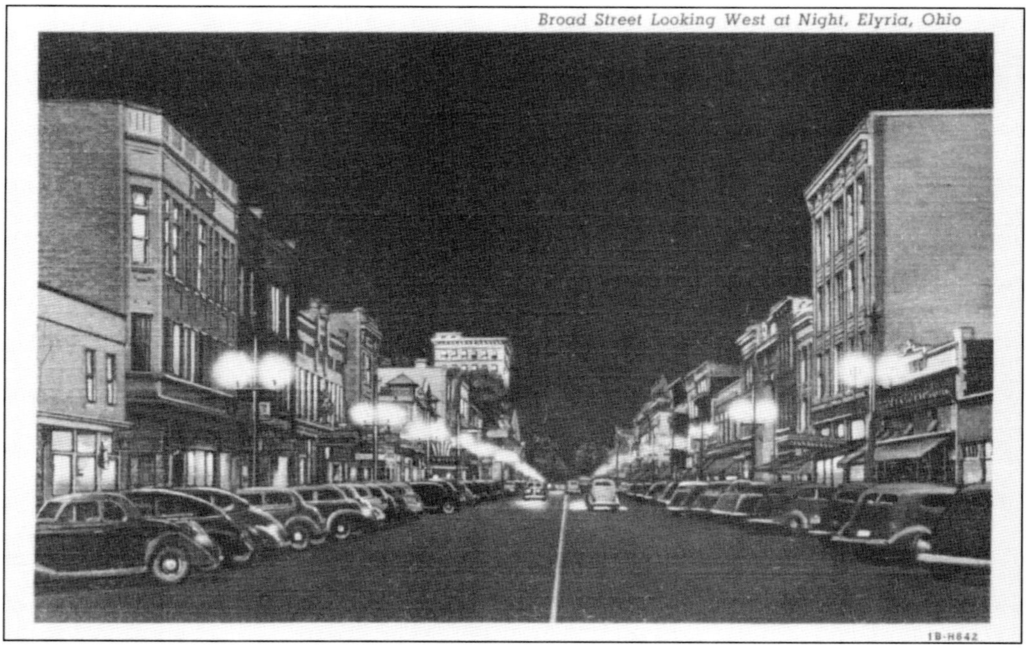

BROAD STREET LOOKING WEST, ELYRIA. Typical of most highways in the first half of the 1900s, Route 20 followed a course through the main business district of Elyria. Many stores remained open into the early evening hours, especially on Saturday nights, making main streets popular gathering places for local residents. This photograph shows a pleasant and busy business district with barely any parking spaces available.

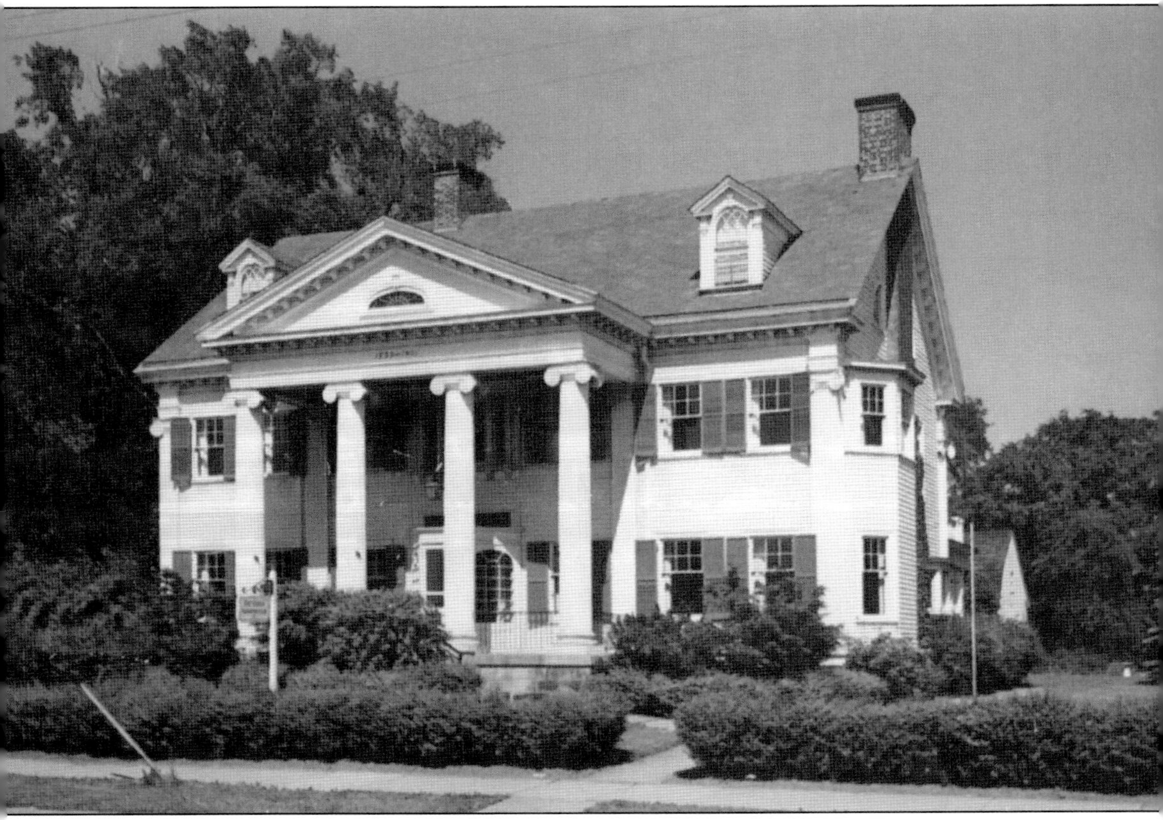

MONTEITH HALL, 218 EAST AVENUE, ELYRIA. Monteith Hall was built in 1835 as the residence of Rev. John Monteith. Before coming to Elyria as the first superintendent of the high school, Reverend Monteith was an educator and minister in Detroit. He was instrumental in founding the University of Michigan before becoming its first president. An ardent abolitionist, he made his home a station on the Underground Railroad route extending from Oberlin. A tunnel that ran from the basement of his home to the Black River was used to help slaves escape to Lake Erie. Reverend Monteith managed the network on the southern shore of Lake Erie and aided fugitive slaves in boarding ships to cross the lake to Canada. Monteith Hall is listed in the National Register of Historic Places.

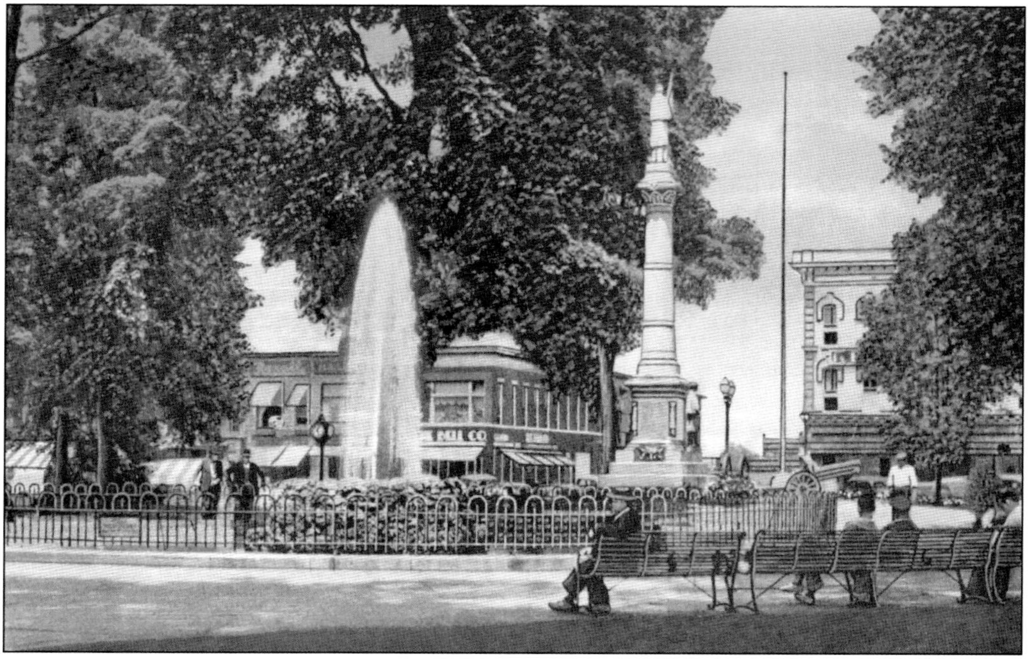

FOUNTAIN IN ELY PARK, BROAD AND MIDDLE STREETS, ELYRIA. This was one of the first electrical water fountains in the country. Illuminated nightly through the years, its ever-changing water displays attracted untold thousands of tourists to Ely Park. The fountain's simplicity and fine natural setting added greatly to its beauty.

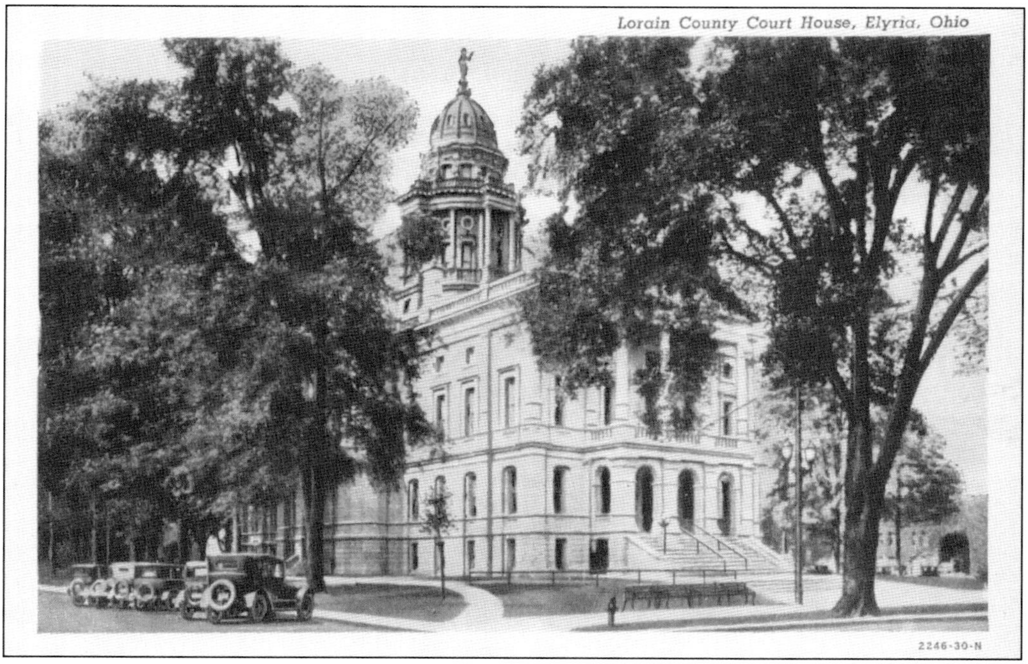

LORAIN COUNTY COURTHOUSE, SECOND STREET AND MIDDLE AVENUE, ELYRIA. The land this courthouse sits on was donated by Heman Ely, the founder of Elyria. The massive sandstone building with a domed cupola for a bell was completed in 1881 and has been the Lorain County government center for more than 125 years.

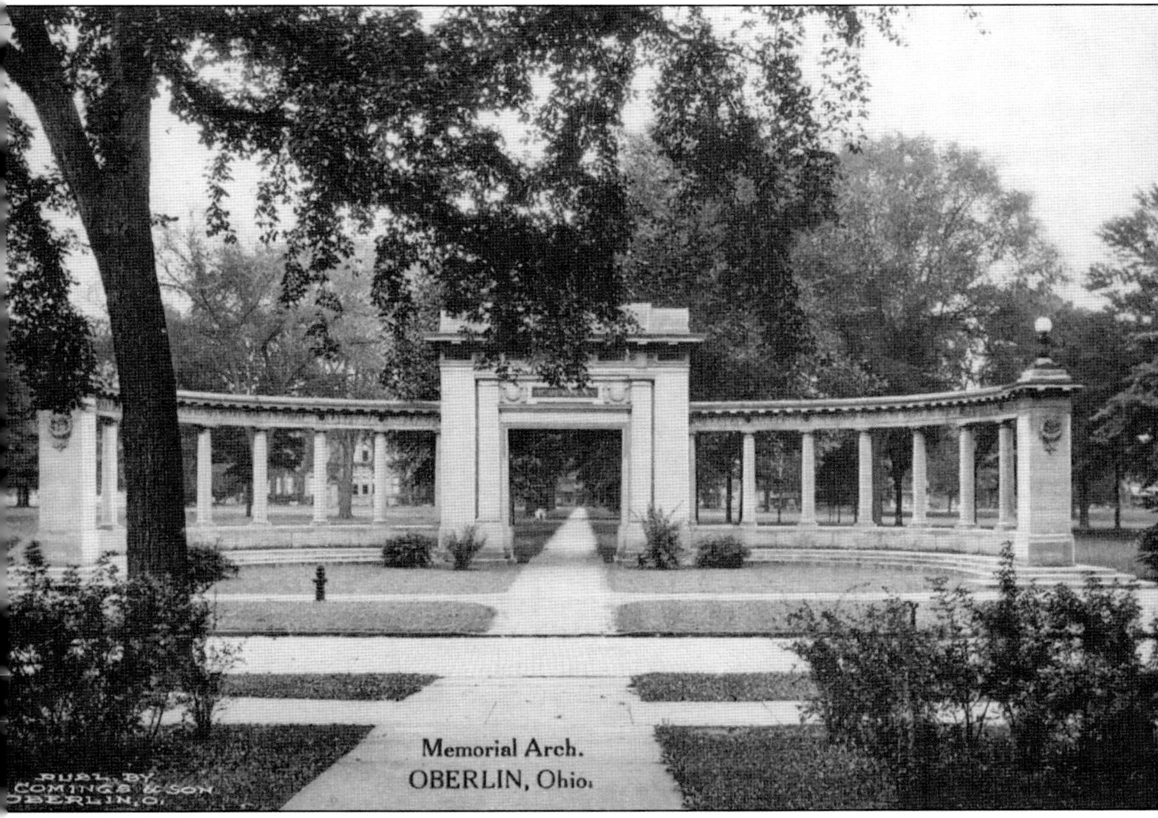

MEMORIAL ARCH IN TAPPAN SQUARE, OBERLIN COLLEGE, OBERLIN. Tappan Square is a 13-acre park that was designed for the specific purpose of connecting the Oberlin College campus to the city. It was named after Arthur Tappan, an abolitionist and benefactor of the college in the 1800s. The landmark Memorial Arch in the center of the square was designed by architect J.L. Silsbee and was dedicated on May 14, 1903. The arch, which serves as the entrance to the college, was built to honor Oberlin College students who were killed in the Boxer Rebellion while serving as missionaries in China. The only other structure in the square is the Clark bandstand. The square hosts many events throughout the year, sponsored by both the college and the community.

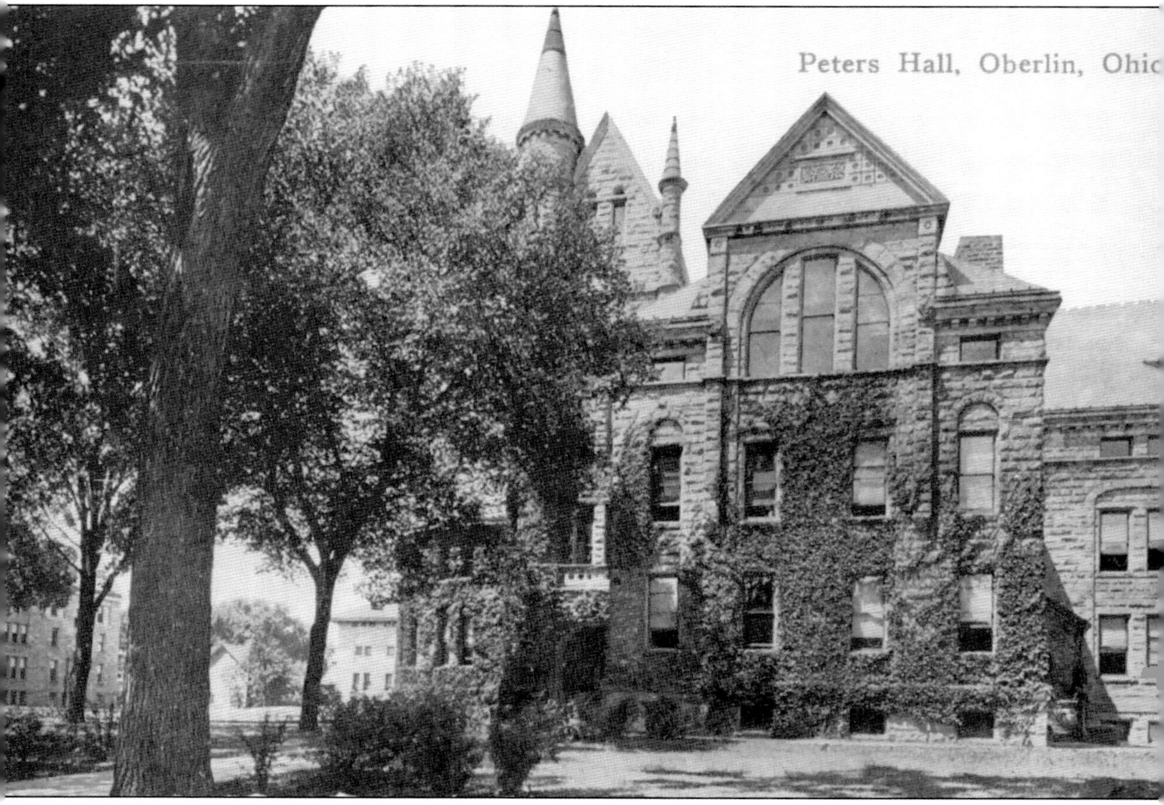

PETERS HALL, 50 NORTH PROFESSOR STREET, OBERLIN. Peters Hall is one of six Oberlin College campus buildings constructed between 1883 and 1887. The building was named for Richard Peters, a major benefactor of the college. Interestingly, Peters had been expelled from Oberlin, together with his wife, when they married during his first year as a student. He went on to become a wealthy lumber merchant in Michigan but never lost his affection for Oberlin. Peters Hall, designed by architects Frank Weary and George Kramer and built at a cost of $75,000, was the college's principal classroom building and an important place for students to gather and socialize. Throughout its long history, Peters Hall was slated for demolition on several occasions, but it always survived because of protests from students and alumni. The building was listed in the National Register of Historic Places in 1978 and completely modernized in 1992.

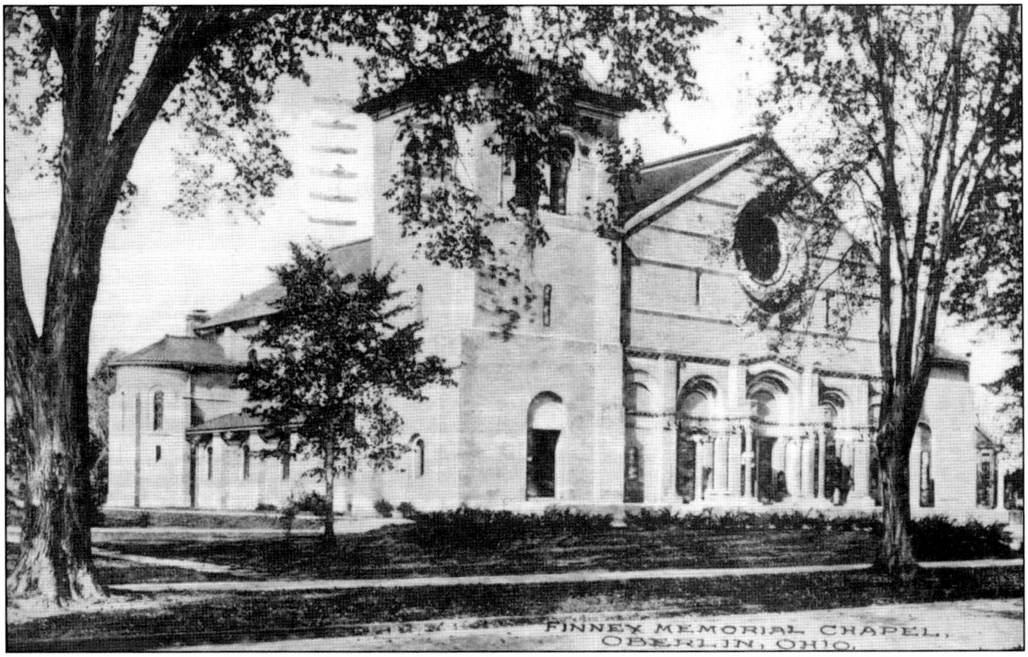

Finney Memorial Chapel and Allen Memorial Art Museum, Oberlin College, Oberlin. Oberlin College is graced by two significant buildings designed by famed architect Cass Gilbert, whose other works include the US Supreme Court, the Woolworth Building in New York City, and the Minnesota State Capitol. The chapel above was built on the site of former Oberlin president Charles Finney's residence and has been a focus of the campus since it opened in 1908. The Allen Memorial Museum, below, ranks among the finest academically based art collections in the country. The collection consists of more than 12,000 works from virtually every culture and spans the history of art. The building honors Dr. Dudley Peter Allen, a distinguished graduate and trustee of Oberlin College.

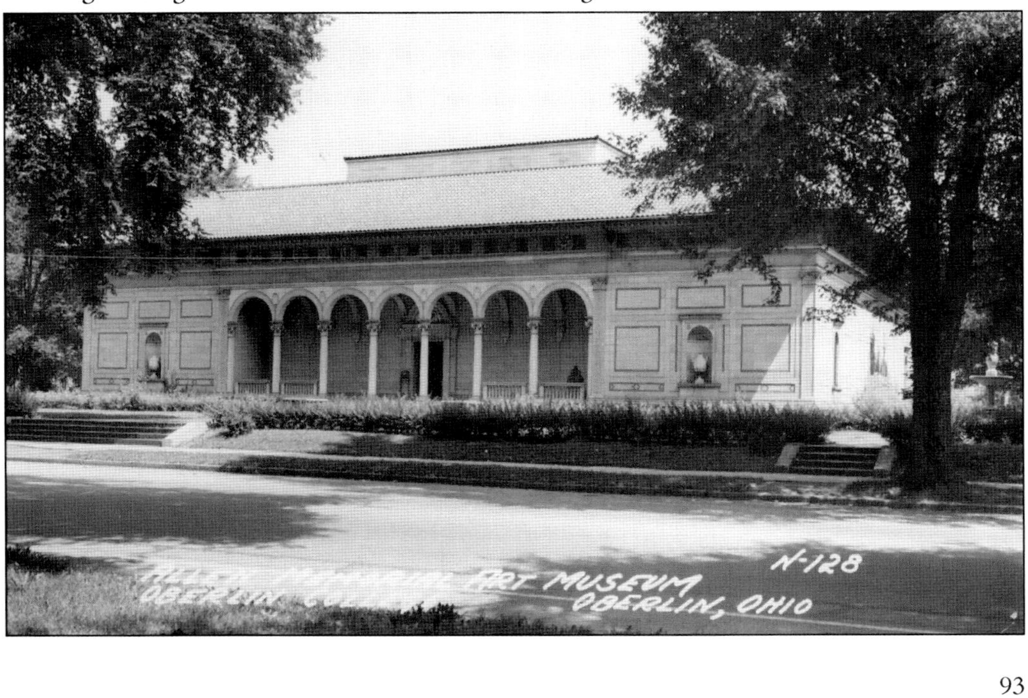

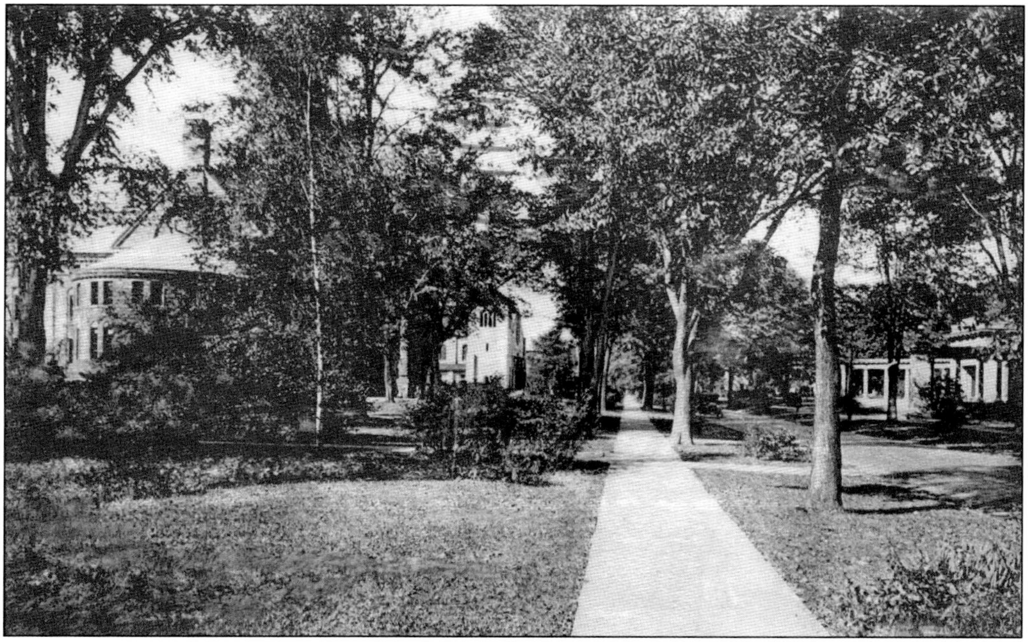

Oberlin College Campus at North Professor Street, Oberlin. North Professor Street intersected with historic Route 20 at the center of the campus. As in many small college towns, the campus and neighborhoods blended together along streets lined with graceful shade trees. The sender of this postcard, a student in 1937, told her younger brother that she had just arrived safely by bus and suggested he shoot off fireworks if he was bored.

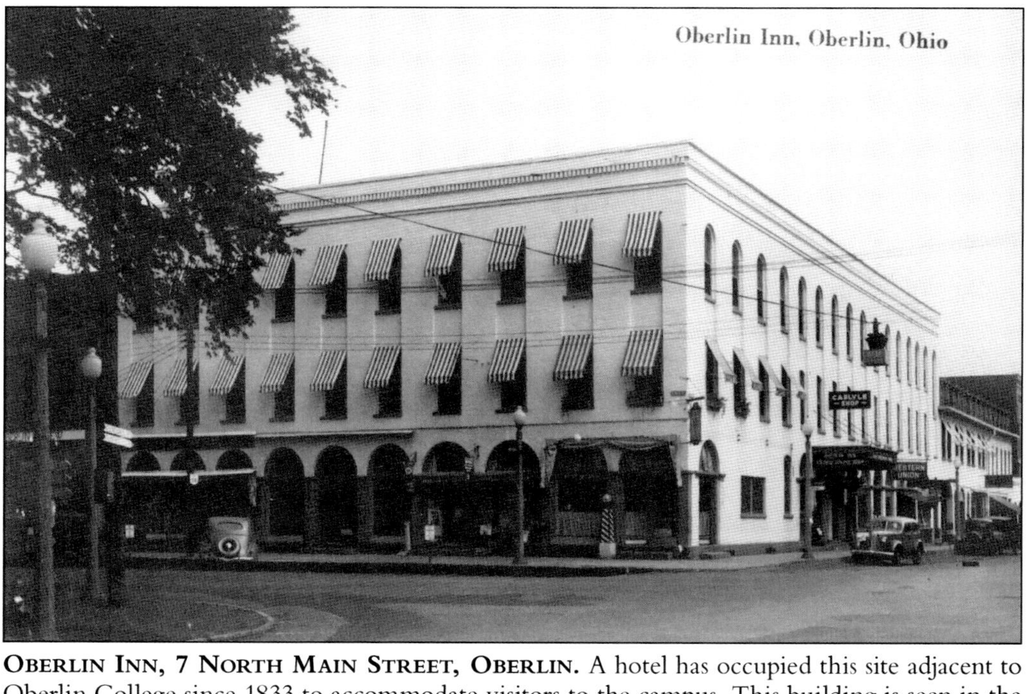

Oberlin Inn, 7 North Main Street, Oberlin. A hotel has occupied this site adjacent to Oberlin College since 1833 to accommodate visitors to the campus. This building is seen in the 1930s, when Route 20 passed directly through the town. Originally called the Park Hotel, it was renamed the Oberlin Inn in 1927. The building was later replaced by a more modern structure.

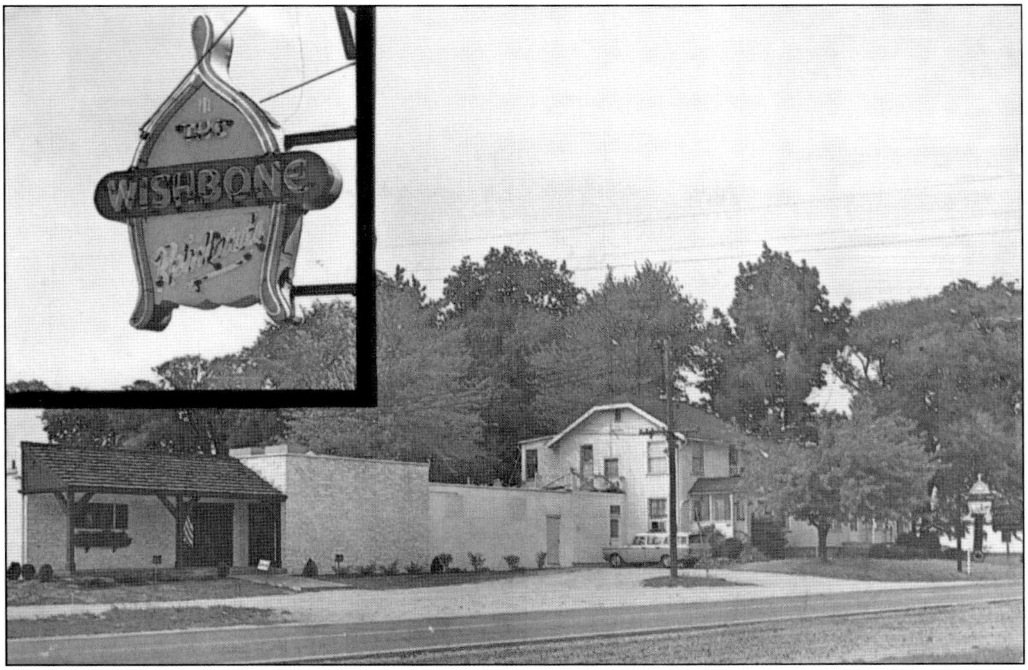

Wishbone Dining Room and Lounge, Route 20, Oberlin. The unusual architecture of this restaurant suggests that rooms were added sequentially as business improved. Diners wanting American fare could select the standard steaks, chops, and seafood. Those desiring more continental cuisine could choose from a menu of specially prepared Hungarian-style dishes.

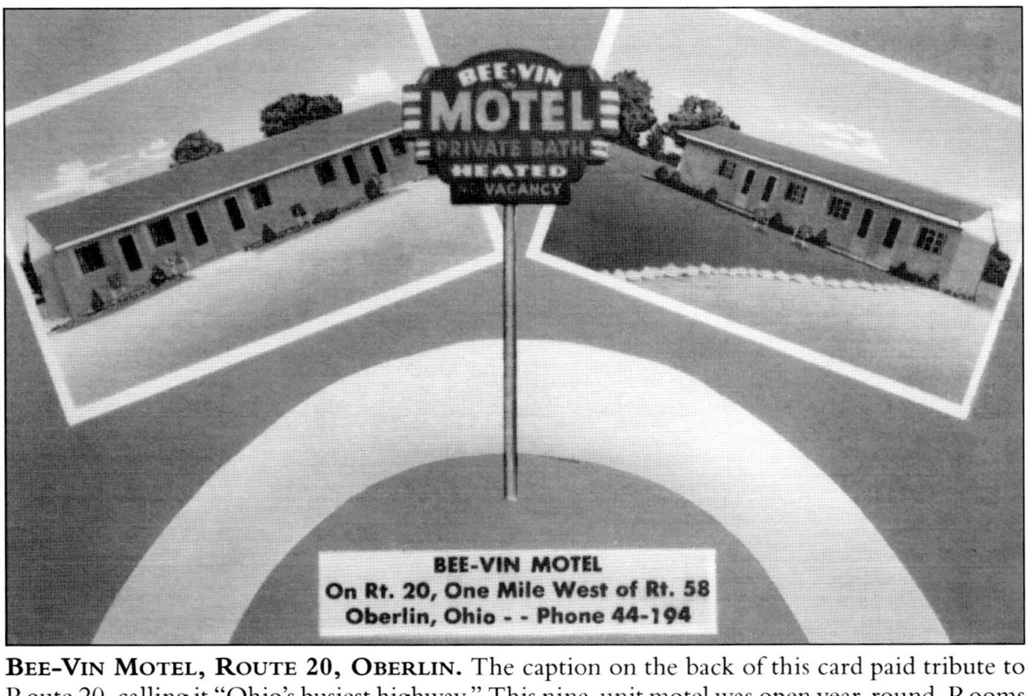

Bee-Vin Motel, Route 20, Oberlin. The caption on the back of this card paid tribute to Route 20, calling it "Ohio's busiest highway." This nine-unit motel was open year-round. Rooms were centrally heated and all contained private baths. Single rooms and family accommodations were available.

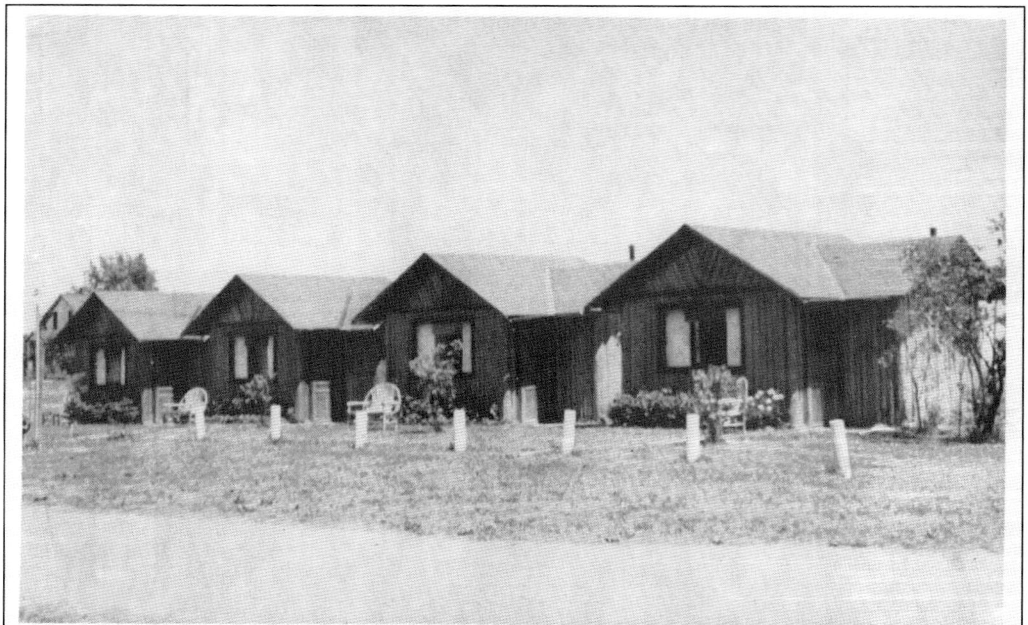

GIL'S TOURIST CABINS, U. S. ROUTE 20, OBERLIN, OHIO

GIL'S TOURIST CABINS, ROUTE 20, OBERLIN. Located 2.5 miles southwest of Oberlin, Gil's Tourist Camp consisted of individual rustic log cabins. They were described alliteratively as "clean, cool and comfortable," and each had a complete bath. In winter, they were heated with oil. Tourist rooms also were available in the owner's spacious home.

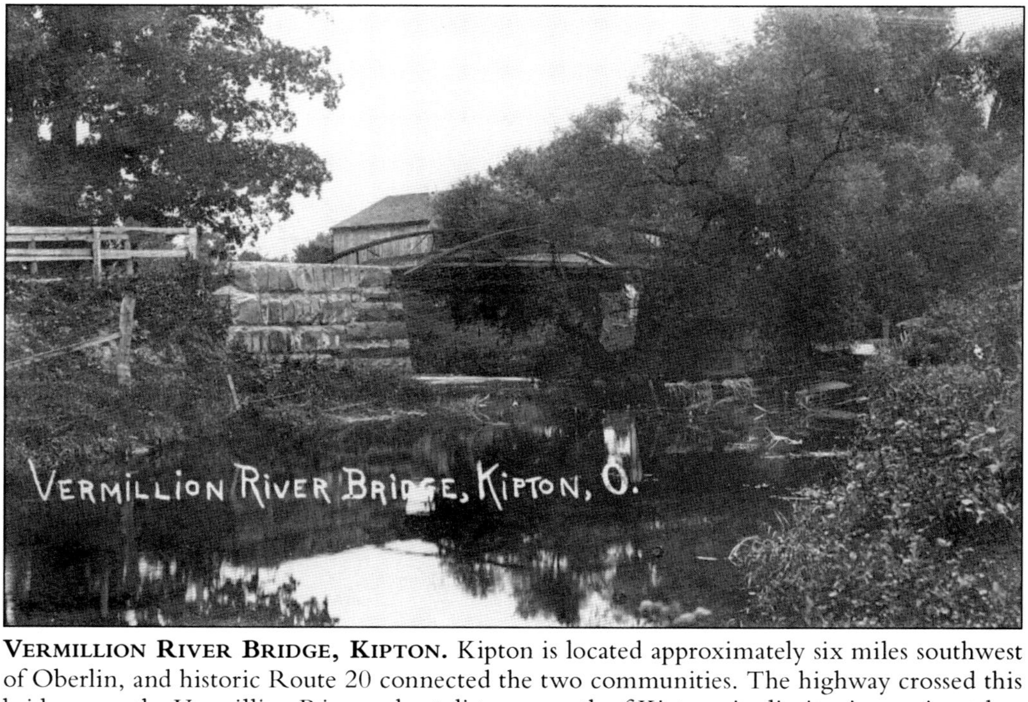

VERMILLION RIVER BRIDGE, KIPTON, O.

VERMILLION RIVER BRIDGE, KIPTON. Kipton is located approximately six miles southwest of Oberlin, and historic Route 20 connected the two communities. The highway crossed this bridge over the Vermillion River a short distance north of Kipton city limits. Approximately a half mile south of Kipton, Route 511 (original Route 20) rejoins present Route 20 and continues toward western Ohio.

Five

The Firelands

Soon after leaving Oberlin, original Route 20 rejoins the present highway south of Kipton, where it enters Huron County. Much of this county is part of a unique historical section of Ohio known as the Firelands. On July 11, 1779, the British burned Norwalk, Connecticut, to the ground. As compensation for the losses suffered by the townspeople, the federal government gave a tract of land in Ohio's Western Reserve, south of Lake Erie, totaling approximately 500,000 acres. The resettlement area came to be known as the Firelands and was also referred to as the Sufferers' Lands. The westward migration from Connecticut to Ohio began shortly thereafter.

All of the Route 20 towns in Huron County—Wakeman, Norwalk, Monroeville, and Bellevue—owe their existence to the Firelands' grant. Each developed into small but thriving communities surrounded by prime agricultural land. Norwalk is now the county seat of Huron County. Farther west, in Sandusky County, Route 20 connects the communities of Clyde, Fremont, and Woodville at the extreme western end of the Firelands.

Ohio has been called the "Cradle of Presidents" because eight have hailed from the state. Fremont is noted for being the home to the 19th president, Rutherford B. Hayes. Hayes practiced law in Fremont before becoming a hero in the Civil War, being wounded five times and rising to the rank of major general. He then served in the House of Representatives from 1865 to 1867, followed by two terms as Ohio's governor. After completing his second term in 1872, Hayes returned to his law practice, but four years later he was elected to a third term as governor. He was immediately catapulted to the front ranks for the presidency, and later that same year he was elected president.

Hayes's estate, Spiegel Grove, contains the former president's home, as well as the Hayes Commemorative Library and Museum. The latter was established in 1916.

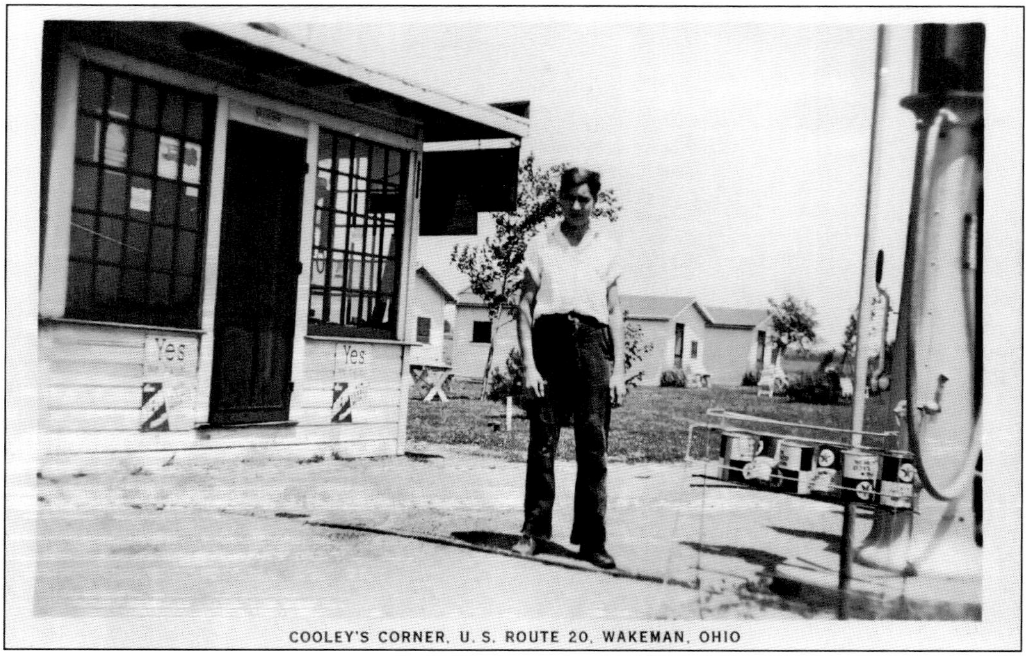

Cooley's Corner, Route 20, Wakeman. Cooley's Corner offered lunches, drinks, candy, cigarettes, and groceries in addition to overnight accommodations in modest cabins. Attendants in many early service stations dressed in snappy uniforms, but Cooley's did not subscribe to that practice.

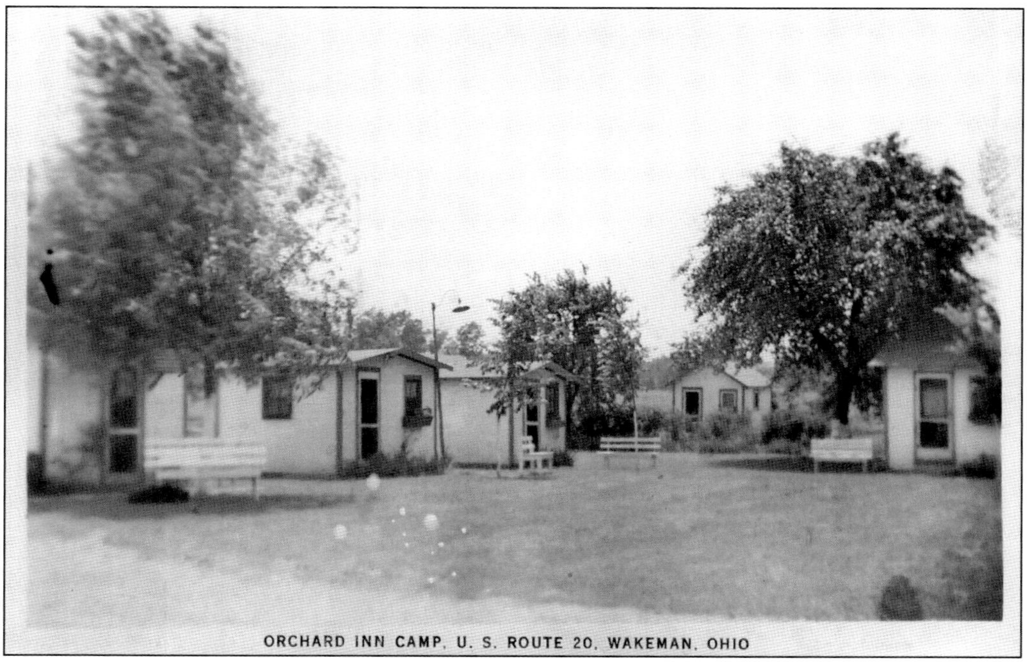

Orchard Inn Camp, Route 20, Wakeman. The sender of this card in 1939 was traveling west. She had stayed at this tourist camp and reported there were rabbits so tame that they came almost to their cabin. She also reported that they were having their oil changed in Gary, Indiana, and on one stretch of their drive they had covered 20 miles in 21 minutes.

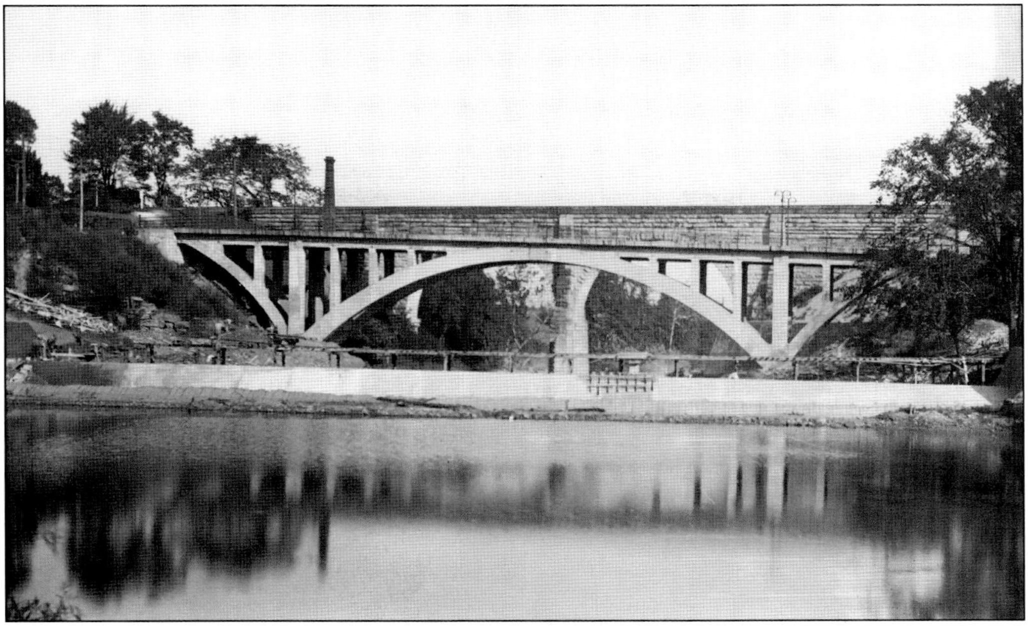

Highway, Railroad Bridges, and Dam, Wakeman. This postcard shows two bridges spanning the Vermillion River east of Wakeman. The concrete-arch Route 20 Bridge is the prominent structure, and the arches of the railroad bridge can be identified behind it. In the foreground, a dam and spillway across the river add to the interest of the image.

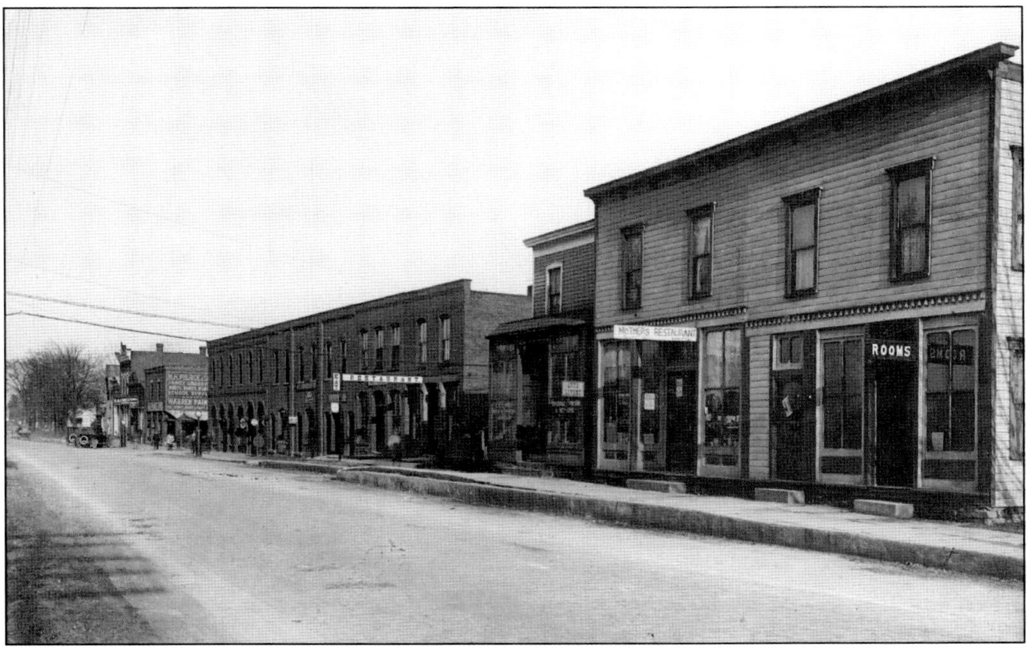

Main Street, Wakeman. Stores fronting the unpaved Main Street in Wakeman in the 1920s provided residents and travelers with all the necessities of the day. Rooms were available above the corner store. Mother's Restaurant was in the same building, and another restaurant was only a few doors away. Wires crossing the street and the shadow of a telephone pole indicate that Wakefield had joined the electrical age.

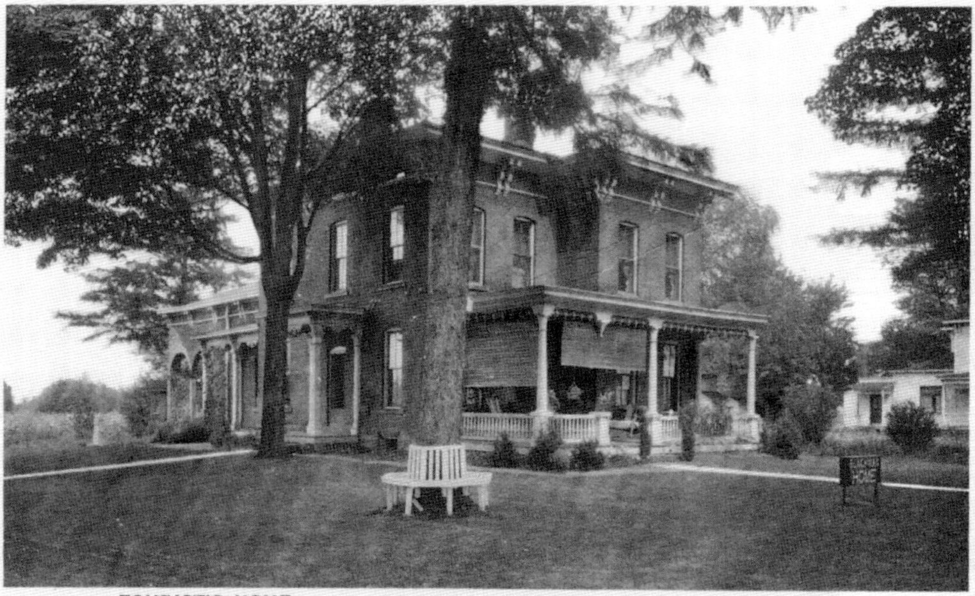

TOURIST'S HOME J. F. BLACKMAN TOWNSEND AVENUE NORWALK, OHIO

J.F. BLACKMAN TOURIST'S HOME, TOWNSEND AVENUE, NORWALK. Route 20 entered Norwalk from the east on Townsend Avenue. The caption on the back of this postcard identifies the location simply as being on Route 20 and further points out that modern rooms, bath, meals, and a free garage are available. Guests could also relax on the large front porch or on the bench on the spacious lawn.

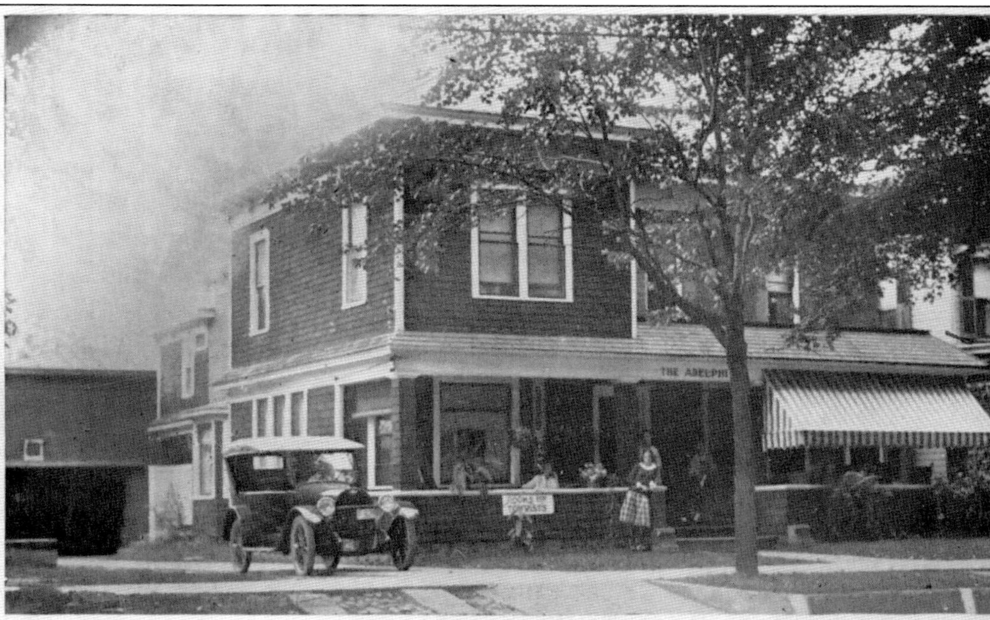

The Adelphi, Norwalk, Ohio.

THE ADELPHI, NORWALK. The sign in front of the Adelphi Hotel reads, "Rooms for Tourists," and several guests are seen lounging on the building's front porch in the 1920s. The woman in front wearing an apron and carrying a tray was likely an employee catering to the guests' needs.

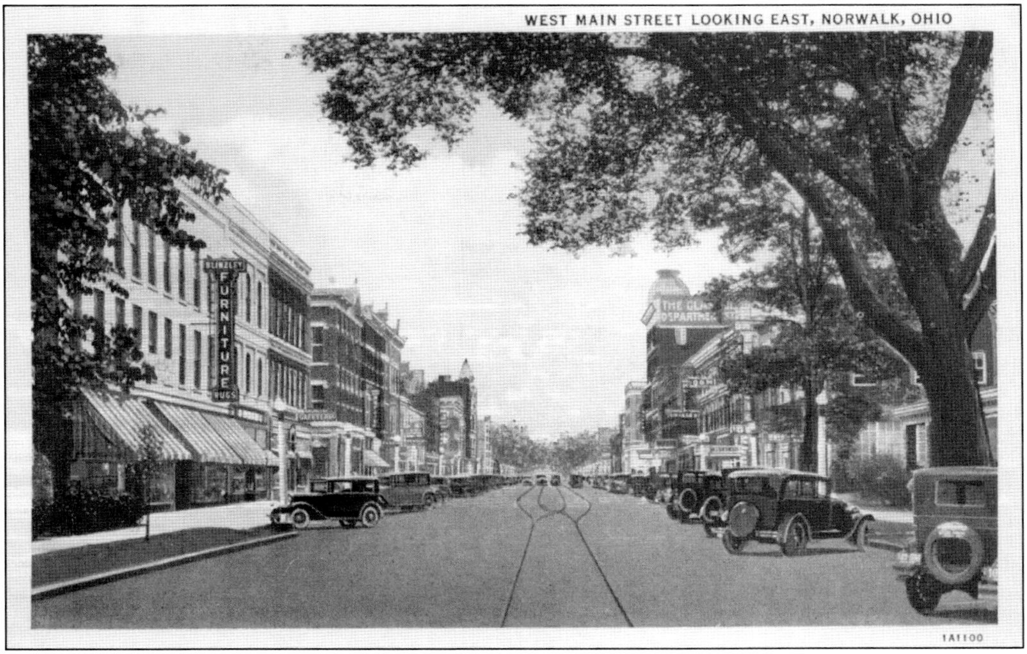

Main Street, Norwalk. These two views of Route 20 passing through Norwalk's business district were taken only a few years apart and from approximately the same location. They show a pleasant and thriving commercial area with retail stores on both sides of the street. Trolleys were still in use in the late 1920s when the photograph above was taken, but they had been removed or paved over when the postcard below was made in the 1930s. Main Street stalwarts, including a furniture store, a cafeteria, and a department store, are identified by their signs, and Norwalk's landmark Avalon Hotel is on the right below.

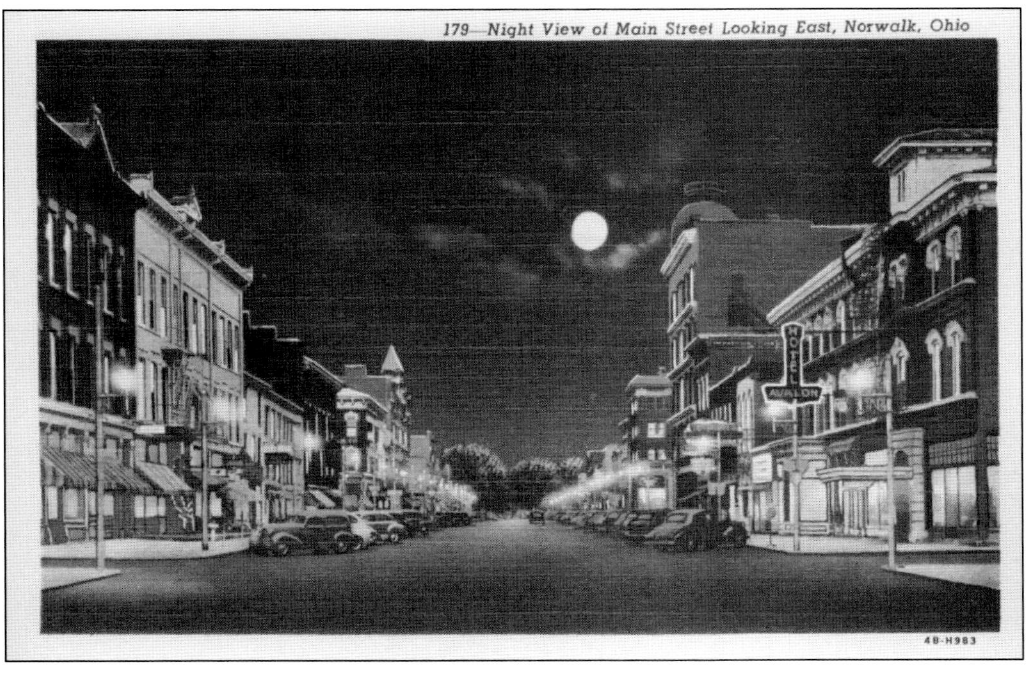

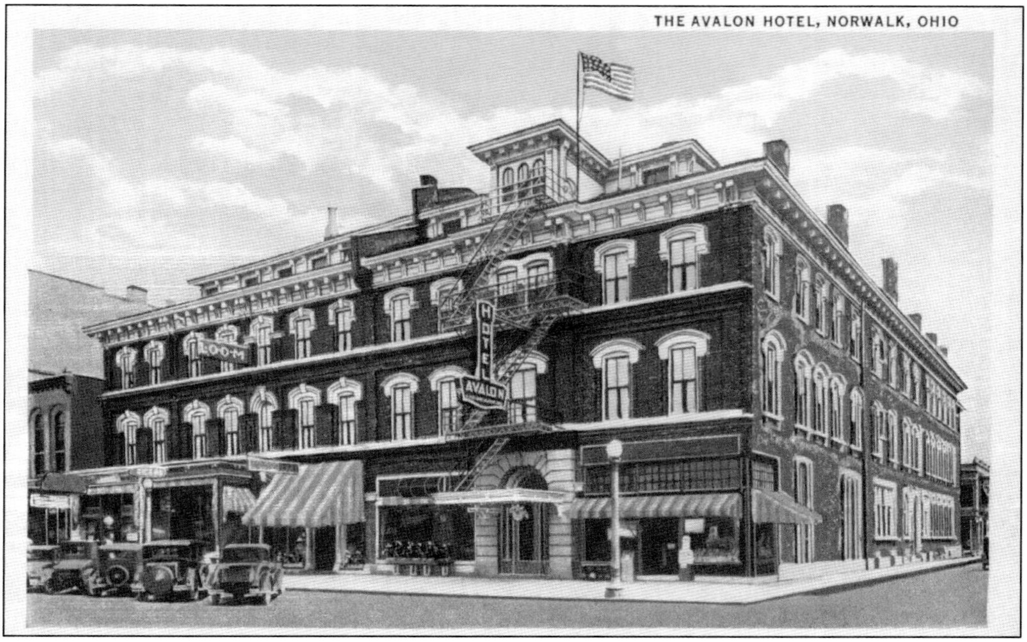

AVALON HOTEL, NORWALK. The Avalon Hotel occupied its prominent position on Main Street in Norwalk since the mid-1800s. Formerly called the St. Charles, it was the leading hotel in the city for almost a century. Early travelers took advantage of the hotel's convenient location, directly on Route 20 in downtown Norwalk. It was also a center for business and social activities of the local community.

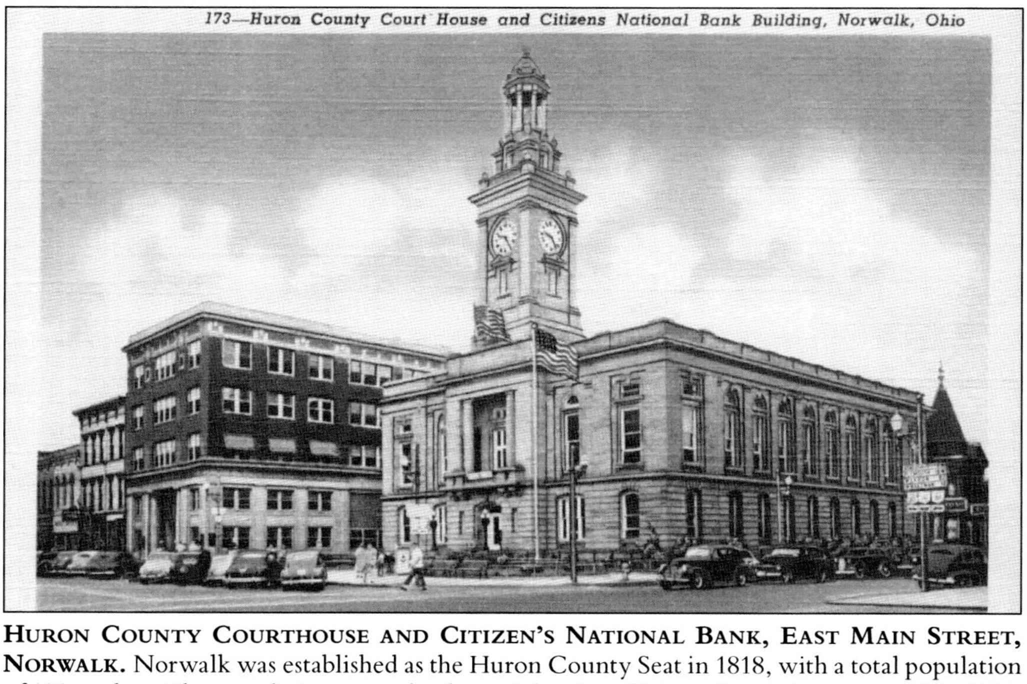

HURON COUNTY COURTHOUSE AND CITIZEN'S NATIONAL BANK, EAST MAIN STREET, NORWALK. Norwalk was established as the Huron County Seat in 1818, with a total population of 109 settlers. The population grew slowly, and the city of Norwalk was incorporated in 1881. Seats of both government and commerce are seen here in the 1930s. The bank and courthouse have served Norwalk since 1865 and 1882 respectively.

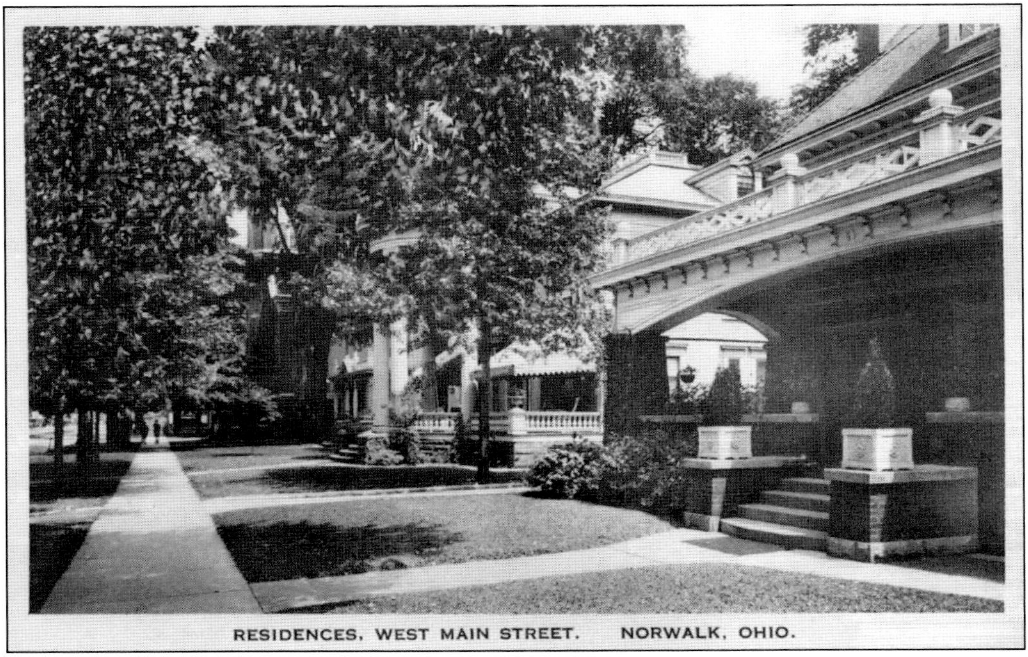

Residences, West Main Street, Norwalk. Stately homes lined original Route 20 on the west side of Norwalk. The city is known locally as the "Maple City" due to the abundance of maple trees that adorn the streets. Many of these trees were planted by the city's founder, Platt Benedict, in the 1830s. The trees and large front porches provided relief from the heat prior to the advent of air-conditioning.

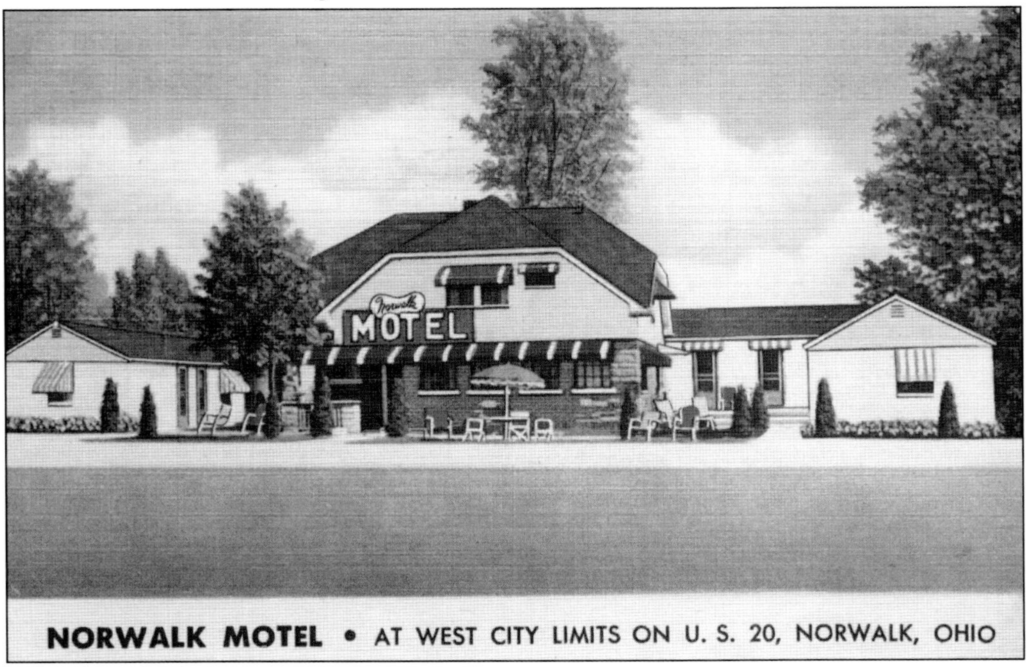

Norwalk Motel, Norwalk. This colorful 12-unit motel was a half mile west of downtown Norwalk. Some of its selling points were the two good restaurants and a tavern nearby. Guests could watch Route 20 traffic from the chairs on the front lawn.

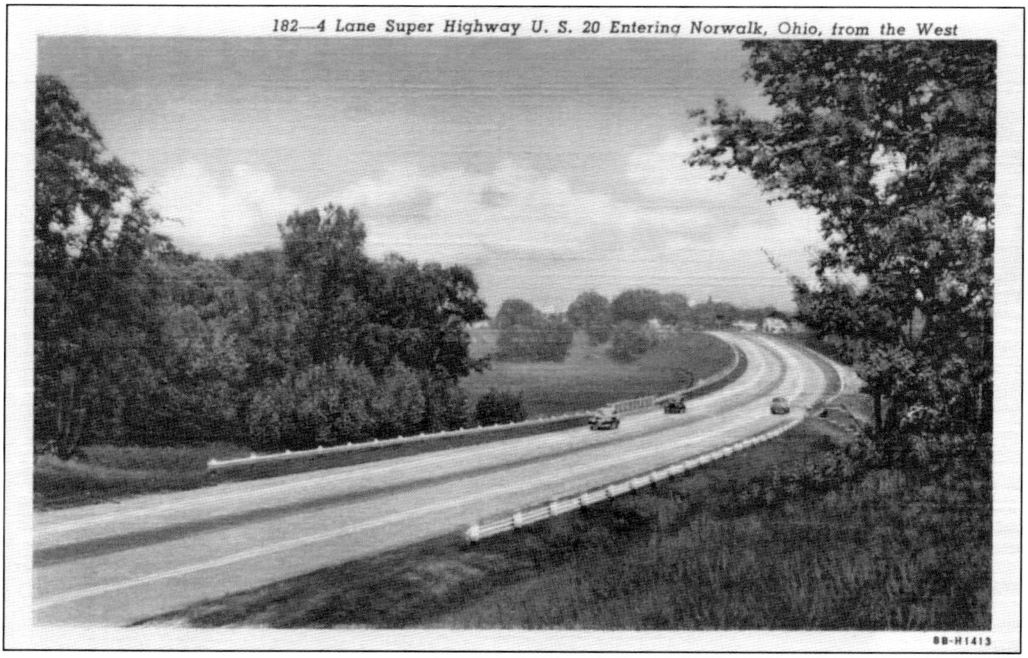

FOUR-LANE ROUTE 20 SUPERHIGHWAY, NORWALK. This postcard was produced in the 1940s. Although the Interstate Highway System was still years in the future, drivers on this section of Route 20 were given a taste of what was to come. These early four-lane roads were a great improvement over the typical two-lane configuration and provided the model for further improvements in highway design and safety.

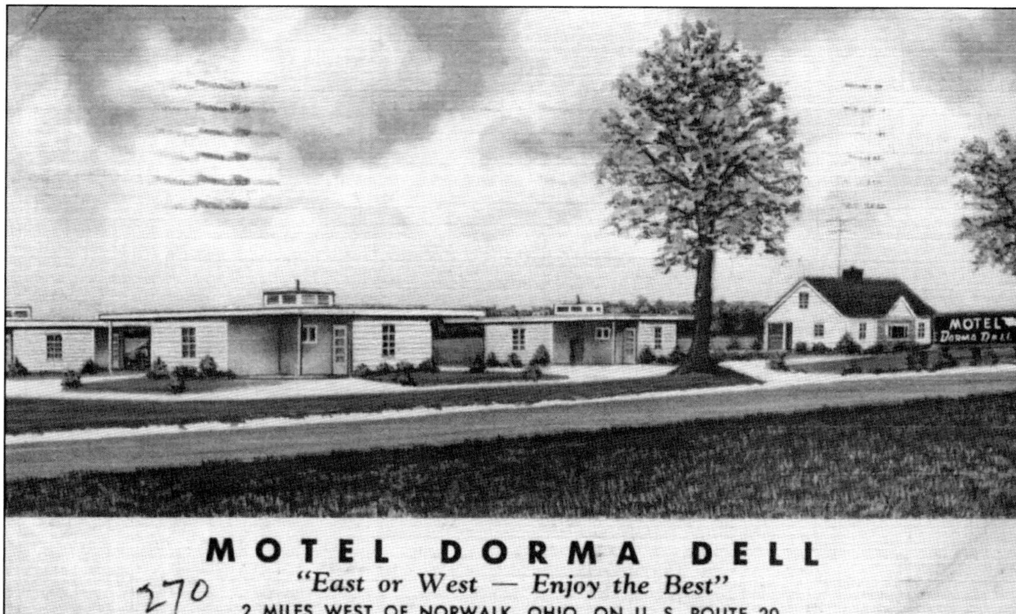

MOTEL DORMA DELL, ROUTE 20, NORWALK. "East or West, Enjoy the Best" was the motto of the Dorma Dell Motel, located directly across the highway from "a good restaurant and an outdoor theater." Guests no doubt appreciated the carport provided with each cabin, although that amenity was short-lived in motel design.

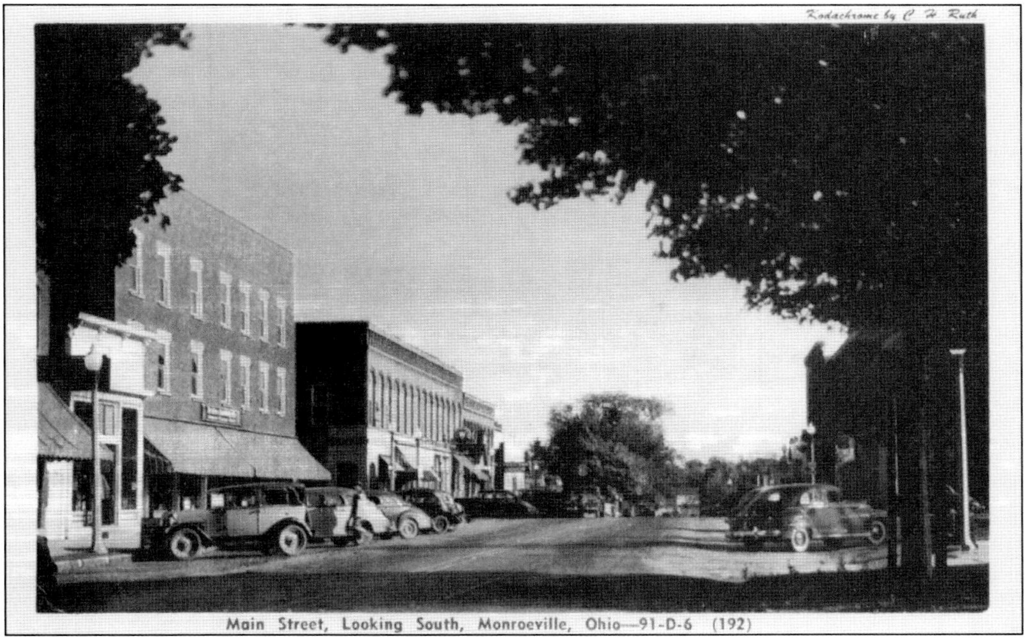

MAIN STREET LOOKING SOUTH, MONROEVILLE. Typical of most small towns in the first half of the 1900s, Main Street was also the route of the primary highway through the community. In Monroeville, Route 20 passed through the pleasant business district, with business establishments interspersed with parks and trees.

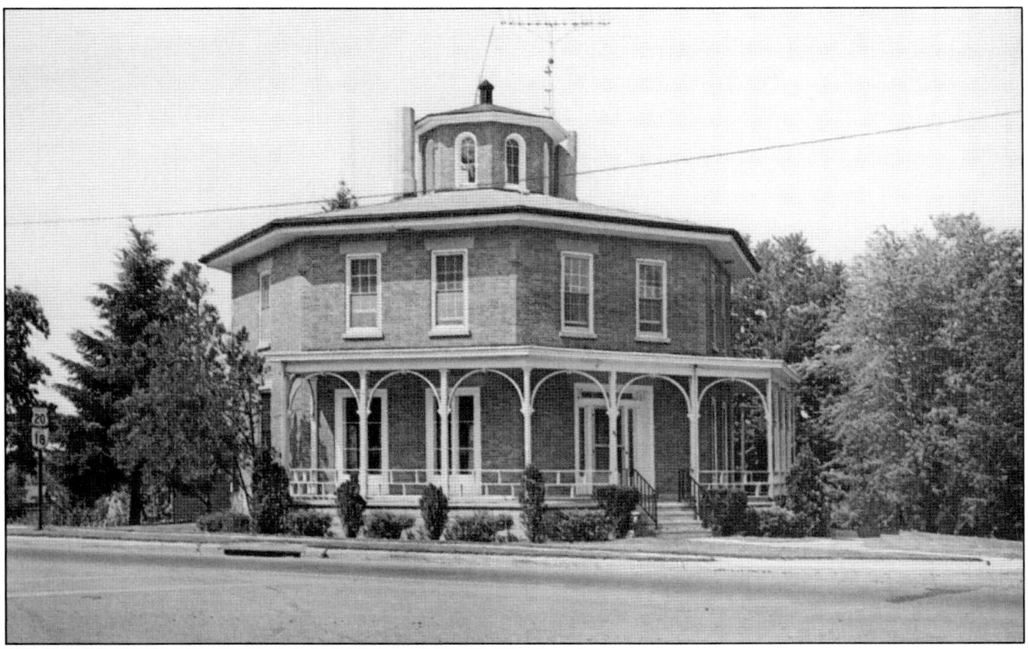

OCTAGON HOUSE, 64 SANDUSKY STREET, MONROEVILLE. This unique house was built in 1860 by John Hosford and has been a Monroeville landmark ever since. Although several octagonal buildings still exist throughout the state, this is one of the best examples of the architectural style in Ohio and the only one that sits directly on Route 20. The house was listed in the National Register of Historic Places in 1974.

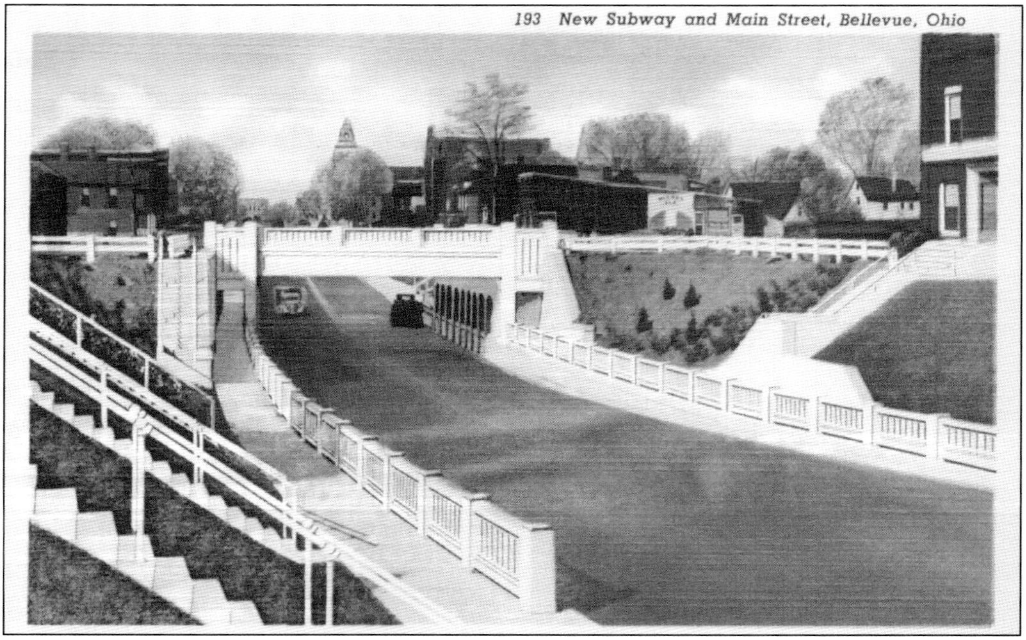

THE NEW SUBWAY AND MAIN STREET, BELLEVUE. Bellevue was a major railroad hub in the 1930s. The Nickel Plate, New York Central, and Pennsylvania Railroads all converged in the city, making traffic congestion a serious problem. This attractive underpass below the Nickel Plate Railroad was only a short distance east of Bellevue's business district. It greatly improved traffic flow on Route 20 and provided safe passage for pedestrians.

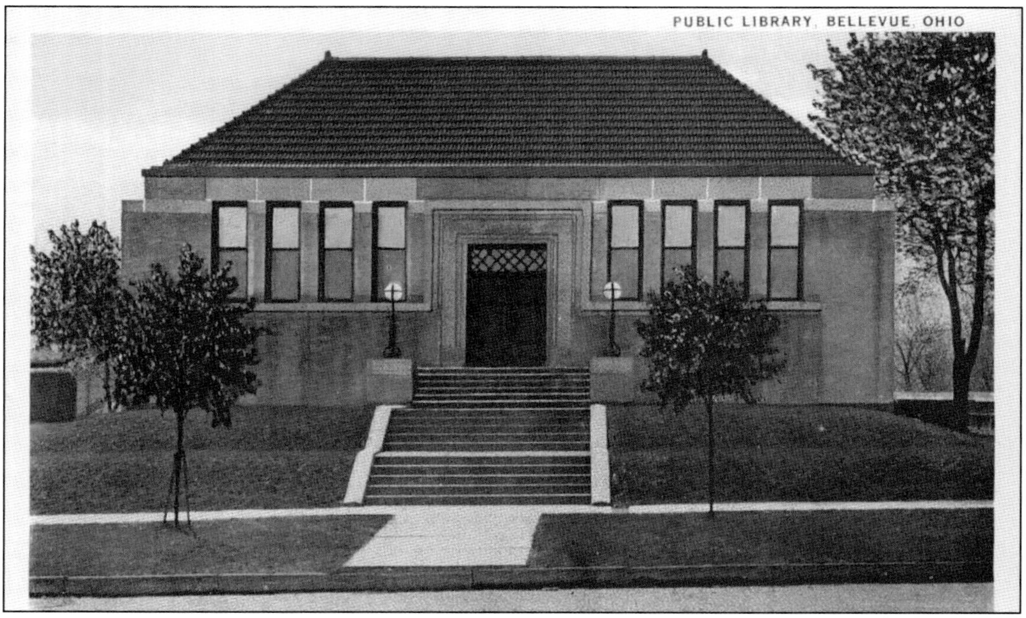

PUBLIC LIBRARY, 224 EAST MAIN STREET, BELLEVUE. The Bellevue Public Library was established in 1905, and like many libraries throughout the country, it was endowed by a grant from Andrew Carnegie. The style of the building, exactly symmetrical in all dimensions, presents a facade that is pleasing to the eye but also projects authority and learning. Additions have been made over the years, but the basic form remains intact.

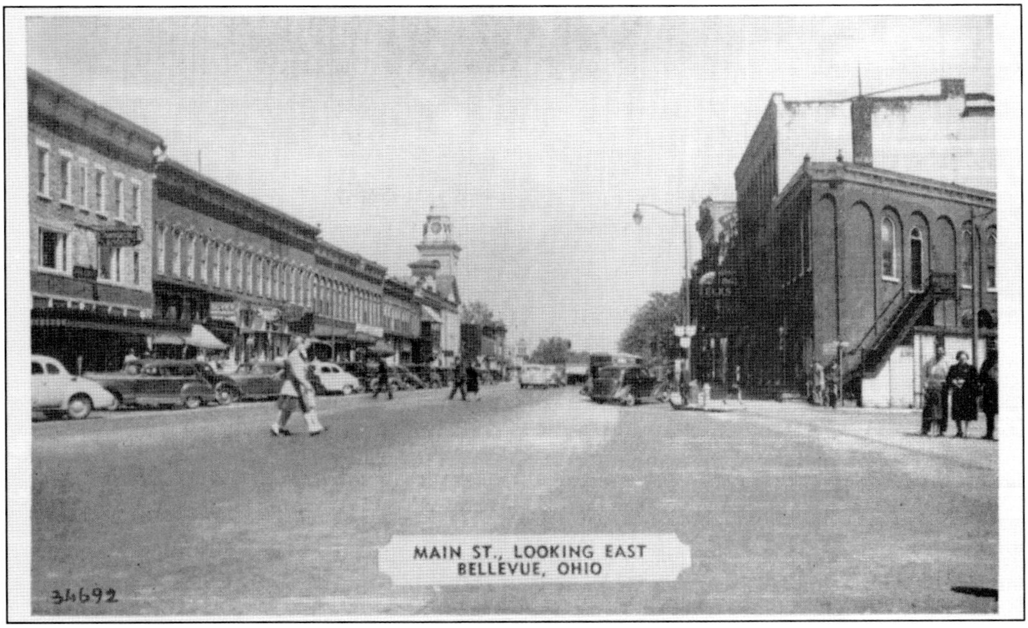

MAIN STREET LOOKING EAST, BELLEVUE. Bellevue is unique for being the only community in Ohio with city limits extending into four counties: Huron, Sandusky, Erie, and Seneca. Here, a Route 20 sign hangs with other road signs on the lamppost on the right side of Main Street. Bellevue was the original home of Henry Morrison Flagler, an American industrialist who, together with John D. Rockefeller, founded Standard Oil.

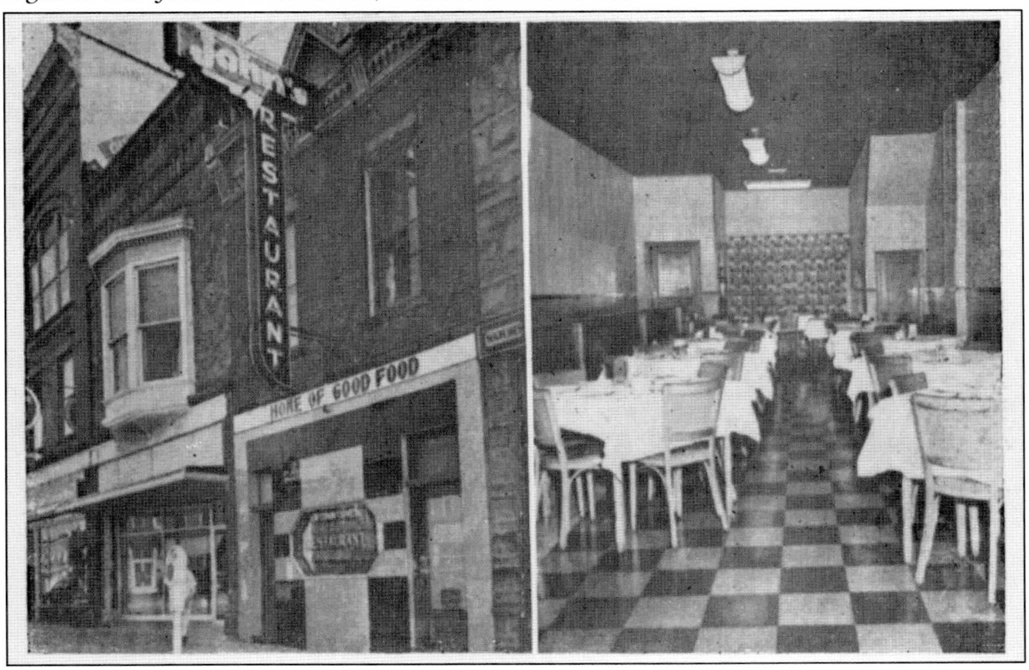

JOHN'S RESTAURANT, MAIN STREET, BELLEVUE. The sign above the door told passersby that John's Restaurant was the "home of good food" on Main Street in Bellevue. The owners of the restaurant were well aware of the commercial value Route 20 brought to their business. The caption states the restaurant was "a favorite dining stop for tourists on U.S. 20 in Bellevue."

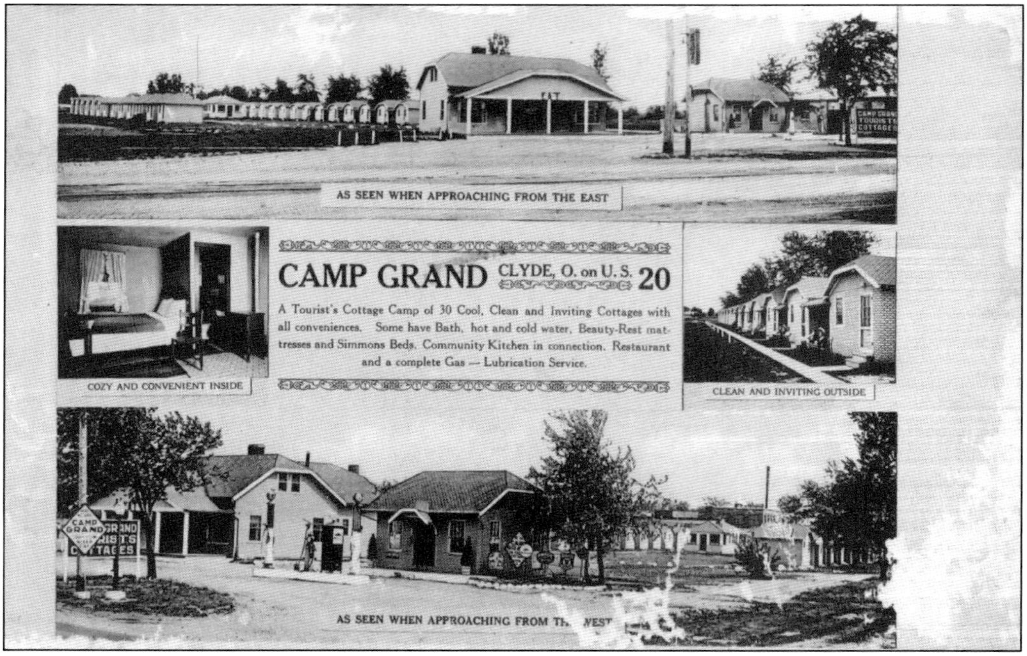

CAMP GRAND ON ROUTE 20, CLYDE. For a 1930s tourist camp in rural Ohio, Camp Grand was quite large. It boasted 30 cabins, some with private bathrooms, and all situated on attractive, well-maintained grounds. A community kitchen and complete gas and lubrication services were available. The postcard above shows the views approaching the camp from both the east and west. The postcard below shows a well-appointed tourist accommodation of the time. The room is furnished with a Simmons Beautyrest bed and mattress, a linoleum floor, a small table, two straight-backed chairs, and either a wood-burning or gas stove for heat. This cottage has an internal bathroom but only a toilet and a small sink. A bathtub or showers were probably available in a common facility in the camp.

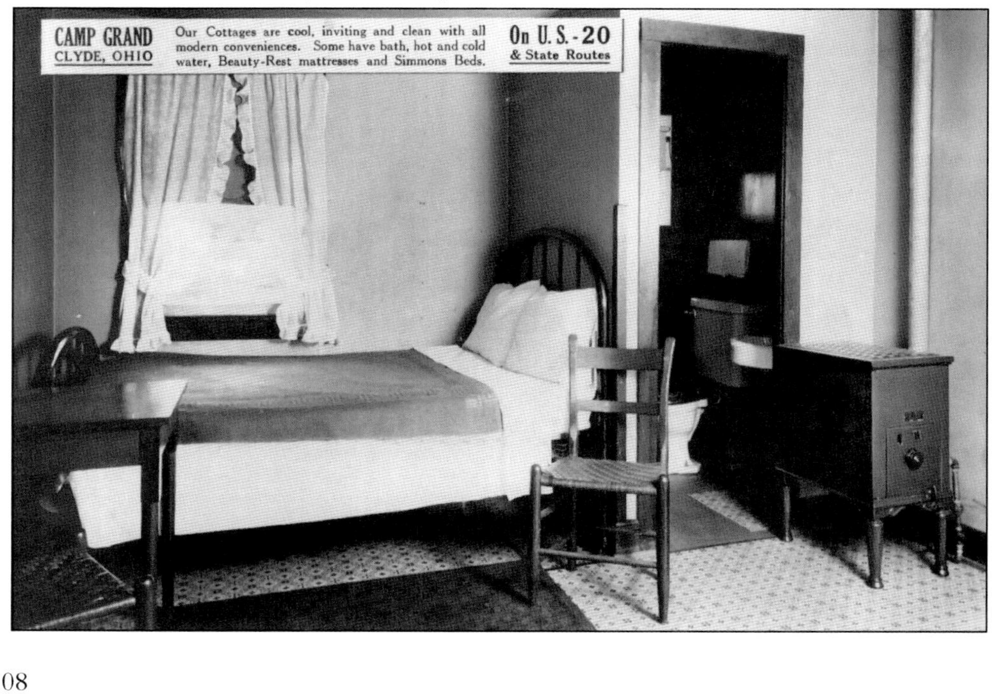

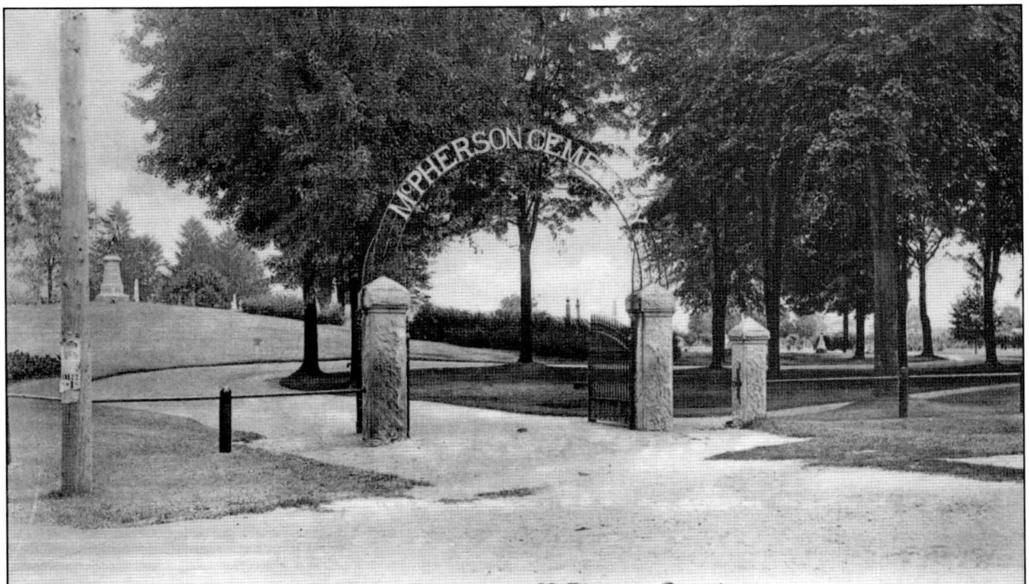

Clyde, Ohio. Entrance to McPherson Cemetery.

McPherson Cemetery, East McPherson Highway, Clyde. Both the cemetery and Route 20 in Clyde honor the memory of native son Gen. James McPherson, a Union hero in the Civil War. General McPherson fought valiantly alongside General Sherman during the Atlanta Campaign, where he became the second-highest-ranking Union officer to die in battle. A statue memorializing General McPherson is located in the left background.

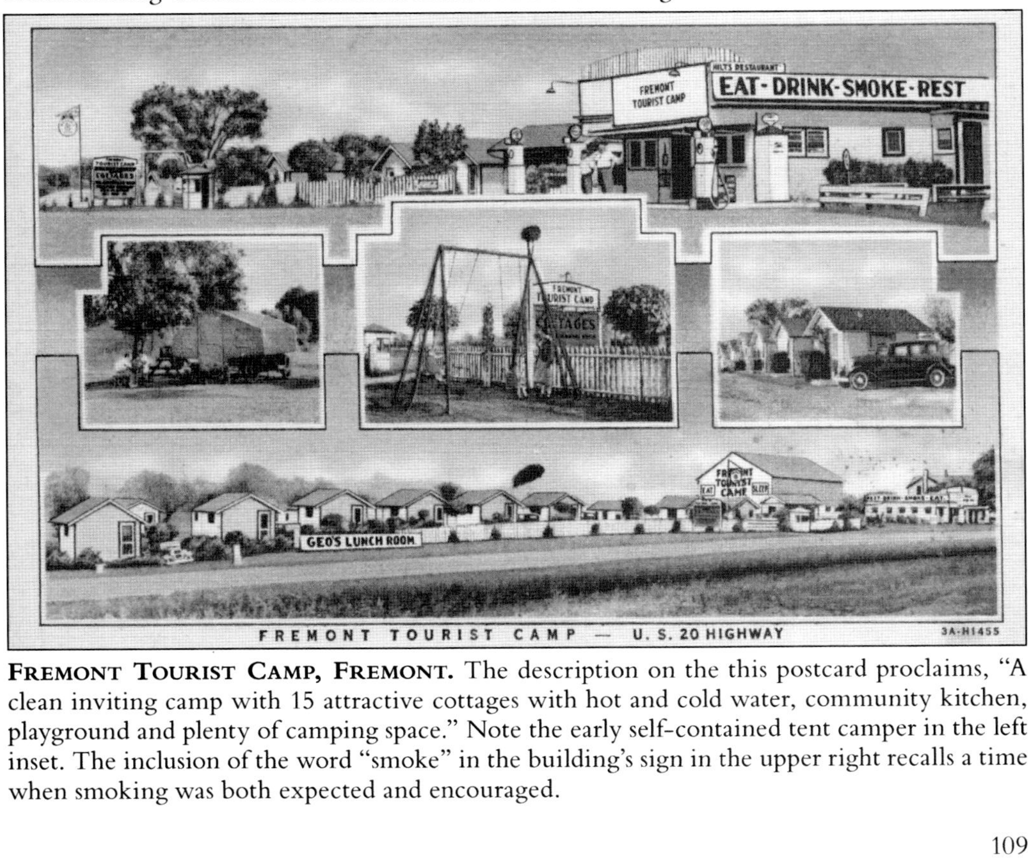

FREMONT TOURIST CAMP — U. S. 20 HIGHWAY 3A-H1455

Fremont Tourist Camp, Fremont. The description on the this postcard proclaims, "A clean inviting camp with 15 attractive cottages with hot and cold water, community kitchen, playground and plenty of camping space." Note the early self-contained tent camper in the left inset. The inclusion of the word "smoke" in the building's sign in the upper right recalls a time when smoking was both expected and encouraged.

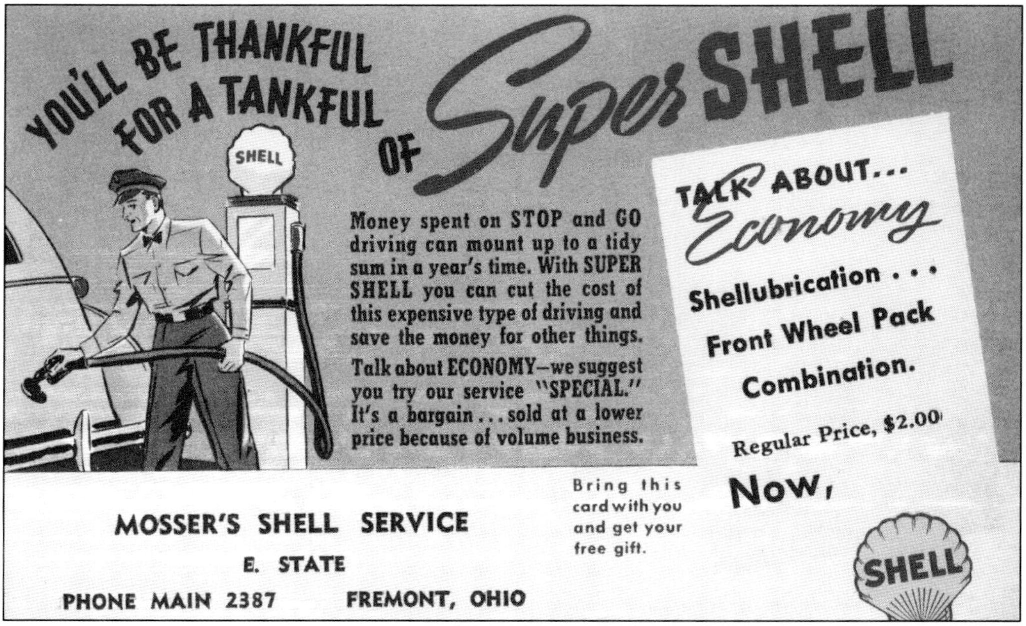

Mosser's Super Shell Service, East State Street, Fremont. This colorful postcard is typical of those produced by businesses in the 1930s and 1940s. Many were mailed to regular customers, and others were distributed to motorists who stopped for service. The free gift mentioned in the lower center was a metal coat hanger to be hooked over the upper edge of window glass, providing a way to keep clothes wrinkle-free on the trip.

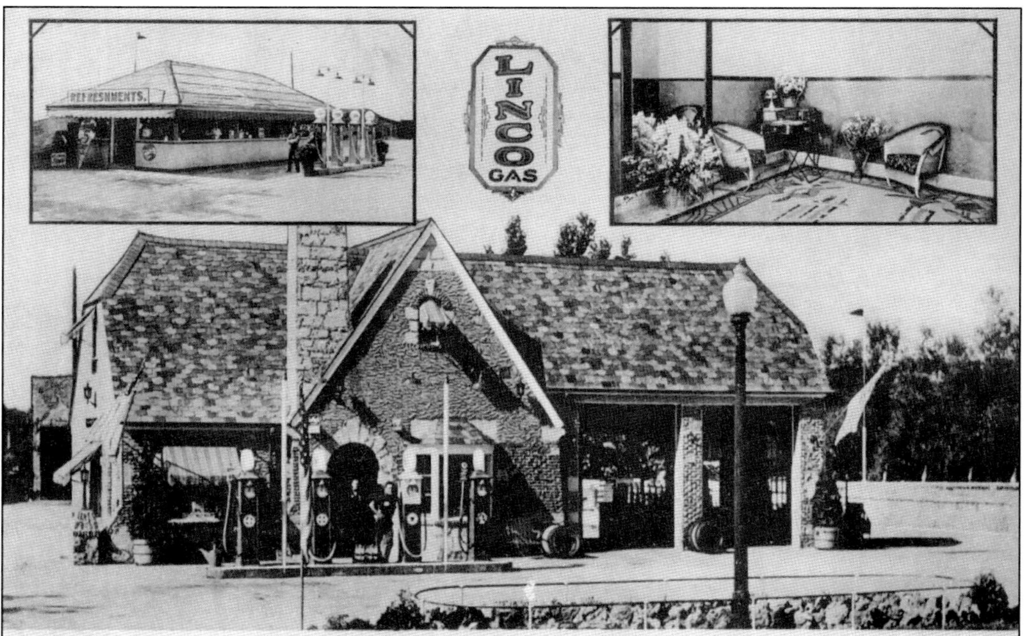

River Bridge Super Service, Fremont. Linco Gasoline was sold at this good-looking brick service station overlooking the Sandusky River. A restaurant was located in a separate building, and although no mention is made of overnight accommodations, the insert in the upper right appears to show either a reception area or a guest room.

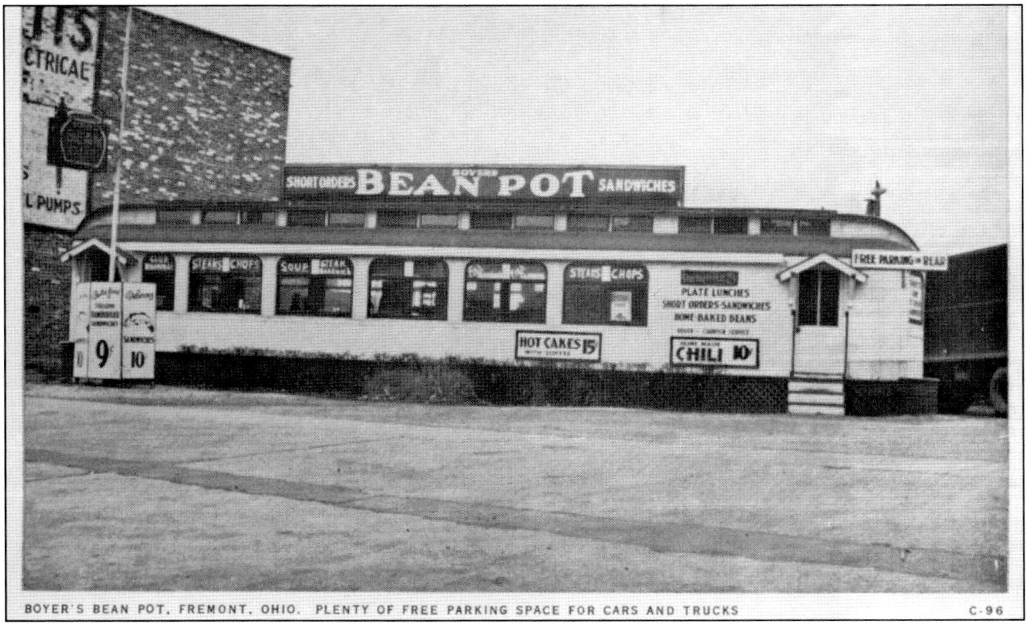

BOYER'S BEAN POT, 117 EAST MAIN STREET, FREMONT. This classic diner was opened by Clyde Boyer in the mid-1930s and continued in that location until the late 1940s before being moved to 941 East Main Street. The Bean Pot offered a wide range of hearty dishes at attractive prices. The sender of the card in 1941 reported that she and "Ralph" had dinner there, but that they did not have beans.

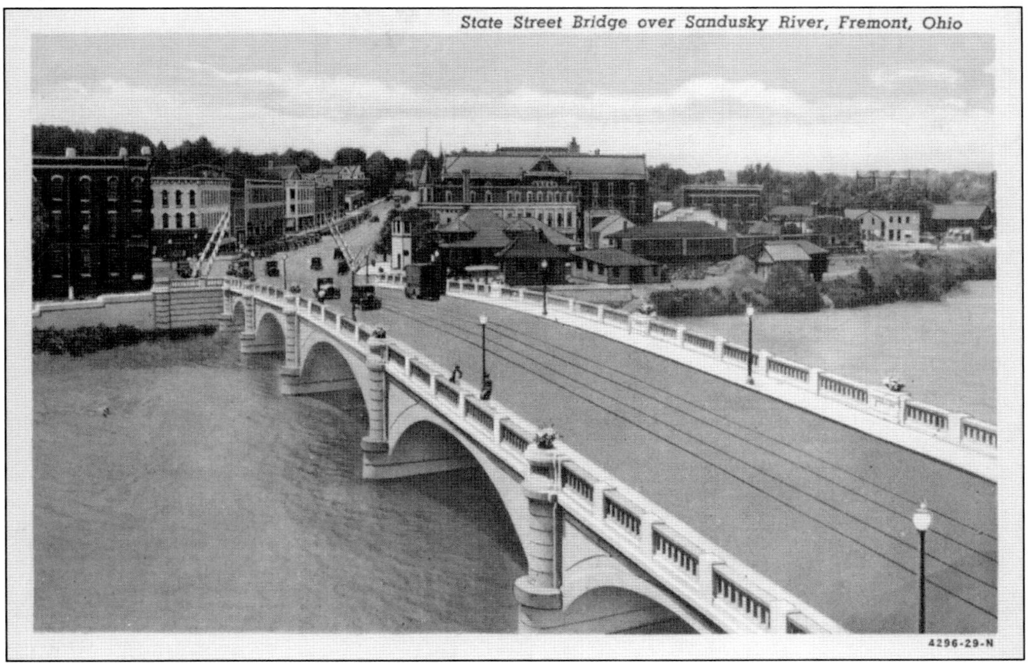

STATE STREET BRIDGE, FREMONT. This bridge over the Sandusky River was another example of the beautiful concrete-arch design that was common along early Route 20. Automobile, trolley, and pedestrian traffic were all accommodated on the bridge, but the railroad crossing at the west end may have impeded the smooth flow of traffic into Fremont's business district.

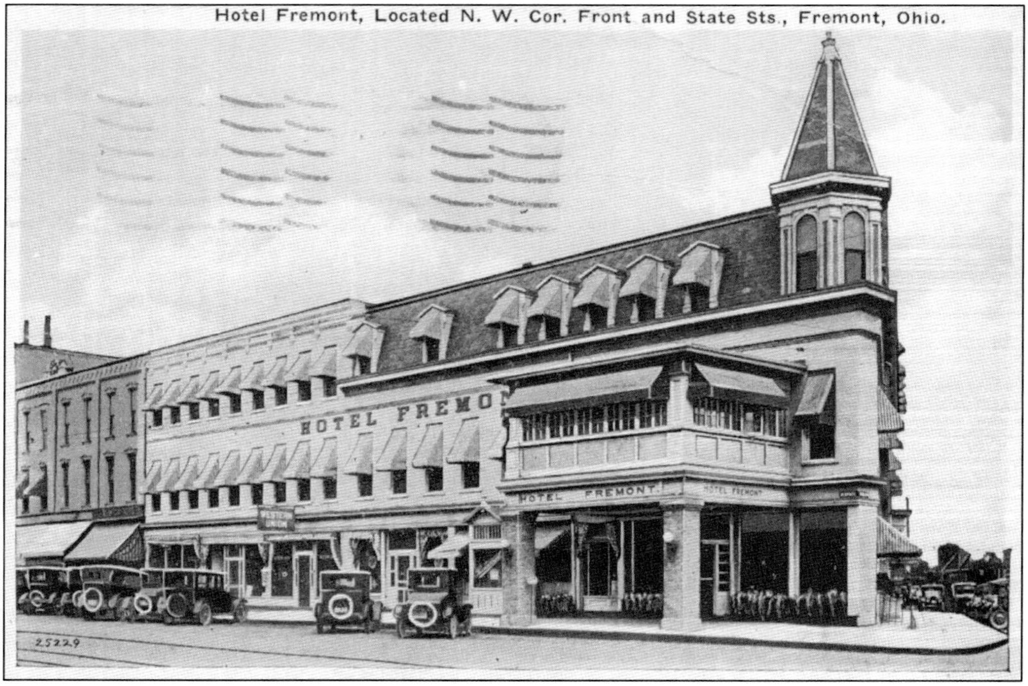

HOTEL FREMONT, FREMONT. The Hotel Fremont, seen above in the late 1920s, was ideally located at the intersection of Routes 6 and 20 with Routes 12 and 53 in the heart of Fremont's business district. For decades, it was the center of the city's social life, as well as a residence for vacationers, business representatives, and dignitaries visiting the nearby Rutherford B. Hayes Presidential Center. The three-story building was notable for its Mansard roof and steepled turret, which was among the tallest structures in the city. Three theme rooms, beautifully decorated in early American style, are seen below. These rooms provided the setting for dining, business meetings, and receptions. A special room above the porte cochere provided a view of Main Street.

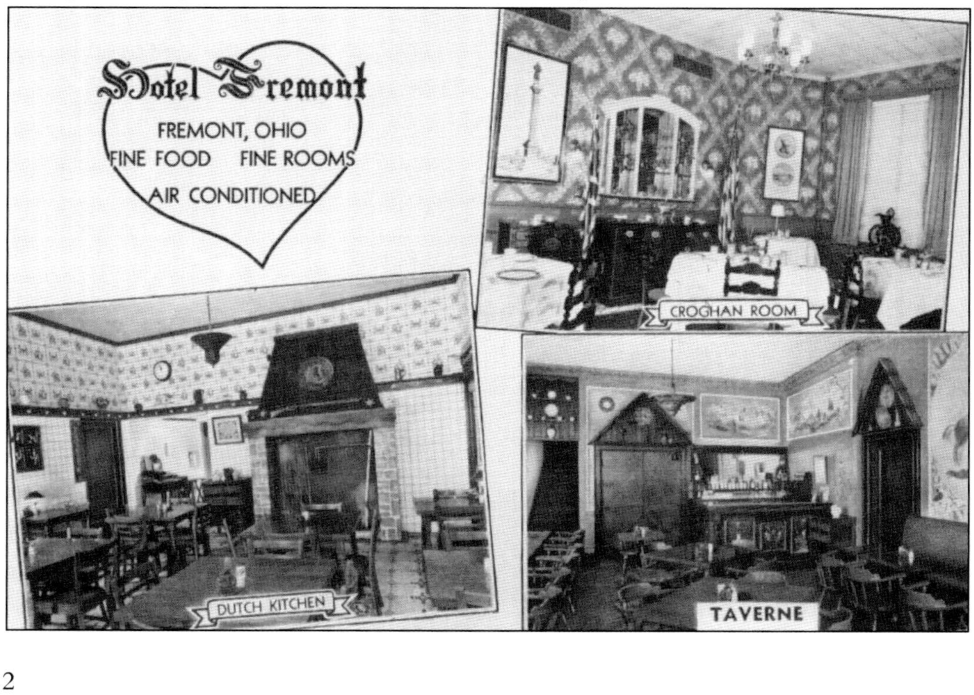

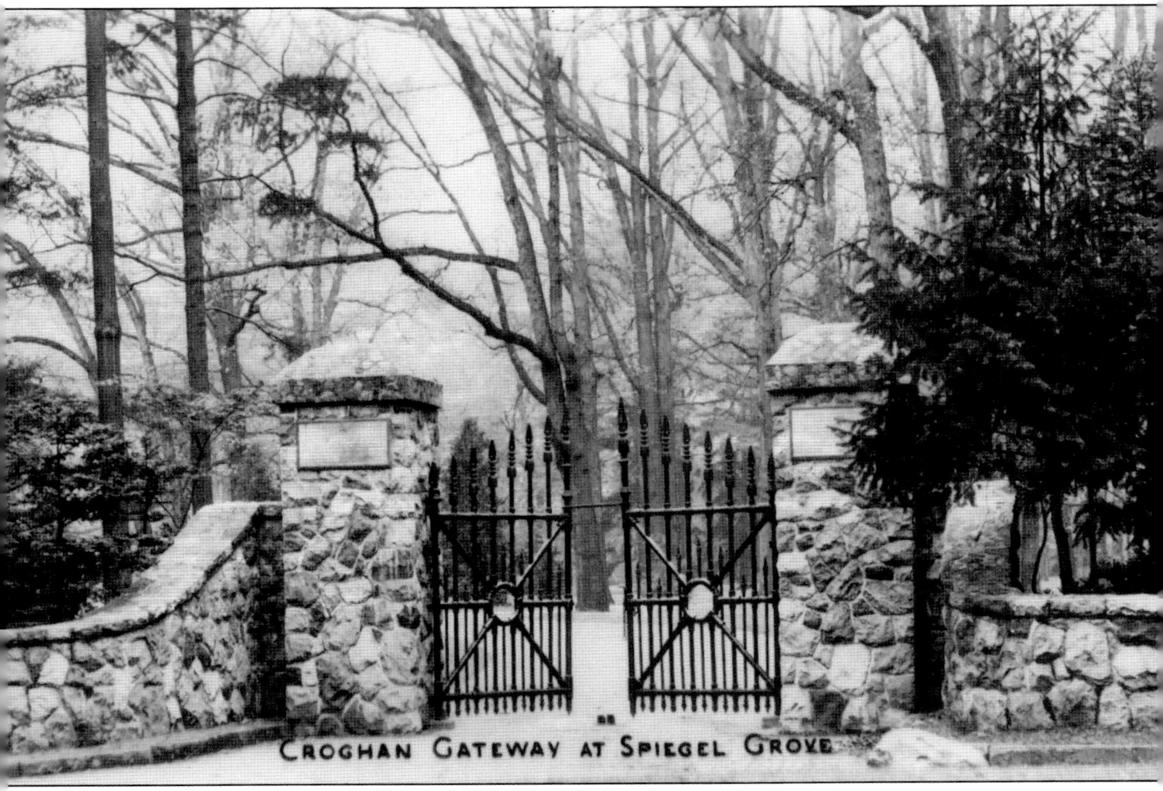

SPIEGEL GROVE, RUTHERFORD B. HAYES PRESIDENTIAL CENTER, 1337 HAYES AVENUE, FREMONT. Pres. Rutherford B. Hayes inherited his estate, Spiegel Grove, upon the death of his uncle and guardian, Sardis Birchard. Spiegel, which means "mirror" in German, was reminiscent of the reflections made by puddles in depressions on the property following rains. The six wrought-iron gates at the entrances to the 25-acre property had originally served the same purpose at the White House during Hayes's presidency. They were a gift from the government in 1928, when new gates were installed at the White House to accommodate larger vehicles. The tombs of President Hayes and his wife, Lucy, are at Spiegel Grove. Also honored is Old Whitey, Hayes's faithful horse during the Civil War.

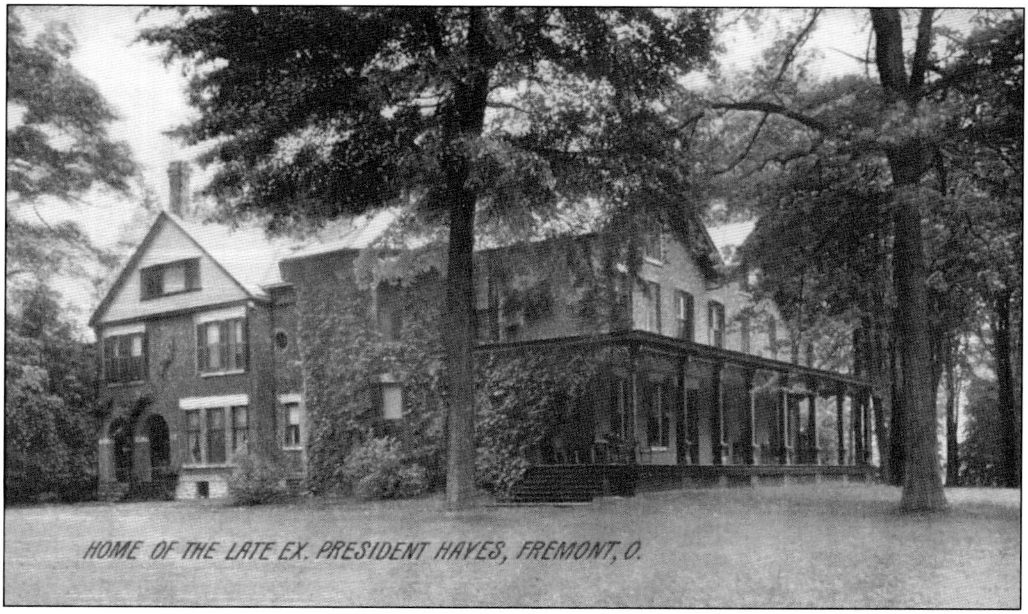

RUTHERFORD B. HAYES HOME AND LIBRARY, FREMONT. The original redbrick home (above) at Spiegel Grove was built in 1860 by Sardis Birchard. The Hayes family lived in the house briefly before Rutherford became the governor of Ohio and then president. They returned to the home in 1881 and enlarged it several times to include a total of 31 rooms to accommodate their extended family. The Hayes Commemorative Library and Museum (below) opened in 1916 and holds the distinction of being the first, as established by the federal government, in the United States. It contains the president's personal collection of more than 12,000 volumes, plus artifacts and documents from his military and political career. Over time, the collections have grown to include more than 80,000 items pertinent to the Hayes presidency and the Civil War. Hayes family descendents donated Spiegel Grove to the state of Ohio in 1965.

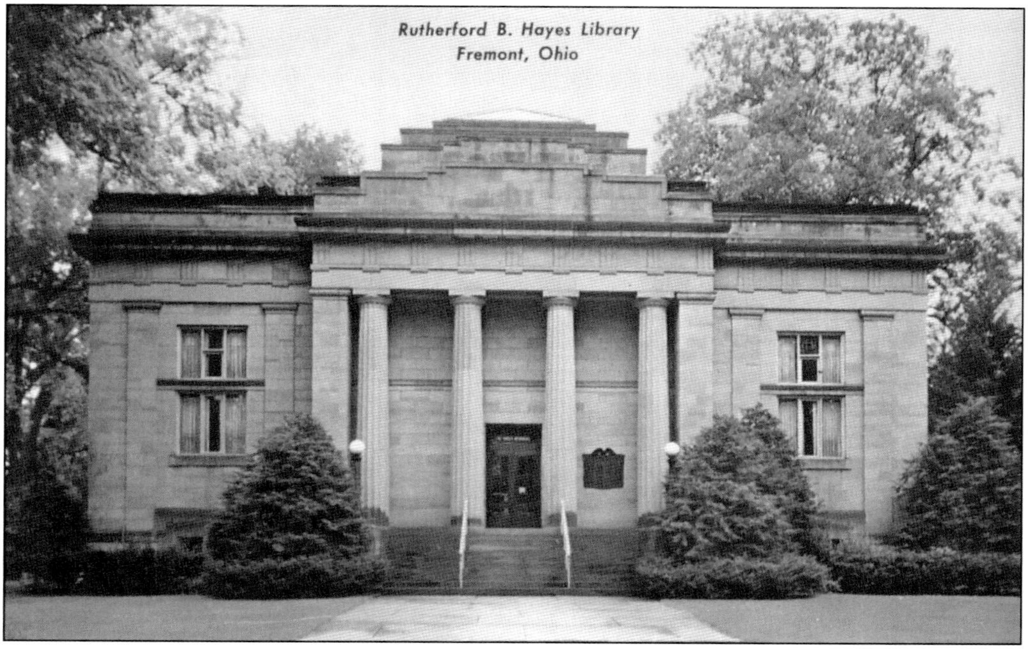

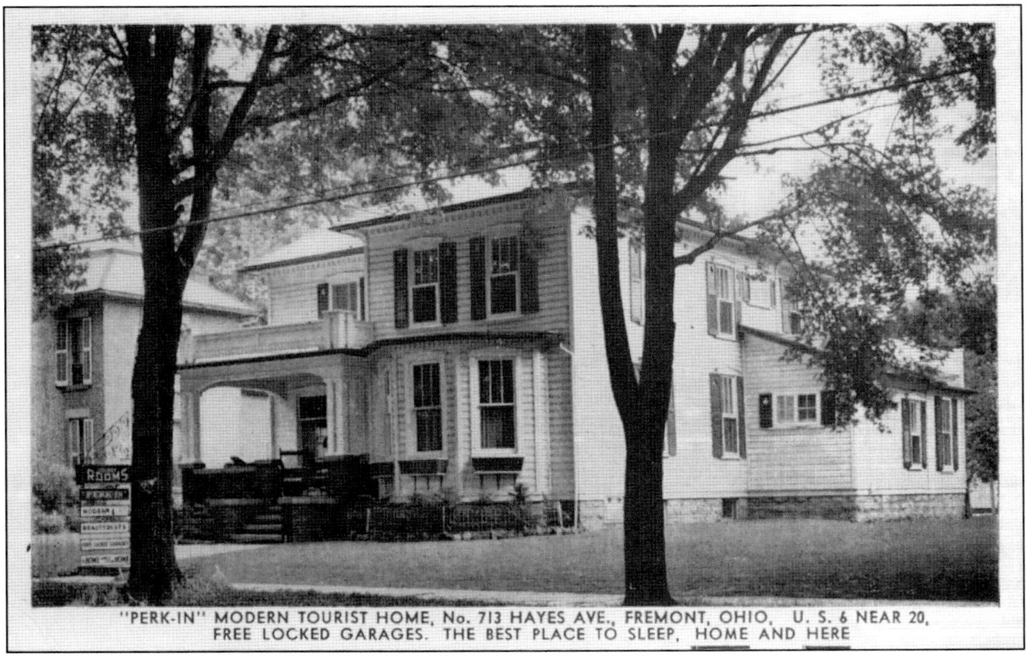

PERK-IN, 713 HAYES AVENUE, FREMONT. The sign in front of this cleverly named tourist home proclaims, "Beautyrest mattresses, free locked garages, a home away from home." The sender of the card appears to have been a guest here while she was nursing her ailing father. She reported, "Dad fell and broke his hip last Sunday, but we think he is improving."

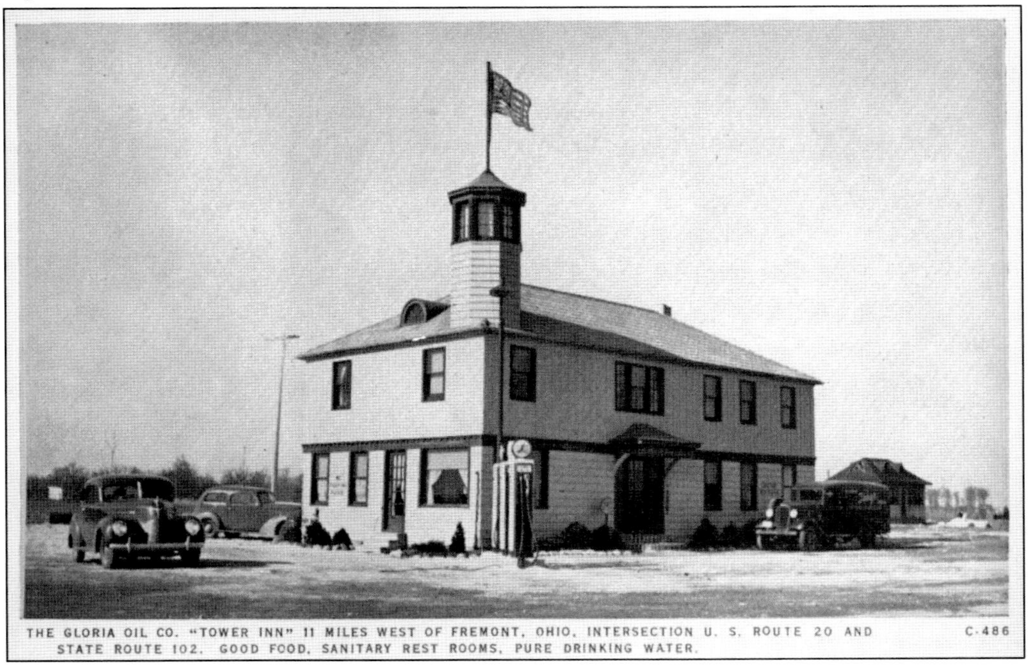

THE GLORIA OIL COMPANY "TOWER INN," ROUTES 20 AND 102, FREMONT. The tall tower with the American flag on top made this aptly named roadside business visible for miles around. Early travelers probably welcomed the gas station, clean restrooms, and the restaurant, which served "good food and pure drinking water."

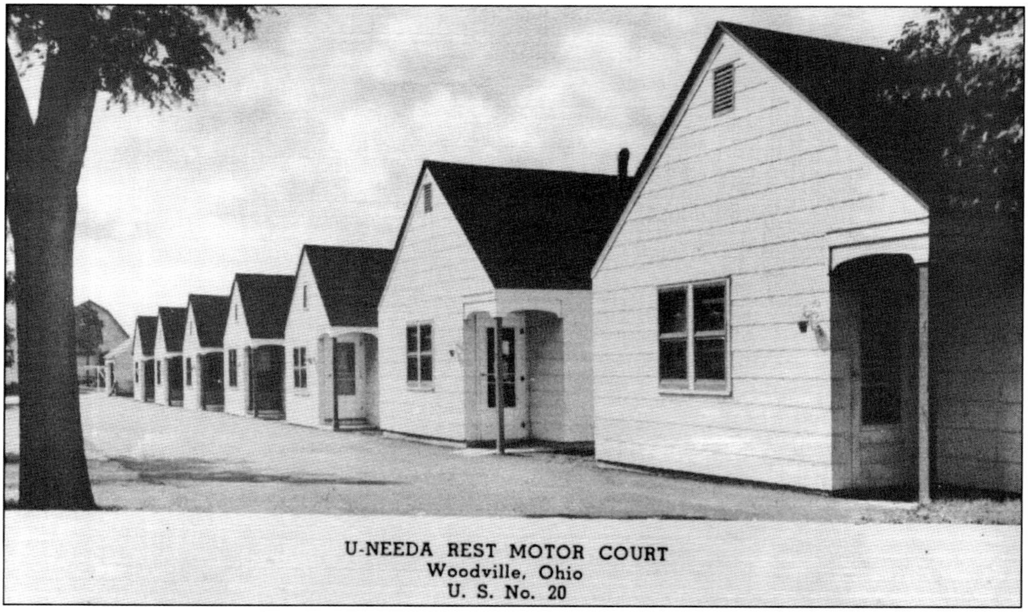

U-NEEDA REST MOTOR COURT, ROUTE 20, WOODVILLE. This aptly named tourist court was 100 miles west of Cleveland and 260 miles east of Chicago. For those traveling east during the early days of Route 20, the distance from Chicago would have been an average day's drive. The camp offered attractive cabins, a restaurant, and a gas station. Reservations were encouraged by mail or telephone.

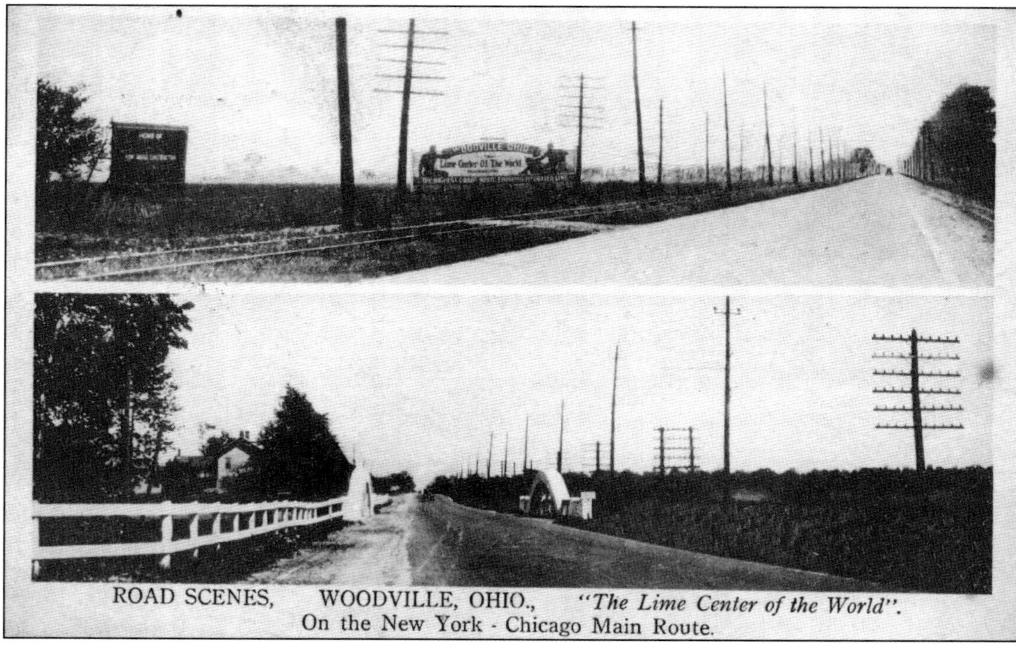

ROAD SCENES, WOODVILLE. The "New York–Chicago main route" promoted on this 1920s postcard was Route 20. The large sign in the upper view proclaims Woodville to be "the lime center of the world, producing the highest quality white hydrated lime." The sender of this card was not interested in the lime; instead, he wrote about his farm. He reported that all of his hay was cut and mostly in.

Six

The Maumee Valley and West

The Maumee River and Toledo present a natural geographic location to begin the westernmost section of *Along Ohio's Historic Route 20*. The highway did not go directly into Toledo but rather skirted the city to the south and west, beginning in Perrysburg on the east bank of the river. A memorial to Commodore Oliver Hazard Perry, the person for whom the city is named, is on Front Street near the river. A hero of the War of 1812, the 28-year-old Perry commanded the Lake Erie fleet, which defeated the larger and better-armed Royal Navy in the Battle of Lake Erie, effectively securing the entire lake. His message at the end of the battle, "We have met the enemy and they are ours, two ships, two brigs, one schooner, and one sloop," ranks among the most famous statements in US naval history.

Leaving Perrysburg, Route 20 crossed the Maumee River on the beautiful concrete-arch Fort Meigs Memorial Bridge and entered the city of Maumee on Conant Street, which it followed for several blocks through the city. Uniquely, from Maumee almost to the Indiana border, motorists could choose a second, slightly shorter option officially designated Route 20 South. In 1935, that designation was changed to Route 20A, and this route still exists. The road went directly west from Maumee, passing through several small villages before merging again with historic Route 20 in Williams County near the Indiana border.

Route 20's 1926 path joined Toledo's Reynolds Avenue and continued north through Toledo's western neighborhoods before turning west toward Indiana on Central Avenue. Historic Route 20 went west from Toledo approximately five miles north of Route 20A. Like the alternate route, it passed largely through agricultural land, with only a few small towns interrupting the idyllic landscape. In its earliest days, the road zigzagged to include a few tiny villages, but subsequent straightening has left the villages a mile or two north or south of the present highway. After approximately 55 miles as separate highways, Routes 20 and 20A merged southwest of Pioneer.

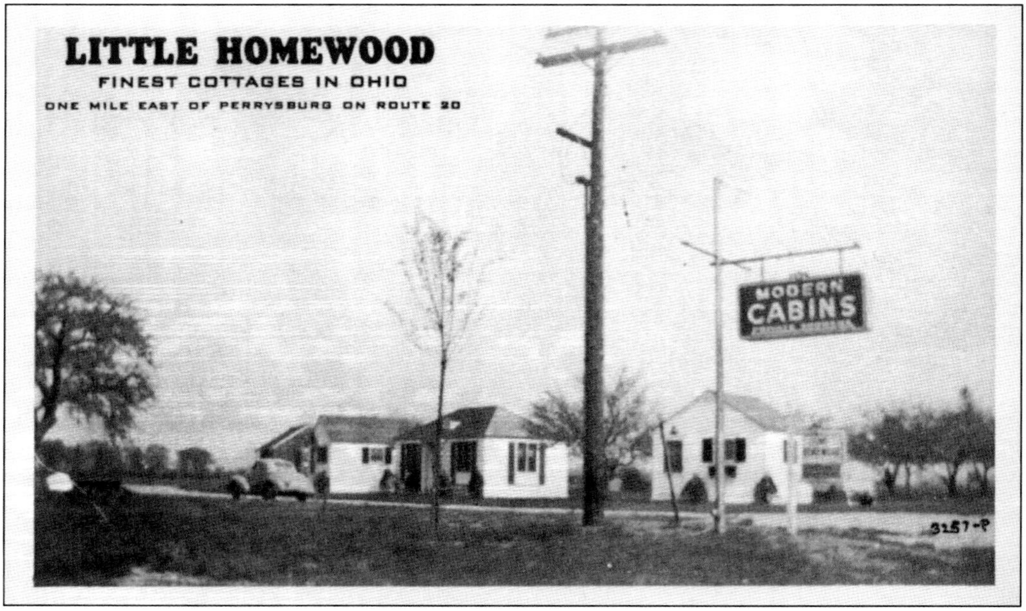

LITTLE HOMEWOOD, ROUTE 20, PERRYSBURG. Little Homewood, on the outskirts of Perrysburg, claimed to offer the finest cottages in Ohio, which were modern and up to date. At that time, "modern" simply meant that the cottages had indoor plumbing. The car in front of a cabin is a mid-1930s coupe. That type of automobile was a favorite of traveling salesmen because of their large trunks, which were convenient for transporting samples.

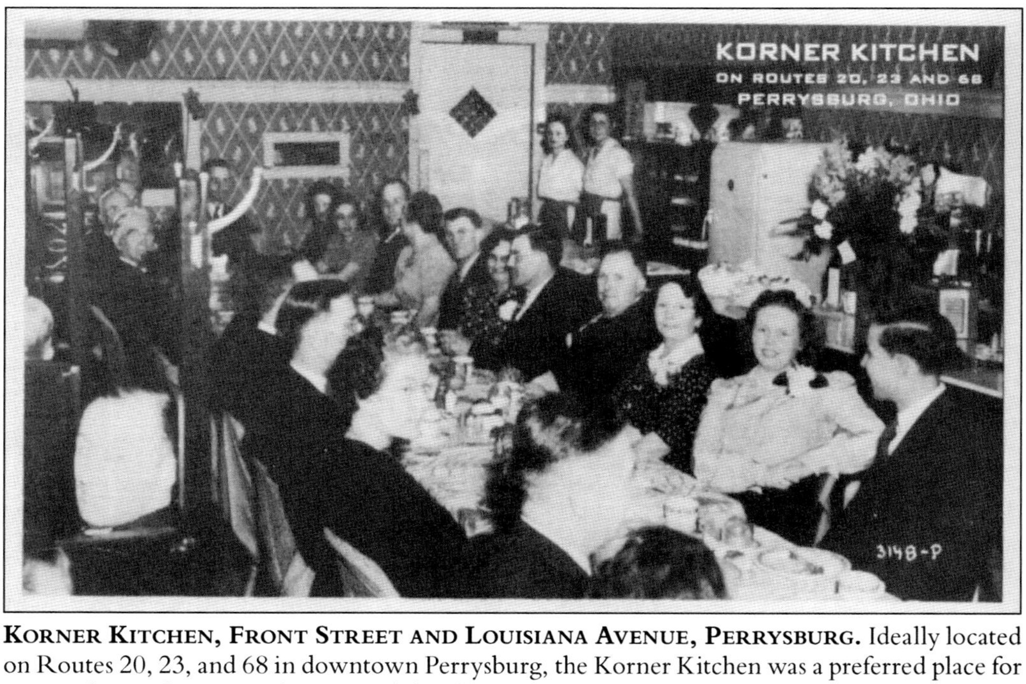

KORNER KITCHEN, FRONT STREET AND LOUISIANA AVENUE, PERRYSBURG. Ideally located on Routes 20, 23, and 68 in downtown Perrysburg, the Korner Kitchen was a preferred place for a quiet dinner for two or for a special family occasion. The attire of the guests at this gathering, together with the ample number of flower arrangements, suggests that this might have been a wedding reception or birthday celebration.

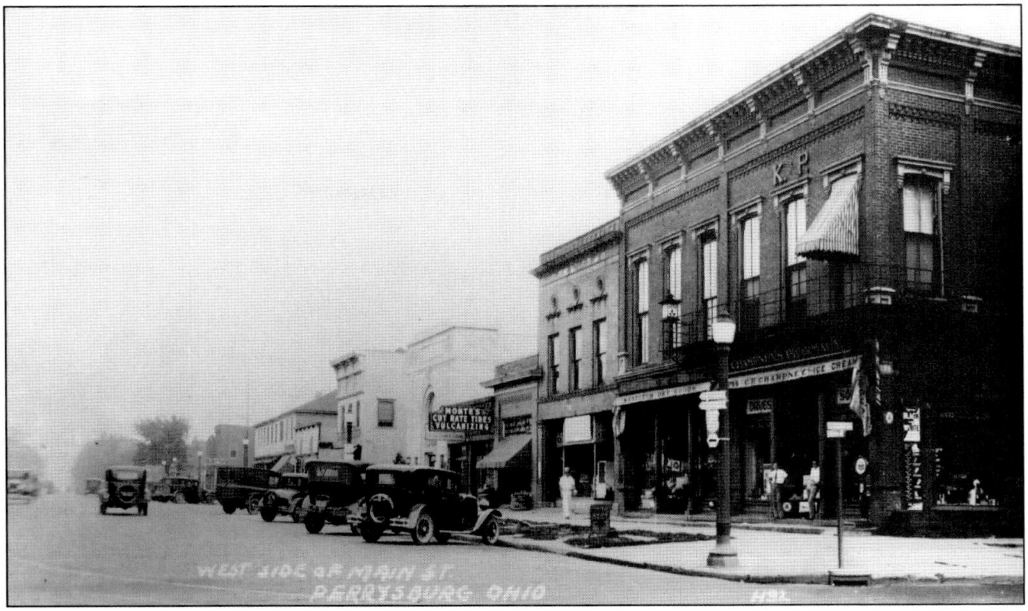

MAIN STREET, PERRYSBURG. In spite of the Great Depression, the early 1930s saw a great increase in the popularity of automobiles. In this postcard of Perrysburg, this is evidenced by the number of cars parked at the curb in the business district. A Route 20 sign is visible on the telephone pole in front of Champney's Pharmacy. The Knights of Pythias hall is on the second floor of the building.

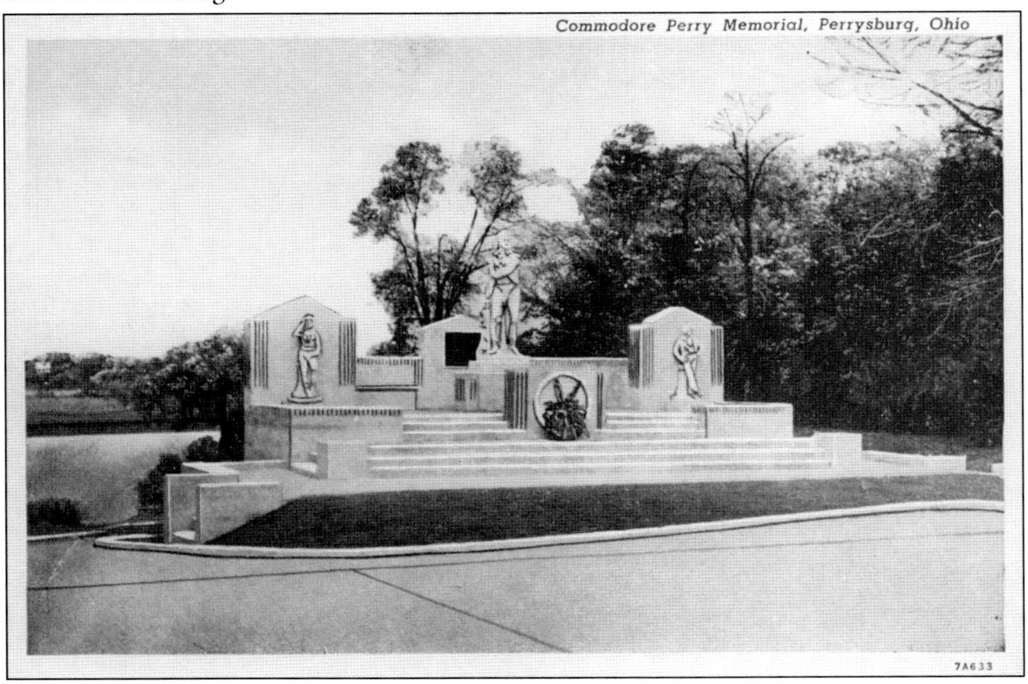

COMMODORE PERRY MONUMENT, PERRYSBURG. A bronze statue honoring the heroism of Commodore Oliver Hazard Perry during the War of 1812 was presented to Perrysburg by the City of Cleveland. The original memorial was erected in 1937, but due to age and weathering, it was moved to a museum in Put-in-Bay in 1991. It was replaced by the memorial seen here.

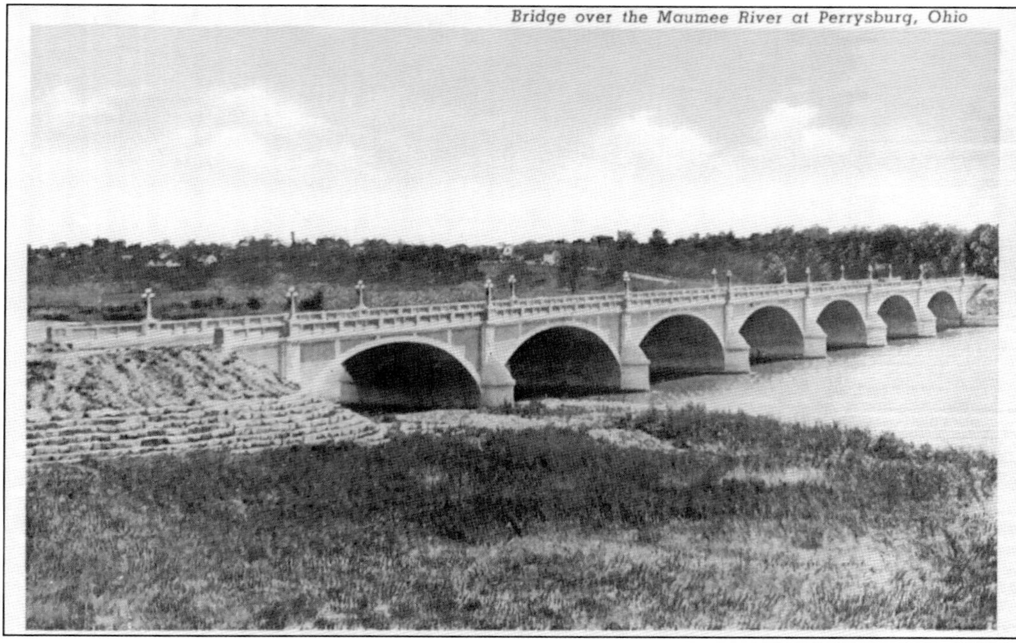

Fort Meigs Memorial Bridge. This attractive seven-arch concrete bridge carried Route 20 traffic over the Maumee River, connecting Perrysburg and Maumee. The bridge opened in 1929 and originally had four traffic lanes, but as the bridge aged, traffic was reduced to two lanes with pedestrian walkways on either side. This venerable Route 20 bridge was demolished in October 2002 following the completion of a new bridge just upstream.

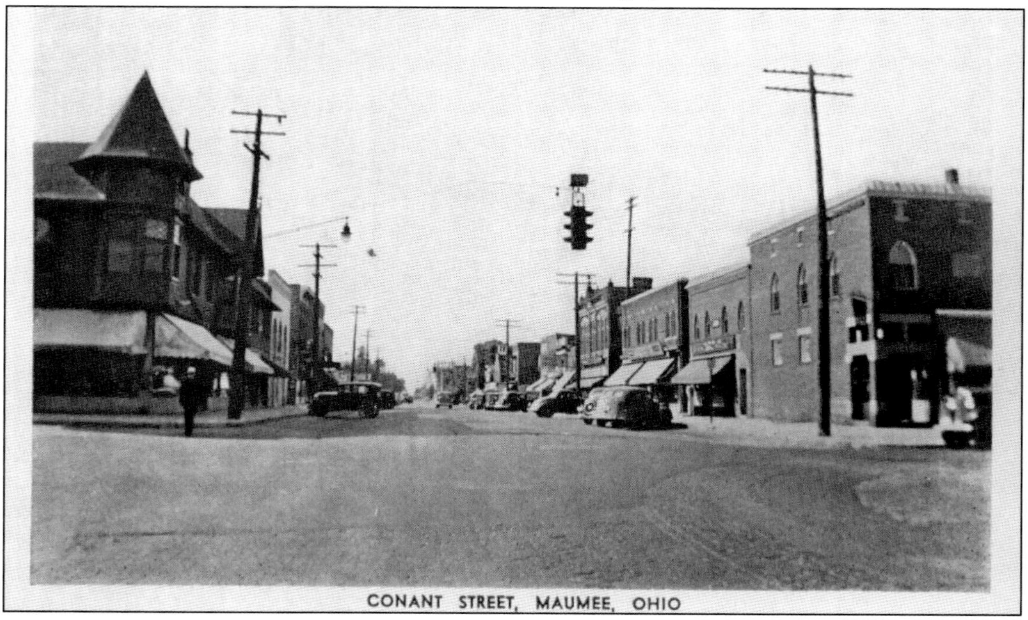

Conant Street, Maumee. After crossing the Maumee River, Route 20 entered the city of Maumee, a southern suburb of Toledo, on Conant Street, seen here in the 1930s. It continued through Maumee and connected first with Illinois Avenue (Route 20A) and then with Reynolds Road (Route 20) after approximately two miles. Route 20 then proceeded north through Toledo's western neighborhoods before turning west toward Indiana.

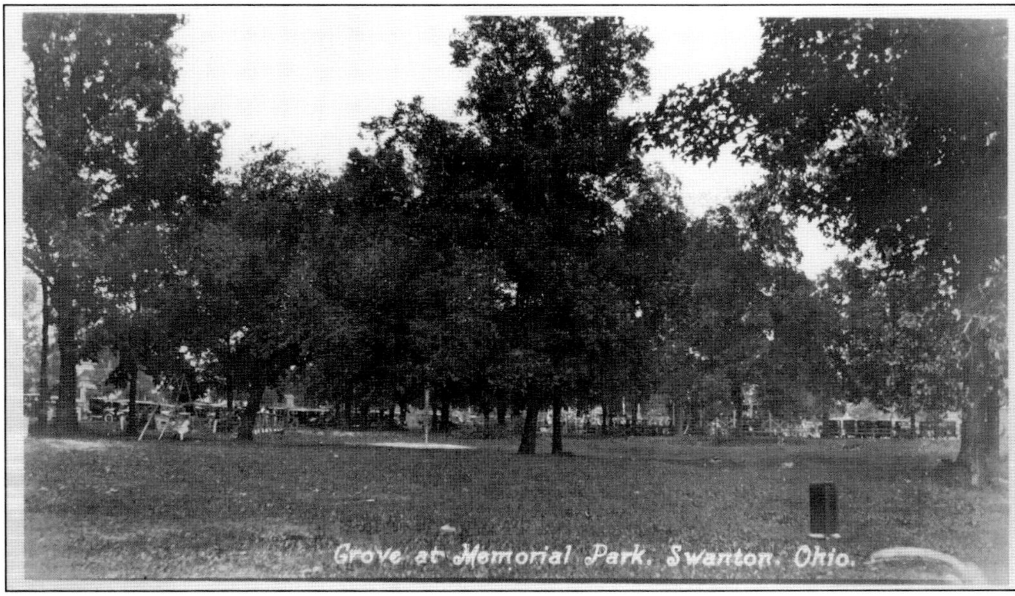

GROVE AT MEMORIAL PARK, SWANTON. Westbound travelers on Route 20A followed Illinois Avenue from central Maumee. Farther west, in the outer suburbs, the name changed to Maumee Western Road. Swanton was the first community Route 20A passed west of Maumee. This park, located just north of the highway, was a convenient place for motorists to take a break and possibly enjoy a picnic.

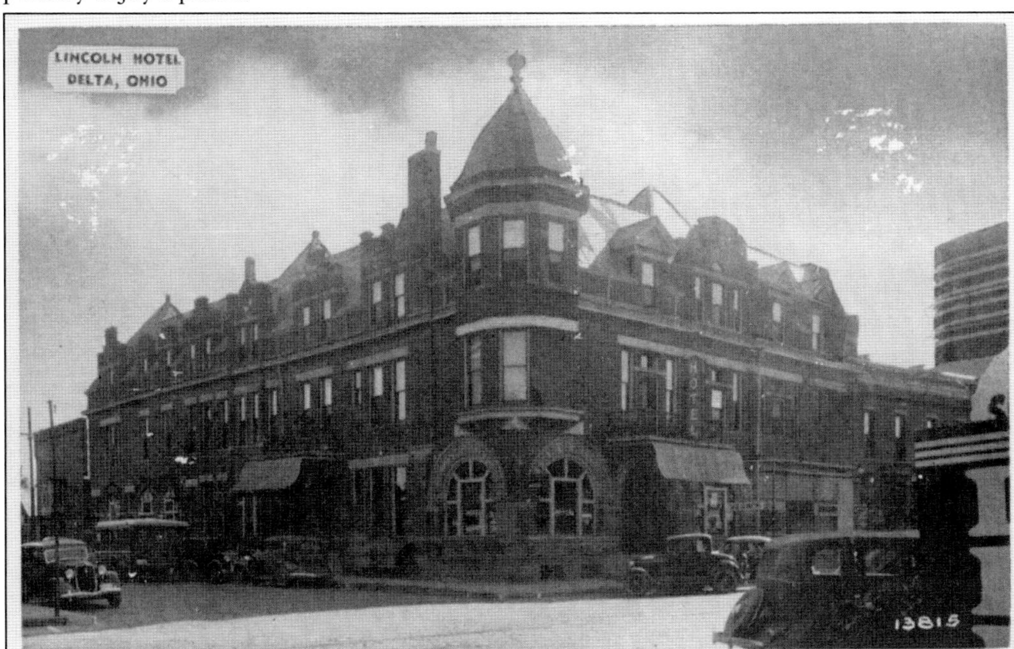

LINCOLN HOTEL, DELTA. The ornate Lincoln Hotel dominated Main Street in Delta, approximately 20 miles west of Maumee on Route 20A. The three-story building opened in 1901. It contained guest rooms, a restaurant, a bar, and meeting facilities and was a center for business and social activities. The cars in this photograph are from the 1920s and 1930s, an era when Lincoln Hotel was at its peak.

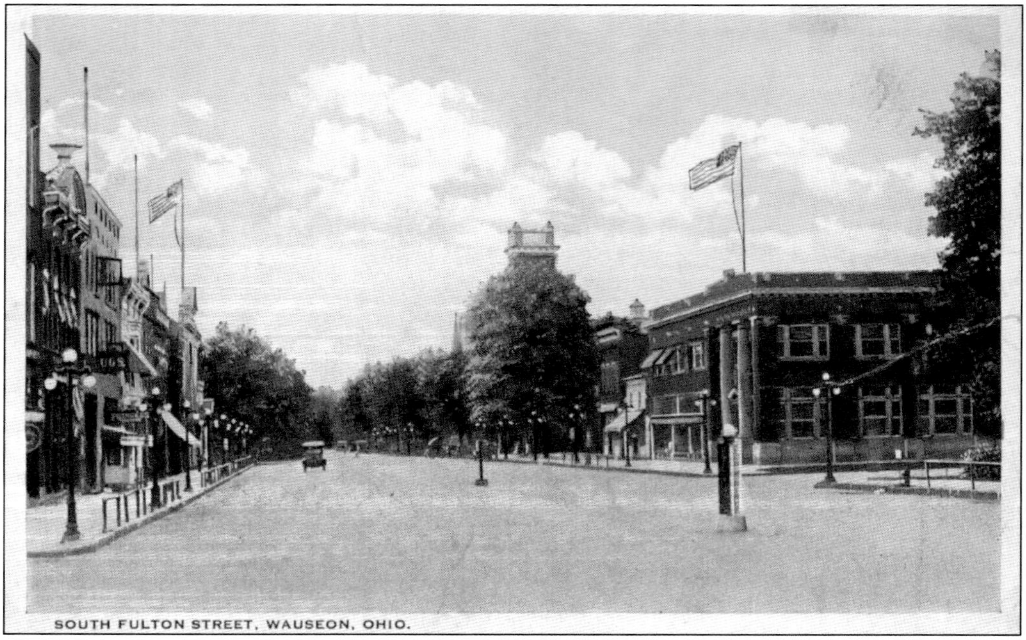

SOUTH FULTON STREET, WAUSEON. Route 20A skirted the northern city limits of Wauseon. This postcard of the business district illustrates the transitions that were occurring in the mid-1920s. A single car is coming down the street, but the curbs on both sides still contain hitching rails for horses. The attractive three-globe streetlamps indicate that electricity has arrived, adding a pleasant ambiance to the scene.

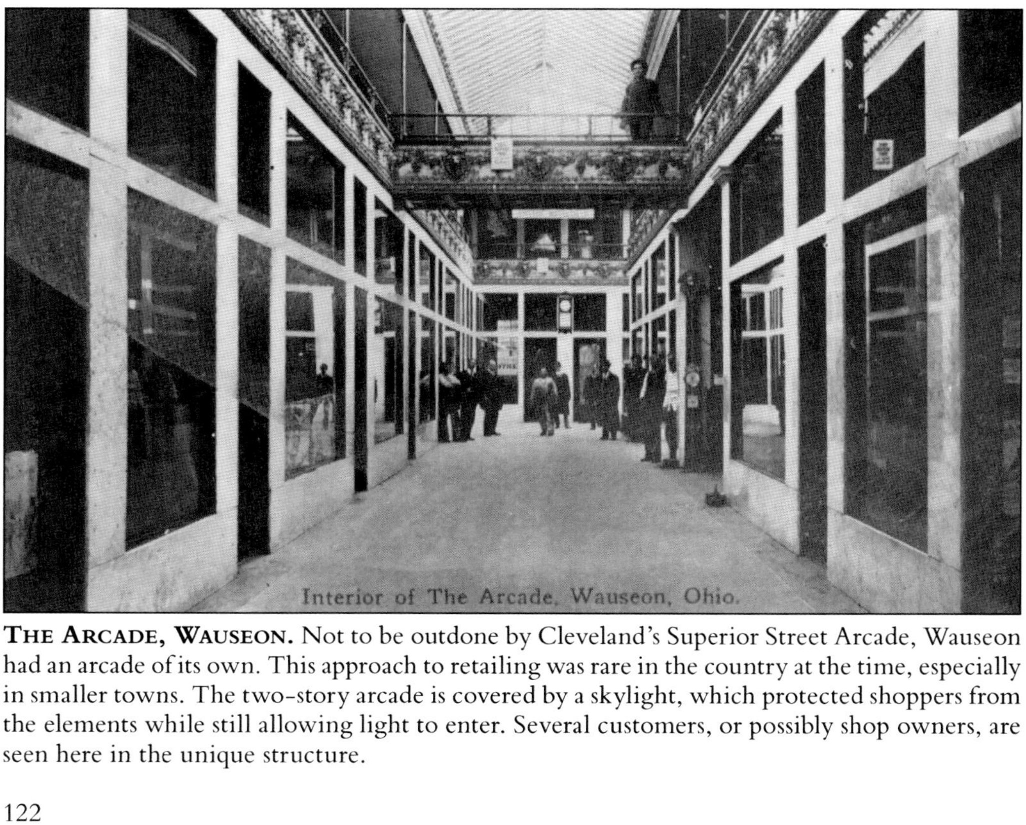

THE ARCADE, WAUSEON. Not to be outdone by Cleveland's Superior Street Arcade, Wauseon had an arcade of its own. This approach to retailing was rare in the country at the time, especially in smaller towns. The two-story arcade is covered by a skylight, which protected shoppers from the elements while still allowing light to enter. Several customers, or possibly shop owners, are seen here in the unique structure.

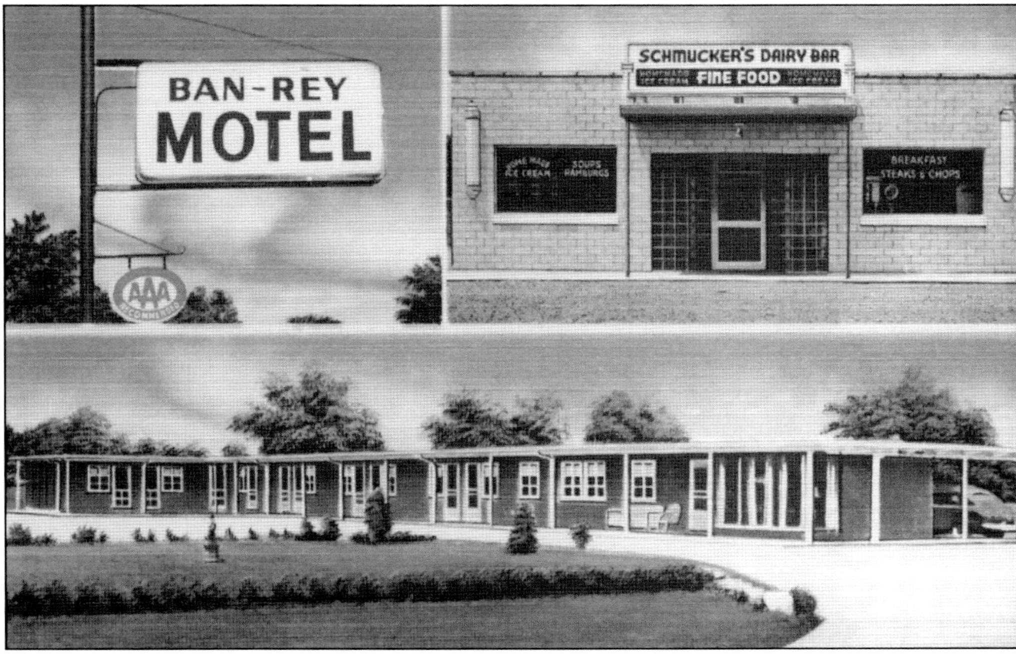

BAN-REY MOTEL AND SCHMUCKER'S DAIRY BAR, 2117 REYNOLDS ROAD, TOLEDO. Drivers on Route 20 continued along Reynolds Road through western Toledo. This 1940s combination motel and restaurant offered a bath in every room and Simmons Beautyrest mattresses. The dairy bar was noted for its excellent food and complete fountain service.

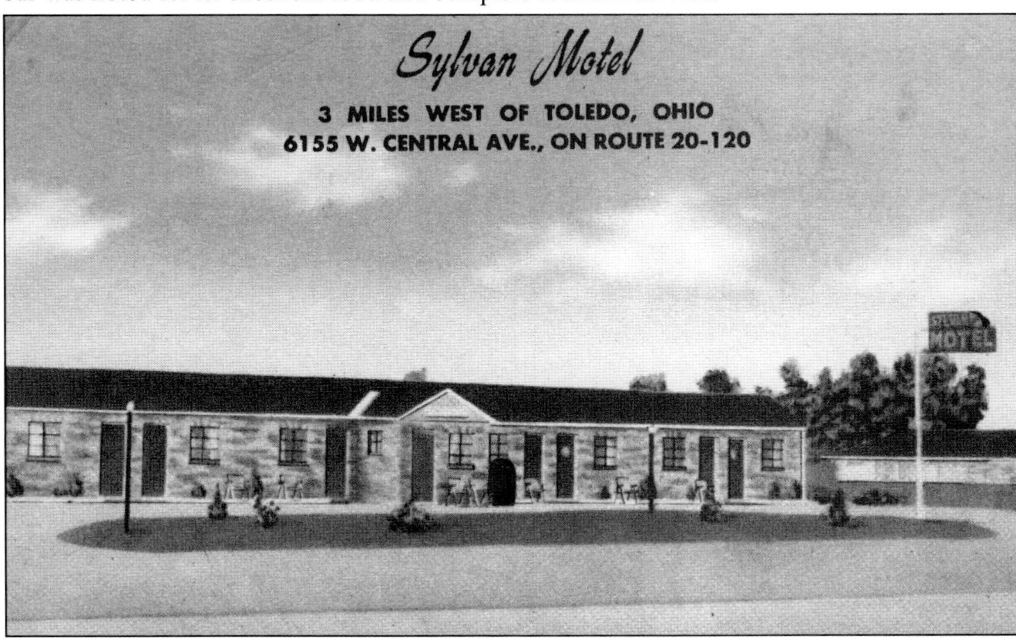

SYLVAN MOTEL, 6155 WEST CENTRAL AVENUE, SYLVANIA. Reynolds Road intersected with West Central Avenue near the suburb of Sylvania, and Route 20 proceeded west from there. This motel was one of the first where a westbound traveler might have stopped for the night. The caption proudly points out that the motel was constructed of the man-made product Permastone, which contributed to its being soundproof and fireproof.

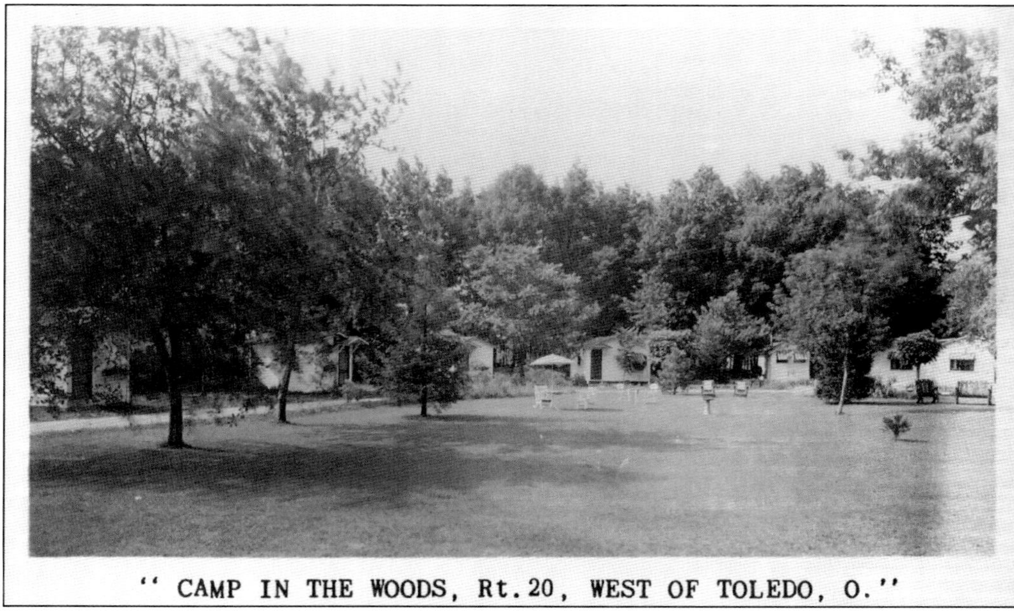

CAMP IN THE WOODS, ROUTE 20, TOLEDO. This 1930s tourist camp was aptly named given its location in a wooded grove. The spacious lawn furnished with comfortable chairs and umbrellas made it a pleasant place for early travelers to spend a night on the road.

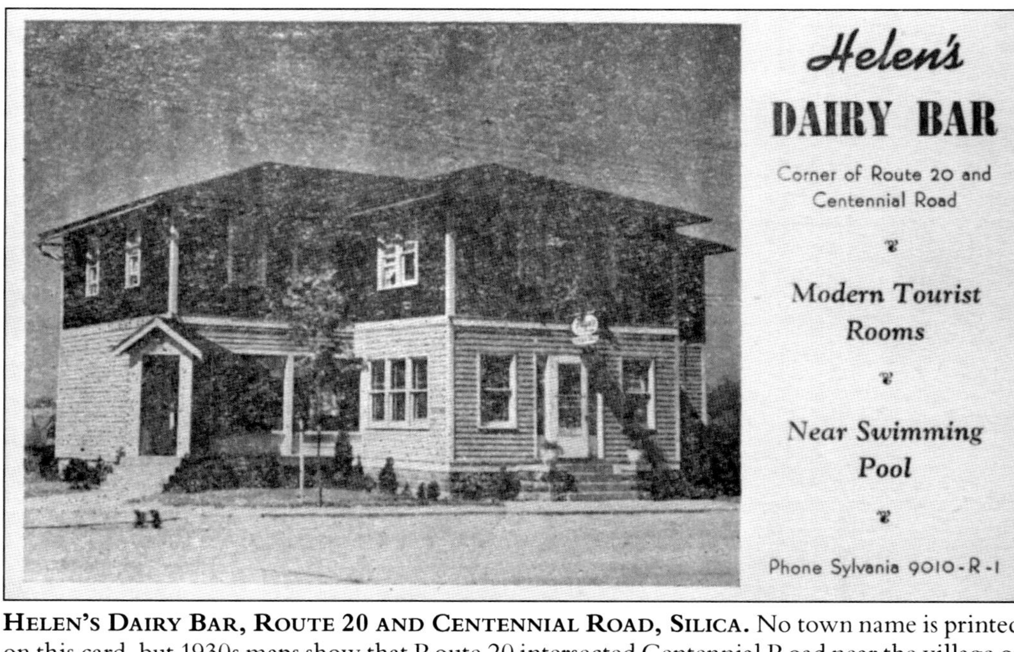

HELEN'S DAIRY BAR, ROUTE 20 AND CENTENNIAL ROAD, SILICA. No town name is printed on this card, but 1930s maps show that Route 20 intersected Centennial Road near the village of Silica, in Sylvania Township approximately eight miles west of Toledo. The Sylvania telephone exchange noted on the postcard also provides assurance that Helen's Dairy Bar was in Silica.

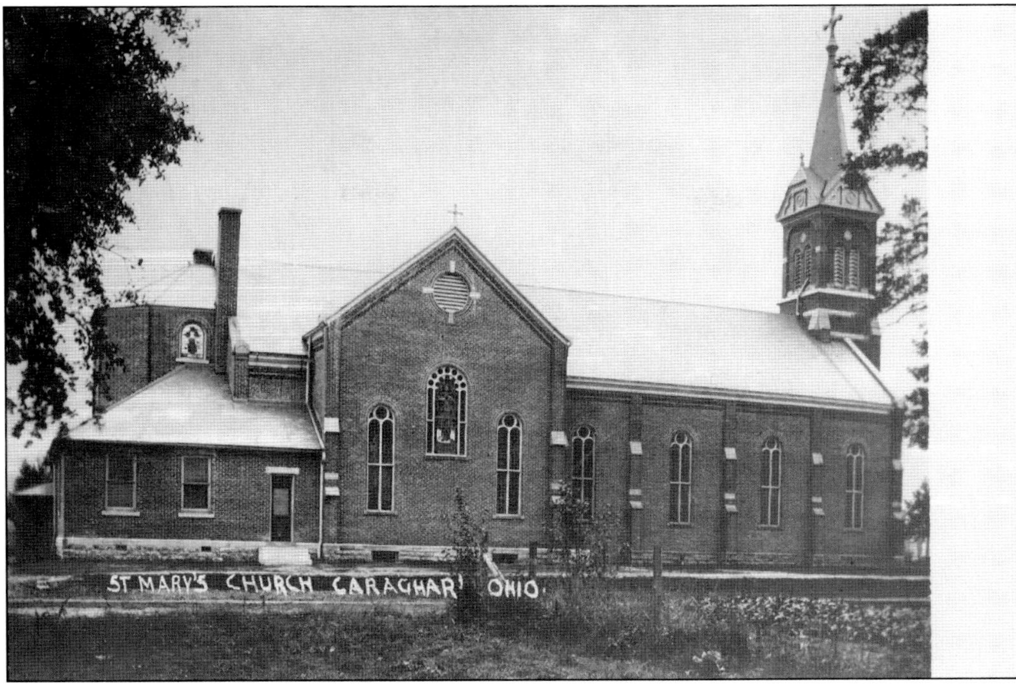

St. Mary's Church, Caraghar. Approximately 20 miles west of Toledo on Route 20, Caraghar has undergone several name changes since the mid-1800s. It was known as St. Mary's Corners in the 1840s, then Caraghar Corners, and then Caraghar for varying periods until 1942, when the name was changed to its present name, Assumption. St. Mary's Church has been the focal point of the community since 1906.

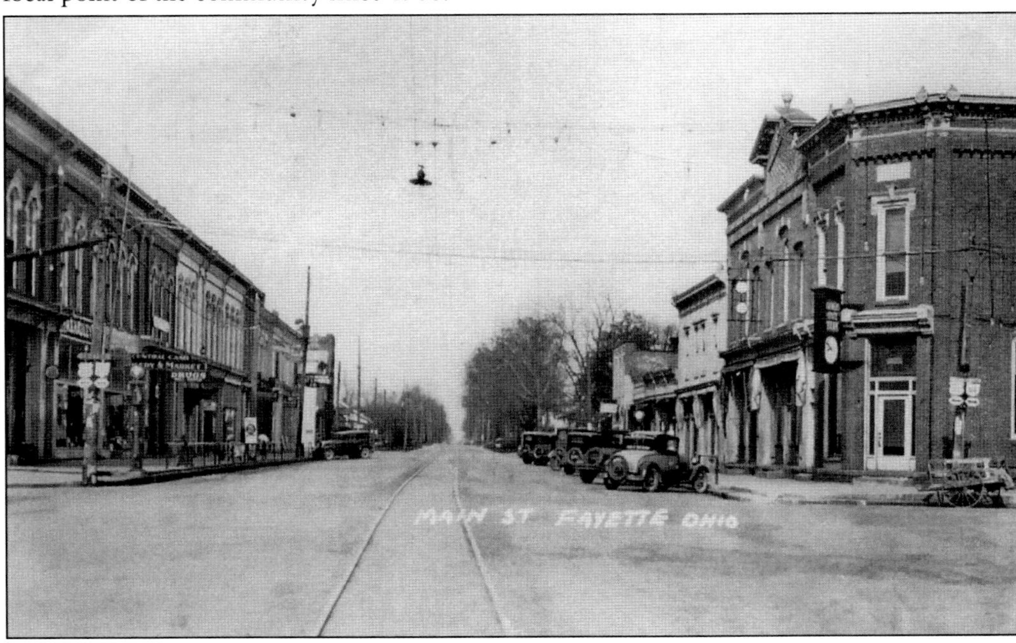

Main Street Looking West, Fayette. Fayette's attractive business district indicates how America was changing in the 1930s. Trolley tracks are still present, but more people have turned to the automobile for transportation. Route 20 signs are on both sides of the street.

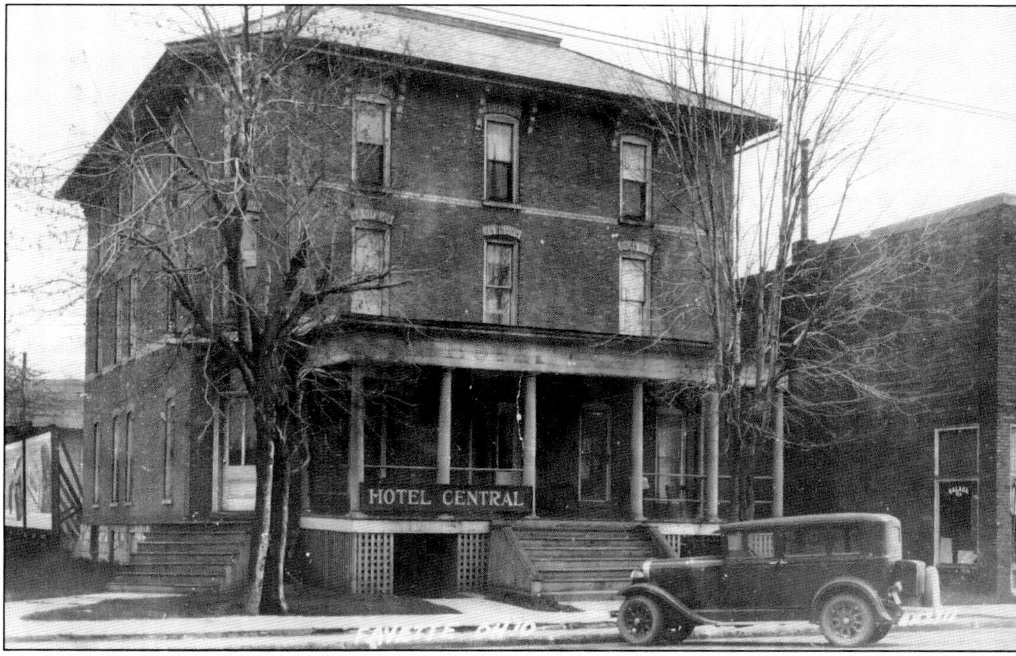

Hotel Central, Fayette. As it was on the main east-west highway through northwestern Ohio in the 1920s and 1930s, the Central Hotel in Fayette hosted many travelers. The sender of this card, writing to a friend in Pennsylvania, reported that they had spent the night here. They also wrote that they were having a very good trip and had covered more than 400 miles.

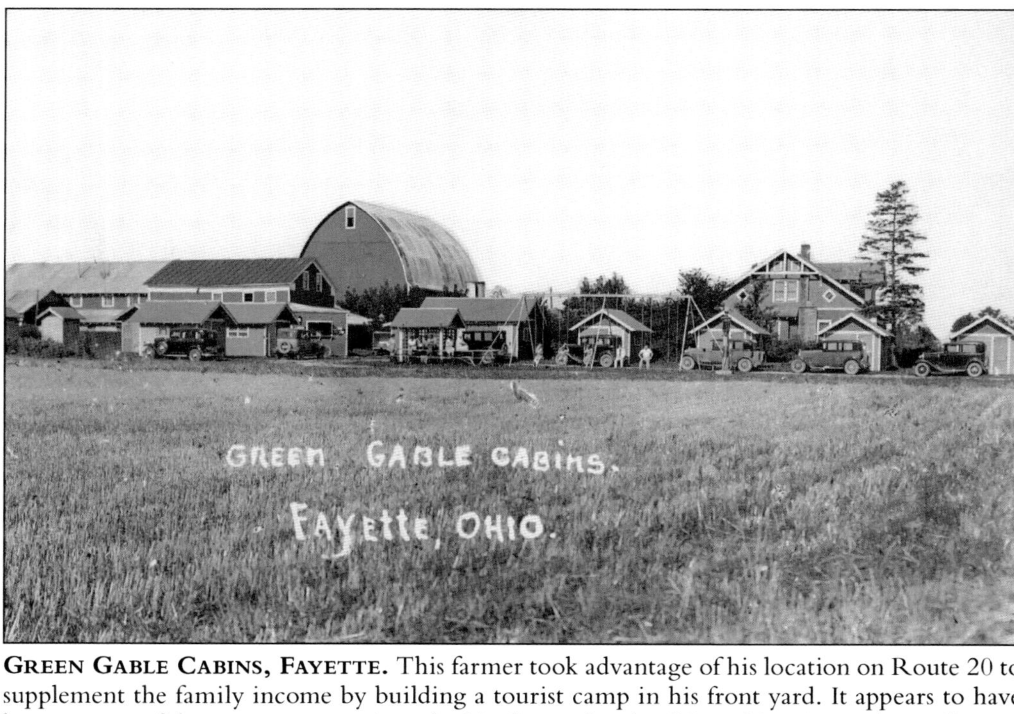

Green Gable Cabins, Fayette. This farmer took advantage of his location on Route 20 to supplement the family income by building a tourist camp in his front yard. It appears to have been a successful venture, as a car is parked in front of each of the cabins. Note the traditional outhouse on the left.

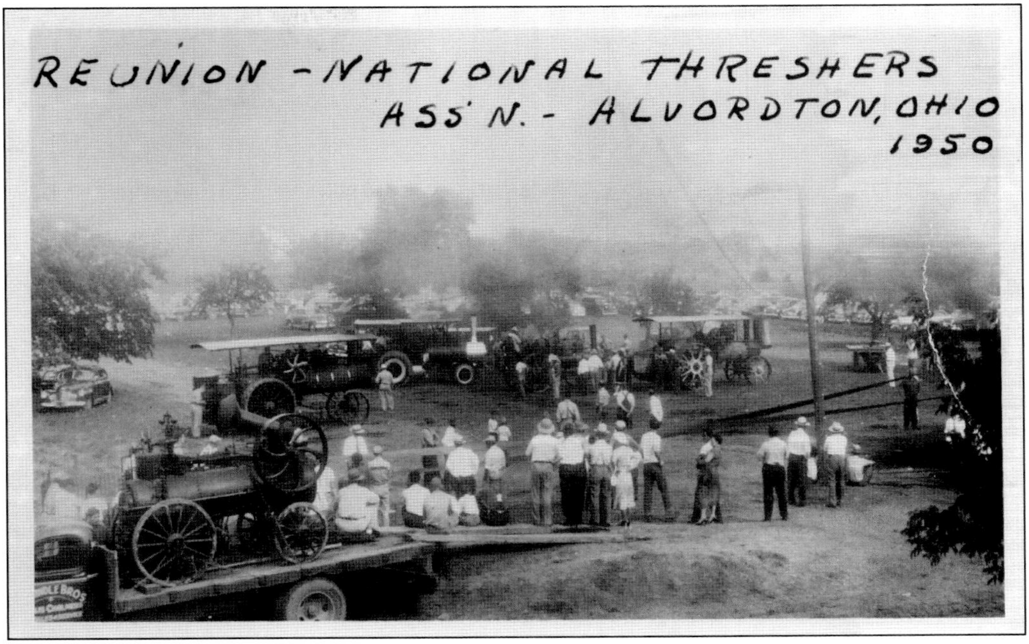

NATIONAL THRESHERS ASSOCIATION REUNION, ALVORDTON. Old-time farm implement exhibitions have long been popular in agricultural communities throughout the Midwest. The date on this card is 1950, but the car on the left and the trucks are of earlier vintage, from the 1930s and early 1940s.

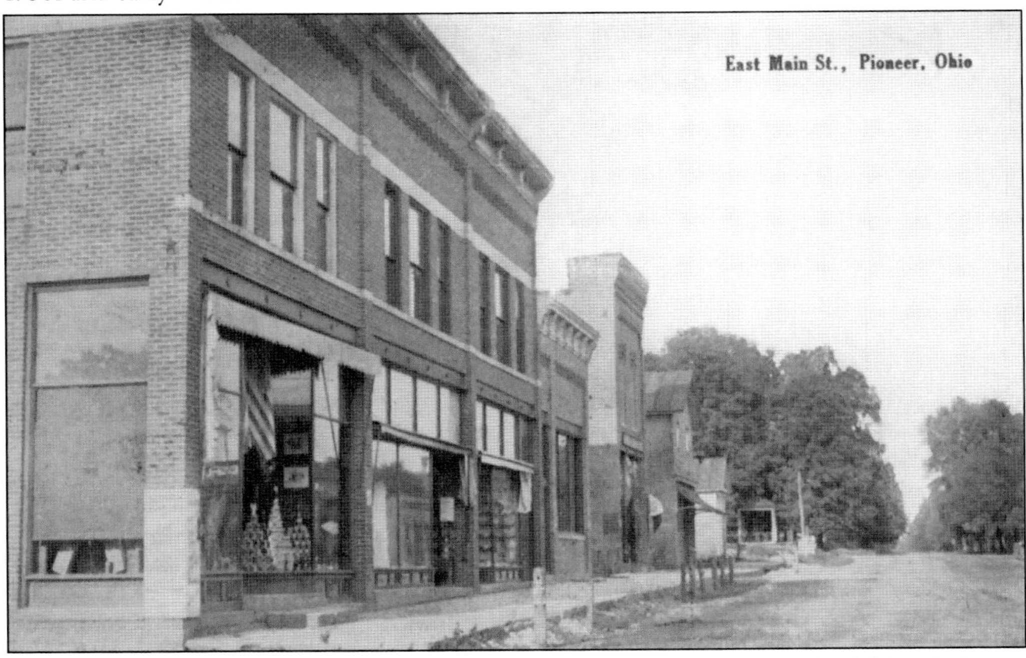

MAIN STREET, PIONEER. Pioneer is the westernmost community along Ohio's historic Route 20. This corner grocery store featured neatly stacked pyramids of canned goods in the window. As was the case with most roads when Route 20 was designated a federal highway in 1926, the street is still unpaved. Routes 20 and 20A rejoined each other again a few miles southwest of Pioneer and continued westward as Route 20.

Ohio

Route 20 was named a federal highway in 1926, and for the first half c the 20th century it was the most important east-west road across norther Ohio. Extending from the Pennsylvania border east of Conneaut to it western terminus with Indiana, it made Ohio the connecting link betwee Northeastern and Midwestern states. Fortunately, Route 20 has remaine virtually intact and can be traveled much as people did in years past Postcard History Series: Along Ohio's Historic Route 20 *celebrate such a trip, illustrated by more than 200 vintage postcards depicting vieu along the way. Town and city scenes, rural vistas, and historic sites tha drew early motorists to the highway are featured. Not to be forgotten a the tourist courts, hotels, diners, and gas stations that made automobil journeys possible.*

Michael J. Till is a retired university professor. He grew up on Rout 20 and has had a lifelong interest in the road. All illustrations are from hi personal collection of more than 2,500 vintage Route 20 postcards.

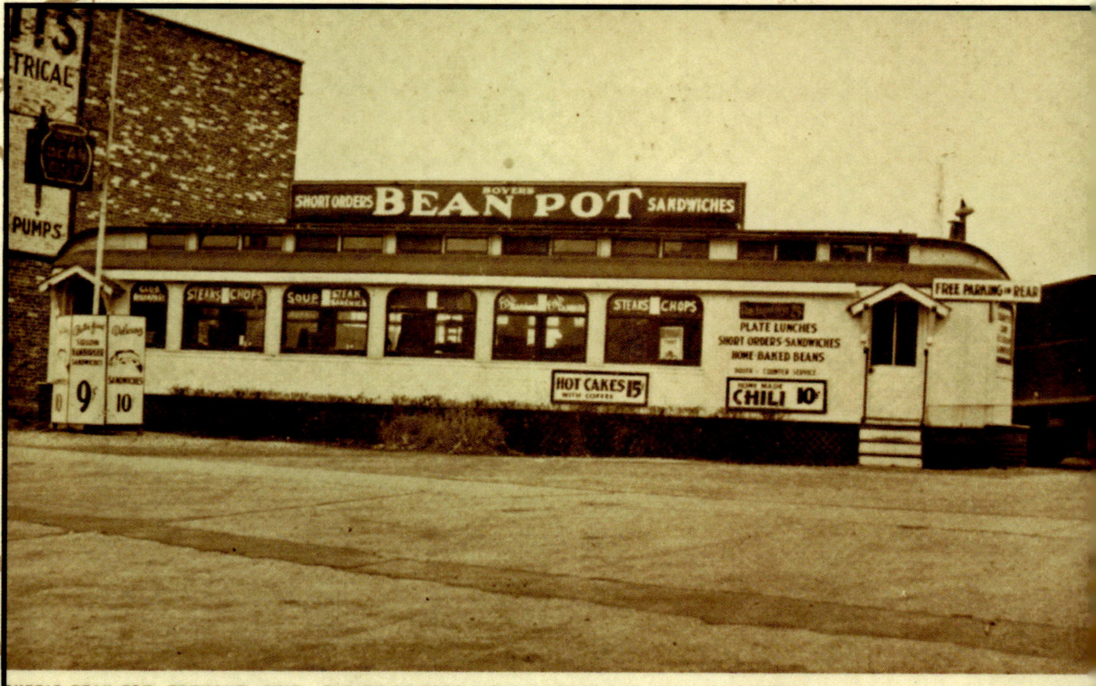

OYER'S BEAN POT, FREMONT, OHIO. PLENTY OF FREE PARKING SPACE FOR CARS AND TRUCKS C-9

ISBN-13 978-1-4671-1042-6 $24.99
ISBN-10 1-4671-1042-6
52499
9 781467 110426

MADE IN THE USA

www.arcadiapublishing.com